FROM SINNER TO SERVANT

One Man's Journey to Becoming a Permanent
Deacon in the Roman Catholic Church

Albert L. Feliu

Bloomington, IN Milton Keynes, UK

AuthorHouse™
1663 Liberty Drive, Suite 200
Bloomington, IN 47403
www.authorhouse.com
Phone: 1-800-839-8640

AuthorHouse™ UK Ltd.
500 Avebury Boulevard
Central Milton Keynes, MK9 2BE
www.authorhouse.co.uk
Phone: 08001974150

First published by AuthorHouse 12/4/2006

ISBN: 978-1-4259-7721-4 (e)
ISBN: 978-1-4259-7720-7 (sc)

Library of Congress Control Number: 2006910012

Printed in the United States of America
Bloomington, Indiana

This book is printed on acid-free paper.

Front Book Cover Photo taken at St. Bernard Abbey Church, Culman, Alabama. Photo by Deacon Kenneth Melvin

Inside Portrait taken by Deacon Kenneth Melvin, Owner-Memories Photographic LLC

Back Photo taken by Jack Kujawa

Deacon Albert Feliu

Dedication Page

- To my family: Cindy – my bride of 22 years, with my children, Christina Catherine and Michael Albert, who gave me the gift of unselfish love and personal strength to follow God's call to service to serve our larger family – the Body of Christ;

- To my fourteen brother deacons and Victor Marulanda who inspired me over five years with their own personal examples of Roman Catholic faith, spirituality and devotion;

- To my spiritual director Father Joseph Mendes, my brother deacons and the numerous priests that I assisted over the last five years; the Benedictine monks in Culman, Alabama: you have showed me how to serve the people of God with unselfish love and fidelity;

- Finally, to Almighty God whose precious gift of His Son Our Lord Jesus Christ has given me every good gift and compassion with the Holy Spirit who I have received through the Grace of Ordination;

This book is lovingly dedicated to you all.

Deacon Albert L. Feliu

Archdiocese of Atlanta

St Oliver Plunkett

December 26th, 2006

The Feast Day of St Stephen – One of the first seven Deacons ordained as recorded in the Acts of Apostles and 1st Martyr of Christianity

Contents

Foreword

*I*magine for a moment a group of men, from diverse backgrounds, educationally, spiritually, emotionally and ethnically, coming together to be formed into men of God for the service to His Church. This is where we start, but it is not necessarily where we end.

Formation is an amazing journey. One would never believe that such a diverse group could possibly get so close that they truly become a band of brothers. Every man has unique gifts and strengths that can be used for the greater glory of God. There is no better or worse – there simply is. Every man benefits from the others.

This book looks a one man's journey and the influences of other men including classmates, spiritual directors, teachers, mentors and others who surround them as they make this unusual journey leading to ordination as a deacon in the Catholic Church.

When men start as aspirants to a vocation, they are generally under the impression that they would grow intellectually. That they would learn Church Teachings, how to interpret the bible, learn about Church law…but they don't come in with any concept that they will also grow emotionally nor spiritually, that they would grow closer to wonderful God and their beautiful Catholic faith.

Some, as the author, experience a rollercoaster of growth and understanding. Their learning and growing takes them to new heights and show them things they never knew, especially about themselves. As they reach these new heights, most experience a special, unbelievable growth and joy. Emotionally, intellectually and spiritually - they come to a closer relationship with Jesus, which leads them to a closer and more nurturing relationship with their family and those who surround them. Their prayer life deepens, as does their devotion to the Lord. Their respect for others also takes on a new meaning. Their lives are basically turned upside down, as the title of this book suggests...Sinner to Saint. This I might add has to be everyone's goal – only saints are admitted into the presence of God.

The men also grow in other area, as witnessed by the author. They come to a deeper understanding of the Mass, Eucharist, Adoration of the Blessed Sacrament, and what service to the Lord really entails. They experience what may be life changing events when they work with the poorest of the poor in Jamaica and in Haiti. They come to the realization that their family is so central in their lives and that placing in Him and not into the materialist world is of prime importance. They also experience something totally unexpected, namely the support they receive from not only their families, but from members of their parish and a totally unexpected group, their co-workers.

The five years our men spend in formation is not lost time. When men enter formation many feel that ordination is a given, or maybe even expected. They learn in a very short period of time that ordination is not earned, it's a gift from the Church for those who are chosen. Many feel they are unworthy, and that is so true, because none of us are. It's only through our love of God and His teachings that we gain some element of worthiness. The worthy are not necessarily chosen, but the chosen are made worthy.

Formation does not end with ordination. Ordination is only one phase of our formation, which is a life long effort. It is an undertaking that continues to allow one to grow in mind, body, and soul. Formation and ordination are both exciting and humbling.

Expectation and the reality start to merge and it is then that one starts a conversion from sinner to saint.

Deacon Loris R. Sinanian
Director of Diaconate Formation
Archdiocese of Atlanta
November 6th, 2006

Preamble:

The reason why I wrote this book

O n February 4, 2006, at the Cathedral of Christ the King in Atlanta, Georgia, fourteen of my classmates and I were ordained as Deacons in the Latin Rite of the Roman Catholic Church.

Although the Archdiocese of Atlanta has been ordaining men since the 1970s to the permanent diaconate, we were the result of the first five-year formation class. During the Year 2000, over sixty men had responded to a prompting from the Holy Spirit to serve the Roman Catholic Church in a very special way. Through the extensive interviewing process that took place that year, twenty-four men would eventually be selected as part of this new formation class.

Actually, we lost one man prior to the first class ever being started. Ultimately, we would lose seven more men during the five years of academics from 2001 to 2005. In a final act of bitter irony, we lost our final brother Victor who would have been ordained with us but he suffered a massive heart attack and died prior to our pre-ordination retreat in January. All of these men were responding to a very unique call: to live their lives beyond their own needs and the wants of their immediate family but to live by giving and serving a greater family: the Universal Catholic Church -- the people of God -- our brothers and sisters in Christ Jesus.

Many people have very different ideas on what exactly **"the call"** is. Some of us can refer to either the Old or New Testament where Almighty God Himself calls to both men and women to serve him in a very unique and special way. In fact, Bill Cosby, for years, did a very credible job using his unique style of clean comedy in trying to get people to understand that when Almighty God calls you, **<u>you need to take that message – right away</u>**! I call it the divine 911 call! Remember the conversation between Noah and God according to Bill? God wants Noah to build an ark and Noah responds "Ok, what's an ark?!" Better yet, God replies and tells him what an ark is and gives him the precise measurements: how high, how tall, and how wide. Noah has only one more question – "What's a cubit?"

Of course, on a more serious note, if you have ever watched the movie **"The Ten Commandments"**, Charlton Heston as the adult Moses has a life-transforming, real face-to-face conversation with Almighty God Himself through the burning bush. The former Prince of Egypt has been humiliated and exiled, he has been purified in the desert heat of Egypt's wilderness, his life humbled to becoming a simple sheppard of sheep – it is a total fall from earthly favor and acclaim. But now, by receiving this divine 911 from Almighty God Himself, Moses is called and empowered to fulfill a greater mission – to lead God's Chosen people out from bondage in the light of God's freedom.

But **"the call"** itself is really just our freely given human response to the Divine God's patient but persistent calling to us -- He is always asking us to serve Him. Contrary to popular belief, all of us have a calling or vocation -- *a unique mission that God calls each and every one of us to fulfill during the course of our human lives.* For many, it may be a vocation to be married: to join the life of one man to one woman and during the course of their married life together, to bring forth or possibly adopt children, to enhance their own lives by living as a family and ultimately our communities flourish from this unified vocation choice.

For others, it is maybe a vocation to join a religious community as a consecrated individual and joining their individual efforts in communal lives of prayer and service through the Roman Catholic Church for the redemption and salvation of the world.

For some others still, it may be a vocation to live a single life until one elects to either to get married or in the case of single Catholic males, to be called into spiritual fatherhood by entering into a seminary to become a transitional deacon and eventually an ordained priest.

But with the conclusion of the Second Vatican Council in the late 1960s, the Roman Catholic Church revived the ability for married men to become servants to their faith communities in a very special way: That vocation is fulfilled by acceptance by the local bishop, to study for a pre-determined period of time at an approved institution or school with an approved curriculum with the approval of the local bishop and then to be ordained as permanent deacons in the Roman Catholic Church.

If you read in the Acts of the Apostles, in the sixth chapter, you read through the evangelist St. Luke, how seven men were chosen, not to the ministry of preaching of the Word but rather the ministry of charity by being the servants to the people of God. The seven men were chosen by the Apostles first, by asking the assistance of the Holy Spirit and then had their selection affirmed with the actual laying on of the hands by the Apostles assembled there. Then these men they called **"deacons"** who were then sent into the local community to attend to the needs of the sick, marginalized, orphans, and widows.

Yet, as you read further in Acts, St. Stephen, one of the first deacons and the first martyr to the new Christian faith, gives a very powerful testimony to those in power. Ultimately, that forceful personal testimony he gave in the

Temple that day sealed his fate with those in power – they sentenced him to die by stoning his body. But St. Stephen shared the ultimate victory when he receives Eternal Life from his Savior – Our Lord Jesus Christ. In his last dying breath, he imitates the action of Jesus at the Cross by begging God's forgiveness for his persecutors and looking to heaven, seeing Jesus sitting at the right hand of His Father – Almighty God.

Twenty centuries later, the local Roman Catholic Church in Atlanta, Georgia, is far from being persecuted by the ancient Romans. Our diocese today is enjoying a surge of population and economic growth that very few dioceses throughout the world could equal or surpass. Because of the great economic engine that the North Georgia region and the Southeastern United States provides, there are many people that come from other parts of the United States to live and work in the metro Atlanta area. Many of our transplants, which I am proudly one of them, come from all parts of the USA -- the Northeast, the Midwest, the West Coast, and the Northwest regions of the United States.

In addition, Atlanta continues to attract a number of workers from outside of the United States, both documented and undocumented, however, all of us are seeking the same things: a safe home to call our own, a good education for our children, economic opportunity for ourselves and a desire to practice our Catholic Christian faith openly and faithfully.

So how exactly does one receive a call to become a deacon today? That answer is as diverse as the men who respond to it.

- **For one of my classmates, it was at the invitation of a religious person who saw he had a very special characteristic and she felt this would be a beautiful thing to share with the Church.**

- **For another, he came to a conversion experience from another faith and, in the process, felt that he was called to do more.**

- Another was a refugee from another country as a young man and was serving his new community with an servant attitude and always placed his faith in the God that delivered him.

- For another still, he came from a family who endured great poverty while living in the Appalachian Mountains; his love of the least of God's people became in him a burning desire to fulfill his faith's teachings on social justice and charity.

As for me, the call came as an extension of the same call that I had responded to throughout all my life: to live a life of service to others. The call to serve was first manifested in my life --

1. as a young altar boy and later as a lector in the Catholic church that I grew up in;

2. then when I served my country by joining the United States Air Force – as a commissioned officer,

3. then as a husband and then, in time, as a father of a small family;

4. then continuing to serve my local community through being a taxpayer, a concerned citizen-volunteer, and then finally;

5. to serve my God in a very special way: to be a servant-leader, a man focused on the welfare of others instead of just my own.

The reason for this book is simply this: in all of my research prior to responding to my own call, I greatly enjoyed reading the likes of the past saints as well as future saints. I like the idea of being able to respond through the example of others and how they lived their Catholic Christian faith. I love reading about those saints' endurance in the struggles that they faced, how they respond to "the dark night of the soul" when they were truly seeking God's face and God somehow was not responding in the manner they wanted but He was always there. Finally, I looked to reading about their final triumphs: how the saint's spiritual lives were increased beyond what they ever expected, how their earthy ministries were blessed, and how they all grew in their faith all the days of their lives.

However, in all of my research prior to entering into diaconate formation, there was not a single book that was written specifically about the formation experience for permanent deacons. To some extent, I wished that a book like this had been available prior to me starting the process. So responding to this unique need, I hope that this book will, at least, provide any future reader an idea of what it's like to prepare for religious formation as a Roman Catholic diocesan deacon in America today.

Like any great object of tremendous personal value, the response to this divine call involves a great deal of sacrifice and perseverance not only at a personal level, but also in my case – also at a family level. My entire formation experience had to have my spouse's permission – from the start – middle -- end. My positive response to God's call could not have taken place without the personal approval and constant support of my spouse Cindy.

I've been blessed with a number of people that have been in my life that assisted me along the way that, hopefully at the end of this book, I can look back with great thanksgiving to Almighty God who placed them in my life to serve His Ultimate purpose. However, in the end, all this book can do is give an accurate mirror about what my experience was like being in formation. But if you are feeling the gentleness of God's constant whispering in your life, my prayer is that you will discover it, acknowledge and positively respond to it. Then, with the help of the Holy Spirit, you will discover the appropriate path for you to fulfill that vocation – that calling – that invitation to serve Almighty God and His people .

In retrospect, going through diaconate formation was similar to my previous military formation when I attended the United States Air Force Academy in Colorado Springs, Colorado, from June of 1980 to May of 1984. There was a saying at the Academy that also rings true when I completed my diaconate formation. That saying is simply this **"there's only two times the place looks good: that is before you get there, and after you leave."**

Now having been ordained, I can now gently look back at my formation time at the Saint Stephen's Center for Diaconate Studies, realizing that time that I spent there provided me with some of the greatest opportunities to learn about my faith – from great, inspirational and spiritual instructors and mentors. This is where I met and worked with my future fourteen brother deacons and where I found my spiritual director. Moreover, my formation also prepared me for the greatest mission of my life: to serve the people of God for as long as I live.

So I am honored that you are interested to read my story – all of the Good, the Bad and the knowing of the touch of the Divine Love of God in my life thus far. It was a joy to write this book for you and your future life of service. It is my constant prayer that this book will be an inspiration as well motivate you to become a fellow servant for our faith – in whatever way Our Lord calls you to use your talents to serve our brothers and sisters in your parishes and in our world today, wherever they may be.

Now, my brother or sister in Christ Jesus, may Almighty God – Father, Son and Holy Spirit -- bless you, keep you and protect you and your loved ones all the days of your life. Amen.

Albert L. Feliu
Deacon -- Archdiocese of Atlanta GA
Lilburn, GA

"Hello Lord, it's me again..."

The title of this chapter is probably the best way to express how I felt in the beginning.

There is a very cute cartoon of a small boy who is kneeling down next to his little bed to pray and he opens his prayer with "Hello Lord, it's me again." So often, as we tried to develop our personal prayer life, we're often just struggling to get started. So the image of a small child starting with "Hello Lord" is almost the perfect way to start. No matter how old we are in this life, compared to the Infinite and Loving God that always existed, we all look small and adorable to Him!

So speaking of starting, please allow me to introduce myself.

My name is Albert Feliu, and this is my story that I would like to share with you now.

I was born on August 9, 1960, along with an identical twin brother Robert in Brooklyn, New York. My older siblings, a brother - Leopold Junior - and my sister - Elina - combined with our parents completed our family. My parents, Leopold Senior and Francoise met when they both lived in New York City in the early 1950s.

Desiring a better life for himself, he left Puerto Rico as a teenager to join his sister who was living in New York City at the time. Leo, as he was called by his friends, did a three-year stint in the newly formed United States Air Force and was honorably discharged in 1953. Now eligible to attend college under the old GI Bill, my dad elected to study chemistry at Saint John University as his undergraduate major. However, because of this course of study, he also had a heavy concentration of higher level of mathematics, Latin and German. My mother Fran was the eldest of six children graduating from high school in Newark Valley, which is located in upstate New York. She came to work in New York City, working as a receptionist/secretary at CBS Television. I was told that they had been introduced by a mutual friend and they developed a serious relationship quickly. After a very short courtship, they decided to get married.

The marriage, however, was very strained from the beginning. It was a combination of not enough money coming in with the combined increasing expenses of a rapidly growing family. My older brother came first and then within fourteen months, my sister Elina was born to this new family. My brother and I came seven years later – completing our family at four children – three boys and one girl.

Growing up in New York City in the early 1960's, as much as I can remember it, was a fairly gentle and safe time. We were not poor but probably, we would be considered on the lower end of the middle class scale. Our city block had about eight large apartment buildings that would look like it formed a defensive perimeter, just like the walls of Jerusalem! Living in New York City even back then, it was a mixing pot of all different people of backgrounds and religions. We lived in a predominantly Orthodox Jewish neighborhood in Brooklyn. On Saturday mornings, we could see our Jewish neighbors walking to and from their temples. On Sunday mornings, they all would see us walking and forth to our church! Additionally, for my mother to be pushing an infant pram with two small but active boys made her the local neighborhood celebrity! I do remember with great affection that in the springtime, my mother's pram would be filled with all sorts of goodies and cookies the older Jewish women had made in preparation for Passover.

The apartment complex that we lived in Brooklyn had a large grass playing field area in the center of the city block that had matching outside water showers that all the kids played under in the summer when the water was turned on. We also had matching playgrounds on the north and south sides at each end. One of the things that I do remember with great clarity was the great 1965 blackout. My mother had taken my twin brother and I grocery shopping at the old A&P grocery store when all of a sudden, everything went black. So after a couple of minutes, we figured out that the electricity wasn't coming back on any time soon and we slowly made our way out of the store and walked home. Since the store was probably only a couple of city blocks away, the walk home wasn't too bad and police officers used to walk a beat so they were out directing traffic – both cars and people. I never felt like we were in any sort of physical danger – even at 9:00 o'clock at night! Finally after getting home, we met a few hundred of our local neighbors that had come out the apartment buildings – all wondering what had gone wrong.

Neighbors were usually friendly and kind to each other, because since we were living in an apartment building, we normally saw them at least once a day. Our family was lucky to have a New York City Fire Department fireman by the name of Joe Lennon with his beautiful family as our very good neighbor and friend. "Uncle Joe", as he was known to us, was a huge fireman, standing over 6'4" who had been married and blessed with two teenage daughters and two sons at that time that we knew them. Joe was lucky enough to walk to work at the local firehouse. I also remember with great affection the time that we actually got a tour of the nearest firehouse while he was at work! As a five-year old, climbing on a huge NYFD fire truck, petting the firehouse dog, and ringing the large brass bell was a great highlight that was not easily forgotten on a small child!

Walking home one time during the summer, one of "Uncle Joe's" best tricks was something he could do with me and my twin brother. We sometimes saw him in the distance and start running towards him. At the very last moment, bending down with his arms wide open, he could scoop me and my twin simultaneously with those two massive arms, flipping us up and plant each one of us on each shoulder and then carry us both back to the apartment building. My mother had kept in touch with his wife after we had moved away in 1966. Ultimately, he had retired from the New York City Fire Department and relocated to Pennsylvania where he died.

Our family had always been Catholic with each of the children being baptized very shortly after birth and attending Sunday Mass at Resurrection Church in Brooklyn, New York. It was also nice that we could walk to church and then either walk back to our house for lunch or go visit my grandmother who lived in Queens. Grandma always had a large box filled with toys and she seemed to put up with her grandchildren quite well anytime we visited her and my Aunt Jean who was living with her at the time!

All in all, living in New York at that time was really quite nice and quite civilized. Kids could go out and play by themselves, the parents used to call their kids by the old-fashioned cellular method – calling at the top of their lungs from the windows of their apartments to the children below! Of course, in the summertime when the ice cream man came around in his white truck, he literally created a small city of hungry children who pestered their parents to no end when he stopped and the ice cream was bought.

My father in 1966 had been hired by General Electric as an industrial hygienist. His specific responsibility was to serve as the official representative for General Electric when the federal authorities inspected GE factories for meeting Occupational Health and Safety Act or OSHA regulations. General Electric had recently moved their corporate headquarters to Easton, Connecticut, from New York City and our family soon moved out of New York City into the suburbs of Bridgeport, Connecticut.

My older brother and sister would start attending Notre Dame Boys and Girls High School – Class of 1969 and 1970 -- in Fairfield and Bridgeport, respectively, and my twin brother and I would attend St. John Byzantine Church School which was a Greek Orthodox Church in Bridgeport. For us twins, it was a family oriented school that could accept us so soon after our move. However, later in time, we left St. John's to attend St. Teresa's Roman Catholic Church in Trumbull, just north of Bridgeport for Sunday Mass and then to attend the school doing the week.

St. Teresa's Church is a beautiful, classic cruciform church that had been built very soon after World War II in response to the large growth of families that resulted in the rise of the baby boomers that were being born at that time. St. Teresa Elementary School was lucky enough to have both priests and nuns that lived on the parish grounds because the elementary school was so heavily attended by parish families. While we were there for 2nd and 3rd grade, classes were taught by predominantly religious sisters with additional female lay people as instructors. Many of the people that attended St. Teresa's worked in the Bridgeport area, which was a very large industrial town from the turn-of-the-century. Bridgeport had grown into an even larger city and a major center of US industrial manufacturing during World War II.

Of course, at that time, the annual celebration of the Sacraments of the Holy Eucharist for the young second graders as well as Confirmation for the sixth-graders was always a very large parish event. Each sacrament had their own dedicated Mass that was always packed to the last seat and sometimes including the choir loft! Regular Sunday Masses were very heavily attended with the expectation was that if your family wasn't in the pews at least 15 minutes before the start of Mass; they were going to be standing for that Mass - period. In addition, St. Teresa's had a beautiful classic organ that was in the choir loft on the second floor. Especially during Midnight Mass at Christmas time, seeing the High Holy Mass from that vantage point was a quite beautiful experience.

I had the opportunity to start altar serving when I was in the fourth grade, and the altar servers at that time wore the classic black cassock and long white surplus. Of course, at that same time, the worldwide conclave of the Catholic bishops being assembled in Rome from 1963 – 1968 known as Vatican II was being concluded. Part of the reforms introduced from that assembly was the new changes to the Mass. As the changes from Vatican II were being shared with the people, I remember the Introduction of the Sign of Peace. As it was explained to us, only family members could exchange a brief kiss with each other, only on the cheek, and with everyone else in the parish, we were politely instructed to only shake hands with our neighbors! We also didn't need to make it look like we were running for office by shaking everyone's hand in sight!!

When I was in middle school, I was able to start training as a young lector. That was a very exciting time because St. Teresa's had a beautiful marble pulpit that was on the right side of the altar as it faced the people. Miss Patty, the parish trainer, who was in charge of all lector training in the parish, was very encouraging to me. I believe that encouragement from her led me to develop some of my skills in public speaking. Of course, once you get trained in the Catholic Church, they actively put you to work! I remember in the springtime season that one Sunday, none of the lectors showed up for their assigned Masses and I ended up doing all four of the Masses that morning.

By the time I walked home, it was 1:30 in the afternoon and my mother was furious with me because she thought I had gone off on my own and not even gone to church that Sunday! Remember, back in 1974, this was well before cellular phones were around and the only way that you communicated with your family was either you told a neighbor to tell your parents for you or you had to use a landline to call home!

Unfortunately, my mother was having some real difficulties accepting some of the changes to the Mass as a result of Vatican II. She ended up leaving St. Teresa's Church to go to a small chapel in Monroe, Connecticut – the next town north of where we lived. This much smaller church that was still saying the Latin Mass in defiance of the local bishop. Ultimately, under pressure, that church would eventually close down and my mother reluctantly returned to St. Teresa's. However, she was always with her crystal rosary and I always remember her trying to pray during the Mass.

She also still insisted on wearing the mantilla which for older Catholics is the lace head covering that women use to wear on their heads when they attended Mass. Of course, if you enter into St. Peter's Basilica in the Vatican or are ever granted an audience with the Holy Father the Pope, women are still required to wear this beautiful article of clothing.

In 1976, as result of my mother's departure and re-entry into the church, my brother and I made our confirmation together at 16. At that time, the normal age for making confirmation was still around 12 or 13 so it was somewhat difficult to make our confirmation around so many younger kids. However, I remember the day as being quite sunny and the bishop at the time, Walter W. Curtis, was rather straightforward with the kids. I remember him reminding us of the importance of our faith and to be prepared to be "soldiers for Christ." At that time, the Catholic Life Teen movement was just starting to come into its own at our parish. I remember wanting to go to Mass at 5:30 p.m. Sunday evenings and then, afterward, pizzas and sodas would be ordered for the teens and we would have an open recreation time period in the school gym.

It was during that time, I also was introduced to the first Catholic deacon in my life. His name was Deacon Martin Ryan, a transitional deacon and he had been assigned to our parish while he was preparing for his ordination to the priesthood. He worked with the young teenagers as part of his ministry with us. In addition, he was extremely personable with a very powerful preaching style. He made the Gospel come alive and that was very appealing to teenagers who came to Mass both on Sunday Mornings with their parents and also on Sunday evenings when Mass was celebrated with us as the primary audience. Also, he had some of the most colorful stoles I had ever seen!

In June of 1978, I graduated high school and at that time felt that I had a calling to go into the military service. My older brother Leo finished his high school education at Notre Dame Boys High School in Fairfield, Connecticut, and went on to Stevens Institute of Technology in Hoboken, New Jersey. He eventually completed his university education and was sworn in as a second lieutenant in the United States Air Force in 1976. Completing training as a navigator, Leo was assigned to a USAF B-52 alert crew within Strategic Air Command in North Dakota until the summer of 1982.

I eventually went to Eastern Connecticut State College in Willimantic, Connecticut, which is approximately 20 miles east of Hartford towards the Rhode Island side of the state. Additionally, I was taking United States Air Force Reserve Officer Training Corps (ROTC) classes at the University of Connecticut at Storrs, traveling to the main campus once a week for classes. This was being done with the expectation that I would apply to go the United States Air Force Academy in the very near future. I would also meet the woman that I would eventually marry, a small and sweet girl of Italian and Polish heritage by the name of Cynthia Ann Lapadula.

We met when we were both taking an American political science class and then started dating soon after that. Since my high school grades were not sufficient to enter into the Air Force Academy directly, my alternate strategy was to show the Academy Admissions committee that I could do college-level work so I concentrated on hardcore basic academic classes only.

However, while on a summer seminar, I had met a first classmen from the United States Air Force Academy by the name of Charles Kelly Buckley who really inspired me to pursue my military career starting from the Academy instead pursuing a commission through ROTC. In addition, during my sophomore year, I also started to be a resident assistant so that I could save a little money on room and board. So by the end of my first academic year, I had met the woman that would become the love of my life, I was making decent grades, and was constantly missing church on a regular basis. Although Eastern Connecticut had the opportunity to have a Catholic Mass said on campus on Sunday evenings, I eventually drifted away from my faith to pursue my own desires of more sleep, Sunday evening movie nights, and enjoying my overall college experience.

In April of 1980, I received the news that I was looking for. I had been accepted to the United States Air Force Academy for the Class of 1984 at Colorado Springs, Colorado, and received a mandatory report date of June 20, 1984. Within a week, I had made preparations to leave Eastern CT with an Associates of Arts degree, saying goodbye to some close friends, and had roughly about five weeks of summer vacation before I had to report.

Cindy had known about my desire to attend the Academy and our final weeks together were both bittersweet and quick. She had been a great and positive influence on my life thus far and we did attend Mass together either in her hometown of Bristol or when she came to visit while I was at school. But going out west and serving my country was really my greatest desire.

However, my academic career at the Academy was not as successful as it had been at Eastern Connecticut. Within a short time, I found myself falling behind my classmates in both academic and military studies, of course, feeling homesick and missing my girlfriend, and generally questioning what the heck I had done to my life! Had I stayed at Eastern Connecticut, I would have graduated within two years, and then receive my commission as a second lieutenant by June of 1982. With the election of President Reagan in 1980, the United States military was surging in both renewal and appreciation from the Nation. So why did I want to languish for four more years at this remote mountain prison? However, cooler heads would eventually prevail, I survived my first year, and eventually I would graduate with my classmates in the Class of 1984 on May 30th with President Reagan as our main commencement speaker.

During that time from 1980 - 1984, my personal relationship to Cindy deepened and we got engaged on Christmas Eve, 1983 and tried to set a time of June of 1984 to get married. Cindy had been asking about getting married at the Academy Chapel, Our Lady of the Skies, but I was dead set against it. I told her that I had spent four years of my life there and the last thing I wanted to do was get married there as well! We eventually compromised and got married at the same church her own parents had gotten married at St. Casimir's in Plymouth, Connecticut. We eventually set a date for June 15, 1984. As a matter of record, I have never forgotten my wedding day because that day was also my first payday as a second lieutenant in the United States Air Force! I received the princely sum of $707 for my first semi-monthly paycheck and felt that I was totally rich.

At that time, of all of my brothers and sisters, I had been the first one to get married and our wedding on that Friday evening was filled with a beautiful wedding Mass and with a very loud and joyful wedding reception.

As a result of our decision to be in the US Air Force, we eventually spent the first five years of our married life together in California for four months, Upper Michigan for 13 months, and eventually England for three years. During that time, our married Catholic faith had been placed on hold. I had been working as a commissioned officer in a security police squadron and had to work weekends and nights. So my attendance at Mass was probably only restricted to special occasions such as Christmas and Easter if I wasn't working on those days. However, in the late 1980s and especially with the thawing of the Cold War relationships between the United States and the Soviet Union, as well avoiding the prospect to being sent back to another air force base in the upper northern United States, I elected to resign my officer's commission and was honorably discharged from the United States Air Force in May of 1989.

We returned back to first Wethersfield and then to Bristol, Connecticut, to be closer to Cindy's family. I would eventually start my graduate business degree program at the University of Hartford in West Hartford, Connecticut, and Cindy went to work at Post College which later became Teikyo Post University in Waterbury, Connecticut. She worked with predominantly the freshman class, doing early intervention for students who were academically at risk. She definitely had a gift working with these young people and she gave herself totally to making sure her kids stayed in school and not leave prematurely. I was completing my graduate business MBA degree program in 16 months while simultaneously working as a full-time marketing analyst at Travelers Insurance in Hartford, Connecticut. I was making better money than the average graduate student at the time but still wanting to make a more professional salary and much more than what I had made in the Air Force.

In 1991, Cindy had reminded me that during our five years in the military, I had specifically asked that we put off having children but she had finally run out of patience with that decision. Celebrating my 31st birthday, we had a great dinner to celebrate my acceptance into business school. Very soon after that, actually on the first day that I started graduate school in September, right after Labor Day of that year, Cindy had announced that she was pregnant! So here I was starting my first day of class, not only as a brand new MBA student, it also has a new father-to-be! Needless to say, I had a great deal of personal motivation for doing well in graduate school. My first child, Christina Catherine, was born on May 13, 1991, healthy and happy, but also in the middle of my finals week of my spring semester.

However, as I said earlier, I had a great deal of energy, and with a little luck, I secured my first civilian job six weeks after graduating from business school. This was a special noteworthy achievement since during that time in 1990-1991, because Connecticut was going through a major economic downturn. But the new job was going to be located in Columbus, Georgia, and February of 1992, I moved in advance of my soon growing family to Columbus. Cindy had elected to finish the spring semester at Teikyo-Post University and remained in our rental apartment in Bristol, Connecticut, while I went ahead and started my new position as a marketing product manager for a large US based-insurance company in Columbus.

As I was getting settled into my new job and hometown, I was looking around for a Catholic parish to join. St. Anne's Roman Catholic Church was roughly about 6 miles from where I will eventually move to and the pastor was an older Irish priest by the name of Father John Kevin Boland. Father Boland was probably my first priest that I developed a great deal of professional and personal affection for since I left St Teresa's in 1978. A humble man of gentle disposition who always enjoyed a good laugh and was constantly asking about your family, he was always prepared on Sunday Mass with a good, insightful homily. In July of 1992, Cindy had also joined the St. Anne's parish staff as their youth minister, so now our faith was starting to take an even greater significance.

In 1994, my family's life suffered a dramatic shift. My mother Francoise who had several heart attacks in her early and mid-50s, had suffered a final massive heart attack and died on Thursday, December 15. A smoker most of her life, my mother had lost about 50% of her heart muscle as a result of her sickness at the time she died. My older brother Leo, who had left the Air Force in the early 1980's and was now living with my mom since her divorce from my dad in 1989, found her outside while she was hanging wet laundry. By the time he reached her, she was not breathing and was starting to turn blue. He called the 911 emergency ambulance response and they tried to resuscitate her as best they could. But ultimately, she was declared dead on arrival. While I had been in the Air Force, she and my father had divorced by the summer of 1989 and the divorce had been extremely difficult and bitter for both of them. My father had eventually relocated out of Connecticut and moved to Winter Park, Florida, a community just outside of Orlando, to be closer to his brother Rueben and restarted his life there.

As adults, it is always difficult to deal with the death of your parents. Under the best circumstances, you can look back to hopefully an example of a life well lived, filled with joy, family, and faith. Unfortunately in my mother's case, her last years had brief respites of joy, but there had been periods of severe bitterness and resentment. She had been attending Mass more often, ultimately reconciling the fact that the Sunday Mass was not going back to Latin and that she would have to adjust to it accordingly.

When I got the phone call at work from my distraught wife, who herself had received the word from my older brother's message on our home answering machine, I was first stunned. My own relationship with my mother had not been the best. She had made it a point of always calling my wife between 10 and 11 o'clock every Saturday morning and Cindy generally look forward to these phone calls. I saw these calls from her as being weekly annoyances and distractions. Although usually the result of my contributions to these conversations was just "yes Ma, things are going fine, hope to see you soon, okay, talk to you next week." My most effective contribution to those phone calls she initiated was about 30 seconds – max. So with her sudden and unexpected death, I had to work the phone and make the calls to try to get us out of Columbus, Georgia, to return back to Hartford, Connecticut. Of course, one of the first things that would stop immediately were those Saturday morning phone calls.

Because of the Christmas holiday season, it was very difficult to get an immediate plane flight out of Columbus that day. However, on Friday, the 16th of December, we flew, through a connection in Atlanta, to Bradley International Airport in Windsor Locks, Connecticut, to join the rest of my family. My older brother Leo was in charge of the initial arrangements and my mother's funeral Mass was going to be on the following Monday.

At this point, I'd started to pray. I don't remember exactly what I was praying for but I do remember for the first time in a long time, I was actually seeking Almighty God's help. My mother had been only 67 when she died, which in today's modern terms, is really far too young for an older woman. She'd taken well to being a doting grandmother and to this day, my only saving grace with her was the fact that we had given her grandchildren to enjoy and love. But it was during this time, I really started to feel God's presence in my life like never before.

He had always been present in my life, of course, but it was now this time of personal sorrow, I was now actively seeking Him.

Your Servant is listening...

s I flew home with my small family, I was trying to think of so many things. Inevitably, when one loses your parents, the first question that pops into your mind is **"Why God?"** She was an older single woman, she had many friends, and her Catholic Christian faith seemed reasonably strong. She tried to make herself available to those who cared about her and she still pursued an active habit of reading many books every year. A person of service herself, she joined with the other retirees in our community, volunteering as an election official during local elections. Always a grandmother, she prided herself on her desire to spoil her grandchildren with many good gifts and often being able to get those items on sale – she never ever paid retail prices!!

Her personal life was also changing significantly as well. Although Fran had been the one that initiated the divorce, she felt that she was finally coming into her own. With all her children now grown and living their own lives, she felt more confident in pursuing some of the things that she had deferred because of her children, like getting some post-high school education at Sacred Heart University in Fairfield, Connecticut. She'd never graduated from college, she had been thrust into the workplace to support herself and own mother who had been widowed at a fairly early age and had been married relatively quickly.

As the airplane approached Hartford, Connecticut, I started trying to start composing what would be her funeral eulogy. I've spoken with my siblings earlier that day and I felt that this was the last gift that I can give her, so I asked if I could do this on their behalf. They were appreciative that they didn't have to do this task themselves. But I truly felt at this time, it was the start of the active work of the Holy Spirit in my life. Although my professional career, at that point in time, I had been reasonably successful, was making decent money, and had the respect of my coworkers and superiors. From my faith's perspective, I tried to at least play a small part in my parish life. With Cindy actively working at St. Anne's, I tried to be supportive of her needs and did what she asked of me. Being a dishwasher at various fundraiser dinners for the kids and teaching the occasional sacramental prep class was the extent of my faith activity. Later, I would be retrained as a lector and serve at the Masses I was scheduled for. But at 34, I was getting restless in my search for personal and professional fulfillment. My mother's death, to some extent, accelerated what I felt was the start of my vocation to serve the Catholic Church. As a result of that gentle prodding; I knew something else was happening.

Cindy's parents, Fanny and Angelo, were kind enough to let us stay with them in their home in Bristol, a city located about 20 miles west of Hartford. Cindy's mother Fanny volunteered to watch Christina and Michael while we traveled from Hartford to Trumbull, about 50 miles away, to attend my mother's wake service on Sunday afternoon. My mother's sister, Suzanne, was the youngest of the six siblings in their family and she came down from Upstate New York to be with our family during that weekend. Suzanne had always been generous to us; she herself had been married to a successful optometrist and had been graced with two lovely daughters of her own. Suzanne always had a bright, bubbly and positive personality. My mother, on the other hand, having been the eldest in her family assumed the position of more of elder sister or proxy mother. However, between the two of them, they shared a very lively relationship and sisterhood. When we traveled to Suzanne's home in Gilbertsville, New York, she always made us feel at home. However, on that day, I began to appreciate the role that Suzanne would play, not only in my mother's life, but also in my own.

We went to Mass at St. Theresa's at 11:30 on Sunday morning, the 18th, and to some extent, I was taken aback. I had not been there since June of 1984 when I came home from the Academy but before I got married. The large church that I had served in as an altar boy and lector, where I had received my first sacraments, and attended elementary school for two years, now seemed so empty. The Mass that would have been filled to capacity by 11:15 for an 11:30 a.m. start time was now roughly about a quarter filled. The high altar had been moved down and even my old pastor, Father Louis DeProfio, was still serving there but was moving at a much slower speed. It almost seemed too out of the ordinary but yet this beautiful church had been so much of my Catholic and personal sacramental history now almost seemed like I was entering into an episode of the "Twilight Zone". However, we found a familiar pew close to the altar and participated in Mass.

At the end of Mass, I had recognized the cantor, Ms. Vivian Burr. Vivian had always had a beautiful voice and it was very comforting to hear that voice once again at that Mass. When I approached her with my wife and my aunt, she was briefly taken aback. She hadn't seen me since I left to go to the Air Force Academy and even though she had not aged a day; she couldn't believe how big I had gotten – her words! She also had been very kind to comment that she had just seen my mother at her assigned polling station during the elections last November. Her most considerate comment was how my mother had always been very kind to her when she saw her.

She asked us if we had selected a cantor for my mother's funeral Mass. My older brother had made some of the preliminary funeral arrangements but we had not made had any confirmation that a cantor was available for her

Mass. She graciously said that she would be more than happy to sing at my mother's funeral. I thanked her, on behalf of my family, and told her that we would be visiting with my mother later on that day for her visitation. She once again offered her condolences and we left to go to the funeral home.

Sunday afternoon was the date for her vigil/visitation and we traveled to the local funeral home that always advertises in the parish bulletin – Cyril Mullins. The people at the funeral home had been extremely generous with us and especially given the time of season that it was, only a week before Christmas, it almost seemed anti-climatic. The holiday season was in full swing, complete with the beautiful Christmas lights on the outside of the building and yet somewhat dark and sad on the inside. Turning to enter into the funeral parlor inside, I looked for my mother's assigned room. My older brother had worked with my aunt on the final funeral arrangements with a suitable choice from her wardrobe selected for her viewing, the staff said that my mother's body was ready for us to be with. As I entered into the assigned room for her, I finally was with my mother once again.

She was wearing a fine dress and she looked immaculate. Her body, of course, was very cold to the touch. The Rosary that she had all those years was in her hands, the crystal beads reflecting the soft light in the room. As tears glistened in my eyes, the only thing that I could keep on repeating to myself was "Oh mom, oh mom, I'm so sorry." At that point, I remember Cindy coming beside me at the casket and offering her support. I felt both shame and loss. I felt the shame because I hadn't always been the best son to her in the last years of her life and now at loss because she would no longer be in my life or the lives of my wife and our children. Some of her friends came to pay their final respects and recalled some of the positive things that she had done for them recently.

Later on that evening, I finished her eulogy. I remember sitting at my in-laws dining room table with some handwritten notes that I had composed and thinking "I hope that this does her justice." Part of the shame that I had felt earlier that day was now being replaced with a sense of hope, knowing that the pain that she had felt in this life could no longer affect her. She had shown some great signs of personal redemption in the latter part of her life, and that she had been surrounded by an army of friends and extended family. The Sunday that had started off as being tragic, was now ending with a sense of relief and purpose. But needless to say, the same voice that I started to listen to on the airplane home, was now the same voice that was giving me the strength in order to be able to give her the honor and respect that I had denied her in her life.

The next morning, we drove from Bristol to Trumbull back to the funeral home. There was a morning viewing period prior to the Funeral Mass and we needed to be there early to receive any additional friends who came to visit. There are a number of people that had not been able to attend her funeral that wanted to at least pay their respects that morning. Several high school friends of myself and my brother, also came. We are now grown up ourselves – married and even with our own children -- came to show their personal support. It was good to see old friends, it'd been at least 20 years since I had seen some of them, and now we all shared stories about our new collective responsibilities as spouses and parents!

The morning viewing time was about two hours and at the conclusion of that time, we had a brief family prayer service at the casket. Suzanne, my brothers Robert and Leo Jr. with myself and Cindy, joined together as family to say three Hail Mary's, the Our Father, and a Glory Be. Unfortunately, a priest or deacon was unavailable to be with us at the funeral home and once again the Holy Spirit gave me the strength to give this gift to my mother.

The funeral home staff gently asked us to start traveling to St. Teresa's Church, telling us that they would have my mother there in about an hour. The casket was then closed for the final time but prior to my leaving; I had placed a small wallet size picture of my new family in her casket. Unbeknownst to me, my wife on that previous Sunday afternoon had done the same thing.

Cindy was showing tremendous strength during this time, but she had shared a great deal about our family with my mother. Her topics included but were not limited to the joys and struggles of motherhood, the personal sharing between mother and daughter-in-law and other things that she kept in her own memories were now starting to flood back. But it was time to travel to the church that we had all worshiped as a family. Now, it was time for us to travel to God's house.

We arrived at St. Theresa's at 10:30 a.m. and Vivian was already in place on the right side of the altar. We had pre-selected a number of hymns with her whom she later sang with great emotion and feeling. My mother's two brothers also met us in the back of the church. The younger one and my namesake, Albert and his wife Janet greeted us first. Jimmy had traveled in from New York City by himself and got there a little bit later. It'd been awhile since I've seen both of these relatives. Albert had been a professional pharmacist in northern New Jersey for a number of years and Jimmy had worked in corporate America after serving in the United States Merchant Marines. Both of them looked extremely worn out. For them, they were coming to grips that their eldest sister had passed and it was taking its toll on each of them. Janet had not met my wife Cindy and we all commented how much older we had all gotten since we had last been together at some family function, probably held at Suzanne's house some years past. Suzanne's home in the country had lots of land for all of us to gather and we could all see each other and, of course, Grandmother and Aunt Jean.

At the appointed time, the funeral hearse arrived and we met the coffin with my mother's body at the rear of the church. St. Theresa has an approximately 300 foot "runway aisle" from the back of the Church to the main altar. It seems tremendously symbolic that the casket that had her human remains was now approaching the altar where our Eucharistic Lord would come into our presence during her Funeral Mass.

Father DeProfio had been my pastor when I was still a young child and for a second I couldn't believe that, outside of his face that I remember, he seemed so much older. Of course, when he saw me and my family, he couldn't believe that I had actually grown up too!

About 75 people came to my mother's funeral Mass and in the midst of this large church, it seems almost sparse. However, all of the people that did show up had strong and personal affection for my mother. Many of her friends, from the local library, the church, the local Republican Party, or anywhere else that knew her and had been part of her life made the dedicated effort to pay their last respects.

Suzanne did the first reading from the Book of Lamentations and my brother Robert did the second reading from the New Testament, one of St. Paul's Letters. Father DeProfio read from the Beatitudes and gave the homily. Once again, I looked in the church that I grew up in and all the memories started flooding back. I glanced at the pew that my mother usually took, remembering how she used to pray with her crystal rosary, I looked at the pulpit that I used to read from, the size of the Main Altar, and also noticed the brilliance of the large gold-finished tabernacle that morning. All of the sights were both reassuring and nostalgic. I could not change the fact that my mother had died, but I could take comfort in the fact that she received all of the graces of the Roman Catholic Church could afford to give her earthly remains and her immortal soul.

Finally, at the end of the prayer after communion, Father DeProfio announced that I had prepared a short reflection for my mother. At that point, I remember rising from the pew where I was sitting and going directly onto the main chair where Father was sitting and bowing down in front of him asking for his blessing. The reason why this is so unusual, is that unbeknownst to me, I was sub-consciously imitating, from years of attending Mass, what I had seen either a deacon or concelebrating priest does before proclaiming the Gospel, by getting a blessing first from the presiding priest.

21

This is also the same action that a deacon does before he proclaims the Gospel to the People of God! I remember him gently asking me to stand up and start the reflection.

The following was her eulogy that I had composed for her as my last spiritual gift for her:

My Brothers and Sisters in Christ:

Before I start this eulogy, I would like to thank both Monsignor Louis DeProfio for celebrating this Mass and Ms. Vivian Burr as our musical soloist, for all their help in honoring my mother today. By being here, in this church again, represents a personal reunion for me. Monsignor DeProfio was my parish priest who I grew up with, I served under him first as an altar boy at 12 and then later as a lector.

If I remember correctly Monsignor, we were both younger 20 years ago when I was first here, but it is good to see you again today. Ms. Burr worked with my mother at various political functions within the Republican Party here in town. In fact, she had mentioned to me that she had just seen my mother at the election polling place, working very hard as a volunteer that day. It is good to see you both again and your collective presence honors our family. Thank you.

To all of you here, on behalf of our family - Lee, Elina, Robert and myself, I want to wish each and every one of you, a very Merry Christmas and a Happy and Prosperous New Year in 1995. We appreciate the time and energy it took each and every one of you to be here and say goodbye to our mother and your sister, neighbor or friend - Francoise. It means a great deal to her for you to be here today.

As we enter into this Christmas Season, I am reminded of an event that happened to me. I am privileged to work for a company called AFLAC in Columbus, Georgia. It was started by a man by the name of John Amos, a good Christian that would start national sales meetings with a prayer, to thank God for the gifts of prosperity, friendship and service to others.

The man who was responsible for first interviewing me into this fine company is a gentleman by the name of Trinidad Villegas. I worked for him for about nine months and it was a pleasure for me personally. Shortly after I had started with the company, his father, Trinidad Senior, suffered a massive heart attack on Good Friday - 1992 and passed away on that day. On Easter Tuesday, at the funeral service, the priest, Father Gerald Schreck, one of the priests at Saint Anne's Parish in Columbus, Georgia -- and my current parish -- said something that struck me. He said:

"There is never a good time to die. But if we are true to our faith and believe the teachings of the Church and of the message in the Holy Gospel, then maybe the most appropriate time to die is at Easter time. Because it is the salvation of the Resurrection given to us by Almighty God through his only Son and the promise of eternal life with our Lord Jesus Christ that provides us with the hope we all will be together with Him forever someday."

I would like to amend that thought for my mother's passing.

If we believe in the Resurrection of the Body and to see the Kingdom of God when we pass from this world to our new home in heaven, then we are able to do so because Almighty God sent down to this fragile earth His only Son, Jesus Christ, in that

23

single event that started our road to eternal salvation --that being His birth to Mary and Joseph at Bethlehem at Christmas time.

So we should, in fact, take comfort that Francoise has achieved - at Christmas time this year - in her passing and receiving what we all will eventually seek and find, being accepted in to the Kingdom of God, secured by the life, death and resurrection of His only Son, our Lord Jesus Christ.

My comfort is that at this special time of the year, we remember that our salvation is a reality because He was here among us and died to lead us on the way to Almighty God's Glory. And His spiritual and physical journey to be among us on this Earth, just as Francoise's journey in death, started at Christmas time.

To those of you that got the regular updates and briefings on our family's progress and was constantly subjected to viewing her grandmother's brag book full of photographs, on behalf of her grandchildren -- Christina Catherine and Michael Albert, I want to thank you for your personal and constant patience with her.

I believe that all the roles she portrayed in her life - daughter, sister, wife, mother, grandmother, friend, and neighbor - as she emerged into the role of being a grandmother, she was in her happiest days. But in that role of being a doting grandmother, she also sought to be connected to the people who mattered most; her family, her friends, and her Church.

Just as sure as she would call you for something or just to chat, she would also call me in Columbus, Georgia, at least once a week and tell me what she had done that week and the people she had seen: her calls and visits to her friends - Joanne Matthews, Mike and Gen Staviff and Jovita Barrett. In fact, her constant attention to these people re-enforced a fact we take for granted - that we cannot both be isolated from other people because it would be easier for our own personal comfort, to not to be involved with their problems and difficulties and be involved with other people at the same time.

In a time where we are constantly being subjected to increasing pressures from work and routines to make more time or just to keep up, we still want to be involved in other people's lives - to feel connected and to be needed.

We all must make that choice to be or not be connected with other people and she wanted to be connected to the people she cared about. Francoise wanted to still be included and to be there for the people she cared most about. And that is what made her special.

So as we leave here today to prepare to lay her into God's eternal rest, it is now time for us to be thankful for the many gifts we all can appreciate: Love, Happiness and Time, with the greatest of that being Time. The time to care and share with loved ones, the time to share with our friends and the time to make this world a better place for all.

Let us bow our heads in Prayer:

Almighty and Eternal God, accept into your keep the soul of your humble servant, Francoise. Grant her the eternal life promised by the Resurrection of Your Son, Our Lord Jesus Christ and with that mission that started with His life beginning on that first Christmas. Remind us that of all the Gifts you gave to us - Life, Happiness, Love, and Joy, the greatest of these is life, because it is through our life we receive the blessings of the others. Bless her and keep her until we all are together in your eternal glory. Amen.

I truly believe with all of my heart – then and today -- that the eulogy that I gave to my mother as a spiritual gift was, in fact, my first attempt at a homily. Now a homily, by definition in Canon Law, can only be given by ordained clergy – a deacon, priest, or bishop after the Gospel has been proclaimed. But given the circumstances and the time of season it was in the Catholic Church year, I felt compelled to try to, not only pay tribute to my mother but to tie in my limited understanding of Catholicism at that time, as well as to try to uplift the spirits of those who came to pay their last respects. As an unofficial feedback for what I had said, I passed the funeral director that was assigned to my mother's funeral, sitting near the pew where my wife was sitting. He looked at me, and smiled, and simply said softly "that was good, really good." As I passed my mother's friends, I also noticed that their demeanor had changed as well. They made eye contact with me, seeming to look a little more relaxed and smiled a little bit easier. They weren't crying as much.

At the end of Mass, her body was brought back to the church's entrance and once again taken out to the waiting hearse. My mother's final wishes had been that she wanted to be buried near her own mother in upstate New York, near Suzanne's home town. Because of the lateness of the year, her body would have to be placed in a temporary holding place in the cemetery in Gilbertsville, New York, which was about four hours from where we lived in Southwest Connecticut. Her body would be returned back to the funeral home for the remainder of that day and then brought up the next day to Upstate New York.

On behalf of my family, I thanked both Father DeProfio and Vivian for all they had done. This had been my first funeral as an adult, but yet the sense of loss that I was feeling was being replaced by a new sense of hope. I had returned back to the place where my spiritual life as a young boy had started. Yet on that day, I continued to feel a stirring starting to increase. I couldn't describe it but I was made aware that it was now present in my life.

My Uncle Jimmy was not so comforted by my mother's Funeral Mass. He seemed extremely distraught and was unable to come back with us for lunch. He left immediately from the church to return back to his home in New York City. Unfortunately, within a relatively short time frame, tragedy would strike our family again. About three weeks later, Uncle Jimmy, while chipping away at frozen ice on his car's windshield, he received the same fate as his older sister – suffering a massive heart attack and died shortly afterward. Unfortunately, he suffered the same fate as my mother and their mother: All had suffered massive heart attacks as the cause of death. He had loved his older sister a great deal and the thought of her loss was too much for him to handle that day.

To travel to Upstate New York the next day was a fairly easy ride. Although there was snow on the ground, the roads were relatively clear and we made the appointed time at the cemetery. The holding place where my mother's casket would be placed was actually hollowed out of the side of the small hill and looked very much like the Garden Tomb in Jerusalem without the large stone covering the entrance. Instead, two large wood doors opened into the large room that served as the final holding place before the bodies at last would be buried. Soon, there would be other coffins joining my mother before the spring thaw. Knowing that in advance, we made arrangements for a small brass plate to be attached to the coffin so that we knew the correct coffin would be selected at the time of her burial, which later took place in May of 1995.

Unfortunately, we could not get any local Catholic clergy to do any sort of prayer service at the cemetery, and once again, we gathered together as a family to pay our final respects to our mother and sister. After saying a few prayers, her sons and friends lifted her casket and placed it upon a holding rack in the tomb. In a few short months, the ground would be soft enough again for her body to be properly buried. Suzanne would make sure that my mother got a proper burial in the spring, but at this time, this was the best that we could do. With her body now safely placed in the temporary holding tomb, we gathered together praying for her soul and for each other and then gently closed the large doors and secured the lock. Safely inside, the earthly pilgrimage of her remains had completed its course and we prayed her soul was with her Creator and God.

As we drove home from the cemetery, my wife was being nostalgic. She had loved the place where my mother would be buried because it looks so peaceful. All I was thinking about was trying to get back to Bristol, Connecticut, and ultimately, to get back to our new home in Columbus, Georgia. It'd been a long week, being both mentally and emotionally exhausting, and with each passing day, it brought us closer to Christmas. Cindy's parents had been really great with the kids, being with our children and their youngest grandchildren. My son Michael was barely 7 months old and my daughter Christina was just shy of her fourth birthday. All in all, they had been given a great grace: their memories of their grandmother would be on their minds while she's still been alive.

My older brother Leo called me the next day with an unusual question. While going through my mother's things, he had discovered a full half closet filled with children's clothing, toys, and other things that my mother secretly had bought her grandchildren over the course of the past year. Knowing that luggage space would be short, I told him that he could just put all the stuff in the mail at his convenience.

Leaving Cindy's parent's house, after being with them for the last five days, our final night in Connecticut was actually spent at an airport hotel at Bradley Field. We treated ourselves to having a nice dinner with room service but I still felt restless that evening. At this point, it was nothing more than I could do for my mother other than pray for her soul, and even that, I felt inadequate to do that. My faith, at that point, had been lax and I had treated my prayer life so carelessly, I barely remembered how to pray the Rosary. However, the only thing that I wanted from my mother was her crystal rosary. My older brother helped me find it after the funeral and securing a small leather satchel, he gave it to me. That night, I just remember having it in my hand, feeling the small crystal beads and the dark metal chain in my palm. I know it always brought her a great sense of comfort, I still remember her fervently praying during Mass, her wearing the white mantilla - the long triangular edges of white lace draping off the side of her face.

Of course, the Bradley International Airport was fully packed by the time that we left about midmorning on Friday, the 23rd of December. While we were waiting for our plane in Hartford, I noticed a woman that had her head bowed down and was extremely modest. Somehow sensing that she was in some sort of pain, I went up to her and asked "Miss, is there something wrong?" She glanced up at me and replied "I'm on my way home because I just found out my father died." Her eyes gently misted with tears on her face. Again, something told me to talk to her a little bit about my experience that week. Quietly, I shared the loss of my own mother and also how my faith had sustained me at that time. For whatever reason, she looked into my eyes and I can see that she was gaining some sort of spiritual comfort in what I said. Turning to join my family, I just quietly said "God bless you." She replied simply "Thank you, and safe flight." My wife looked at me and asked me, "Do you know this woman?" I replied "No, I don't, but I just found out she lost her father and she's flying home to be with her family." Cindy just looked at me and said "I think it's time for us to go."

Eight hours later, we arrived back to our small home in Columbus. As we entered into the living room, the small artificial Christmas tree that she had just been put up in the first week of December almost seemed out of place. Of course, my daughter was thankful that she would be sleeping back in her own bed and she eagerly looked for her room to make sure it was still there! Having dragged all of the family luggage back into the house, I had the opportunity to just sit down and rest on my couch. The final sense of my mother's passing was just starting to hit me. The Saturday morning phone calls that I had resisted as her scheduled intrusion into my life was no longer going to be a problem. At that point, that's why my personal shame was in front of me. She had been constantly reaching for me and I had put her off –even to that last weekend.

Christmas Eve and Christmas Day seemed to come so quickly. As we gathered in the living room now on Christmas morning for the children to unwrap their presents, it just seems so unnecessary – where was the joy? To my surprise, my older brother had slipped some gifts that my mother had bought for her grandchildren into Cindy's suitcase: it was two Barbies for my little daughter and some baby clothes and toys for my son. Even then, I could now start to feel her spiritual presence because this Christmas wasn't about me; it was about the love of small children and the love of Our God towards humanity through His Gift of His Son in the baby Jesus. Even in death, my mother would not be denied a final time for the chance to give gifts to her grandchildren. With the giving, she would have received great pleasure of knowing that she was a significant presence in the life of her grandkids.

The pastor of St. Anne's, Father Boland, was kind enough to accept our invitation for Christmas dinner that evening. Cindy and I had started a tradition of having a very fine Christmas feast dinner and it seemed only natural that our pastor was able to join us. Father Boland is a fine priest, a man always with a very challenging and engaging Sunday homily and a personality to match. His presence in our home was a calm reassurance that even in our personal pain, God had not left us to be by ourselves. By the end of that evening, I can only stop and think how truly blessed I was at that time. My children were safe, love was in our home, and I had the warmth and friendship of many friends. Although I would have to go back to my job soon, it seemed that, at least on that evening, everything was fine in the world.

As the end of that year became a reality, there were new challenges that I was starting to tackle. I had requested a sales management job in the field that was starting to look like it was going to be a reality. It would probably involve a re-location to either California or Texas in the spring of 1995. By April of 2005, I had accepted a sales manager's job in Texas and would soon be moving to Arlington. In the meantime, my pastor would be elevated to becoming a bishop and serving in Savannah. After his elevation and being officially ordained as a bishop, now Bishop Boland returned back to his parish family of St. Anne's to celebrate the Sacrament of Confirmation that year. Afterwards, there was a parish dinner for him and people were being very gracious and toasting him in his new job.

Then I did something that I had never done before. In the process of thanking him for all his hard work that he had done for me and my family, I said "Now you are my bishop and you will soon be responsible for the annual appeal so I want to make your job easier. Please put me down for $1,000 for this year's appeal." My loving wife shot me a look that only a spouse can understand in the translation was "Have you lost your mind? You have never publicly pledged that sort of money for the Church before." I whispered in her ear, "You know he's not going to expect it all at once but we have a full year to pay off. Just trust me." But her final look to me that night was more of real skepticism than blind faith.

Two weeks later, we had another party to attend. The parish staff of St. Anne's threw a small going away party for my wife and I with a "Texas theme", complete with barbecue and straw cowboy hats!! These were all the people that my wife had worked with on a daily basis, and as the night wore on, I could tell that this was going to be a very difficult separation for all of us. These were our friends that had supported us through our family move to Columbus, taken care of our family's needs after the birth of our son Michael, and soon afterwards when Cindy had to be returned back to the hospital because of medical complications after the delivery. They had visited her in the hospital and helped looking after our children when I had to go back to work.

These are the same people that we worked with teaching the young people of the parish about our faith, preparing them for the sacraments and hopefully, preparing them for life. At the end of that evening, it was a bittersweet moment. From a career standpoint, I felt I had to leave Columbus to move forward but yet from a faith standpoint, it was probably not the right thing to do – a potential career mistake. The fact that I started going to Mass on a regular basis seemed like a minor miracle to some! This parish had given me an opportunity to develop a spiritual side of me that had been buried for a number of years before. The opportunity to witness to other people about my faith or really sometimes the lack of it, the occasion to work with three wonderful priests – inside and outside of Mass -- and the prospect to start learning more about my faith had been such an important part of my life in this great parish.

Within the next year, the call that I started to feel at my mother's funeral would gently become more persistent. It was still a whisper but the whisper was not just something that you could ignore or swat away like a stray mosquito buzzing in your ear on a summer night. It was more of the patient but persistent kind of reminding.

Now the question being given to me by God's call was then being presented to me. **"Would I now start responding to it?**

The Call – Given and Finally Accepted...

n the spring of 1995, I accepted a sales manager's position with my company and started to formalize my relocation plans to Arlington, Texas. Texas had been seen as a very fertile ground for my company's present and future growth and it would be a good place for me to be able to cut my teeth in outside sales. Over the spring break, I had flown out to Dallas, Texas, to visit with my future sales manager and to start doing some preliminary transition work. Arlington was a good location because it is right between Dallas and Fort Worth, and this was a very good opportunity to develop sales. My last day at my corporate job was April 28, 1995. As I left the small house building one last time, I started to feel that my life was not going to be the same. Over the next week, the movers had come and packed up all our personal longings and within a week, all of our stuff had arrived at a rental home that I had contracted with. Cindy had decided to go back to Bristol, Connecticut, to visit with her family and this break allowed me the extra time to do some logistic work before she came back with the kids.

As I drove through our new neighborhood in south Arlington, I was filled with a certain amount of personal apprehension. Although I had gone through my company's sales training, I never would've thought before that I would have done this sort of work for my family's livelihood. But I had seen many successful salespeople in my company; inevitably I was making mental comparisons in my own mind "well heck, if they're doing it and making great money, I certainly can be doing that and be making more money too." I had all the tools necessary, was definitely motivated to succeed, and only anticipated that I be doing this for about two to three years - max. Once I showed everyone that I had my sales outside experience completed, then I could go back to the corporate office with even more professional credibility. So with so many advantages and a limited downside potential, this seemed like the best possible opportunity for me to take advantage of. Then real life started to kick in.

Starting with nature, life sometimes has a funny way of showing who's really in charge. On Friday night, May 5, 1995, after being in the rental home for less then four days, one of the most powerful hail storms came through the Dallas-Fort Worth metroplex. Having grown up in the Northeast United States, I was used to seeing snow on the ground but I had never seen golf to baseball-sized hail before! Starting at about 8 p.m. and continuing to almost about midnight, the hail came down all around us. I had left my house in order to find a place to eat and found myself being locked into a gas station. People were suddenly pulling off the roads and driving to any building that had any sort of overhang that could provide cover from the hail storm. For those cars that were unable to pull over, it seemed like they were trying to find anything, even a tree to break up the path of an on-coming hail stone. For those people that were unsuccessful in finding any possible cover for their car, they were leaving their cars outside and running inside to either a convenience store or any other place that offered suitable shelter.

Along with 30 strangers that night, I was in a convenience gas station looking out into the parking lot. This weather was unreal; I was just being amazed that in North Texas, the pavement was covered with what look like at least two inches of snow! Finally, the store attendant said that the storm had passed and that we can all leave – like right now! Seeing that my car was still under cover, and untouched, I started the engine and with a feeling of increasing dread, turned to drive back to my house. Then it hit me, my other car, the Chrysler Concorde, had been out in the open driveway throughout the entire storm. People were telling me, while we were gathered together, about how destructive the hail could be to the exteriors of cars. Now, I was thinking that my car was going to resemble something that had been repeatedly struck by a ball pin hammer! That was going to be a great **"Welcome to Texas!"** greeting if I ever saw one. But as I started to look at the car, even in the pale light of the streetlight at the end of the driveway, the car's exterior and paint job was totally intact and undamaged; just covered with soft hail. Silently, I just said a quick "Thank you Lord" and went inside for that night.

During the next few months, the job was progressing but I was not earning the type of money I expected to be at that time. I had closed some small group deals, but nothing that I had projected for myself to do. My field sales management team was very encouraging and I was doing everything that they told me to do. But I just wasn't closing the number of groups that I needed to do in order to earn the money that I needed. Suddenly, the loss of a positive cash flow was starting to become a real concern. I had dipped into some of my own saving to invest in my new business as well as some other company allowances that I was getting as well. But money started becoming tight and I was becoming more frustrated with my own lack of performance than anything else.

We were fortunate that just up the street from us was a Catholic Church -- Church of St. Vincent de Paul -- and suddenly going to church started to become very important in my life.

Of course, we'd loved our old church in Columbus and going to a new parish almost seemed anti-climatic. But we were now alone as a family and we needed to be around our faith and other families. The parish church was really quite large and even though we were strangers to this local church, we were made to feel quite welcome right away by everyone. Of course with two small children in tow, frequently we would have to duck out when one of them got too antsy. But in the outside hall, there were other mothers with their children in tow as well!

St. Vincent also had a very active Men's Club that met once a month and is also provided me with a great outlet to meet other men and also to hear how men share their spirituality with each other. Like most Catholic parish men's clubs, it's a great mixture of fundraiser for the parish ministries, positive male bonding for the guys, and also being a volunteer workforce for the general parish needs. The men that I met in this parish went the entire spectrum of economics: but the most important thing they shared: all of them had a firm desire to grow in their faith.

One of the meetings that I remember with great affection was when we had a seminarian that was soon going to be ordained a deacon in the diocese. He had come to our men's club to describe about his training thus far but also to ask for financial help for his future vestments that he would need to purchase soon as a new priest. After the seminarian left, the guys talked about the initial request but as they looked at each other, you could almost tell that mentally they were already doing a silent vote. In the end, not only do they give the seminarian everything what he needed, but also $200 more! You could just tell that these guys had a superior attitude of service and generosity. In addition, they were also responsible for the annual parish picnic.

Over a Saturday morning, and only in the great state of Texas, they assembled an apparatus for barbecuing beef brisket that only could be described as a large outdoor, mobile barbeque kitchen. In addition, someone had brought about a hundred quail dove that had been shot in some ranch during the week. All through the afternoon, these guys work together as a team, swapping stories and tall tales as well as preparing, with seemed at that time, some prime Texas meat; probably over 1,000 pounds of beef! That would be their main source of fundraising for the picnic. The beef brisket was cooked with subdued heat so that literally the beef would melt in your mouth when you ate it. After eight hours on Saturday, I left to go home, but some of the guys were staying through the night to go to prepare some more meat and wrap the dove.

The following morning after all the Masses, the parish community came together and had a great Texas style celebration. There was plenty of music, a cordoned off play area for kids and more people were coming in for takeout orders for the beef. Ultimately we probably made over $2,000 over that weekend, but more importantly, these men would start to have an influence on my life. They were good providers, husbands, and they were striving to live their faith as best they could. When they prayed, they prayed as men often do with their hearts lifted up and open hands. In my mind, I knew that at least this was a great outlet for me to be a part of.

However, as the summer progressed and my job progress became more uneven, I struggled with my career choice as well as my family's personal finances. However, the promise that I had made to Bishop Boland was actually coming true. When a sales commission check came in for me, I made sure that I wrote him a check and sent it within two days. Sometimes it was only $25 but over the next few months, I had actually been able to send to him several hundred dollars! However, I was still in a state of professional and economic turmoil. Some mornings, I barely wanted to get out of bed, and in some instances, I created busy work for myself to stay in the office instead of going out, trying to be in front of potential prospects. By Labor Day, things were not looking good and I started to feel that my career choice had been a total mistake. By the end of September, I was starting to feel desperate and my sales management team probably suspected that something was amiss. I remember I was in my home office thinking that something has got to be done and I was fresh out of ideas.

I had been privileged to work with a gentleman who is a great Christian man. He had gone and moved on to another company in the Atlanta area and we made a constant effort to keep in contact with each other. So, finally in my desperation and thinking that I had come to the end of my rope, I gave him a call.

"Hello Ken, it's me Al."

"Hey, how are you? Things going ok?"

"Well actually, things are not going so great." Then, for the next 20 minutes, I told him about all the highlights and the circumstances happening to me in Texas. At the end of the conversation, I told him that I had come to the end of my rope and I did not know what to do.

"Funny that you should say that, because I had just been thinking about you and I was wondering if you'd like to come and work for me." At that point, I felt that my entire life had just been turned upside down once again.

"Now listen Al, I'm not going to guarantee you anything, you got to come and interview with the people that I work with, and you have to give us your best effort, but I think this'll be a good opportunity for you."

Overcome with emotion, I said "Thank you Ken, I won't disappoint you!"

He responded, "I know you won't but you have come prepared. I'll be putting together a briefing book with the materials you need to look at before coming out here. I'll make some arrangements to fly you out here within a couple of weeks and then we'll take it from there."

Instead of despair, I was now feeling a sense of hope. I trusted this man completely and he was a man totally of his word. If Ken told me that he needed me at two o'clock in the morning, the only thing that I would ask is where I needed to meet him and did I need to bring coffee!

In exactly two days, a Federal Express package arrived at my home with a plane ticket and an interview itinerary as well as the briefing materials he promised. Inside that package was my introductory education to the telecommunications industry. I devoured that briefing material like a starving man who is hungry for a new opportunity.

On October 11, 1995, I flew to Birmingham, Alabama, from Dallas-Fort Worth Airport and began a series of interviews with two people: the person that would eventually become my supervisor and a senior executive in my chain of command. During both of these interviews, I probably was a little bit over the top in my enthusiasm for the potential job. But the telecommunications technology was really starting to take off with the Internet and wireless becoming more mainstream to our economy. This industry was poised to doing some pretty innovative things and I felt that this was something that I'd like to be a part of.

The senior executive that I met with was very personable and knowledgeable. He said that he could forget me of the fact that I was a Yankee but he wouldn't forgive if I had an attitude that was not responsive to the company's customers. I told him about my own efforts in the insurance industry and how I personally delivered claim checks to policyholders stricken with cancer. That experience, by itself, had taught me the power of good customer service. He seemed impressed by this fact. As I left his office that day, I was praying that I had not messed up this shot at a new job.

I flew back to Fort Worth that afternoon and came home at approximately 6 p.m. After a nice dinner and constant peppering by my wife on how the day had gone, I went into my basement office to give thanks for the blessings of that day and to just be alone. At 8:30 in the evening, the phone rang.

"Al, its Ken." My wife had picked up on the extension and then I asked the first question "Well, how did I do?" He replied "Now I tried to prep them that you are a very enthusiastic person and needless to say you didn't disappoint them." At that point, my heart sank because I felt intuitively that I had blown it. I had the image that they thought I would be too "high maintenance" to deal with on a daily basis. But I was just dying for this opportunity and I felt that surely more enthusiasm was better than no enthusiasm at all. But he continued. "Actually, they were very pleased about that and Frank was very impressed with your diligence in trying to satisfy customers. So the only thing that I need to know is this: **When can you start?**"

At that point, my wife started crying openly and I can hear her sobbing on the phone. **"Cindy, it's OK, Albert has the job!!"**

"Ken, you just don't know how much this means to me and I promise I will not let you down. I'd like to start as soon as I can. You tell me what works for you."

"Let's do this, why we go ahead and get together sometime next week and then we can go ahead and get you in-processed. Once again, great job today and we'll see you next week."

At that point, Cindy came down into the basement and we shared a long hug. Cindy's only question was "Where are we going to live?" I told her, "The job is based in Birmingham and hopefully I'll start by the end of the month." At that point, I was truly humbled. I knew that this opportunity had not been just a random event. Almighty God had truly been looking out for our small family, and even though I didn't deserve it, God was being very gracious to us all.

Within two weeks, I started working for my good friend and mentor and continued working in Birmingham for the next two years. I had been promoted twice within that time and seemed to enjoy some real career success. However, while we were in Birmingham, my son of 18 months, Michael, had to have major brain surgery in order to correct a genetic defect in the base of his skull. His small spinal column was building up and retaining excessive fluid. We had some misgivings that some things were not right with our son and we had an MRI done to ensure that his brain development was intact. But in the process of eliminating that possibility, we discovered that his medical condition was such that he needed to get the surgery right away. My new company's medical insurance was extremely generous but yet time was of the essence. Once again, I would feel the loving touch of a generous God towards His children.

We scheduled the surgery at Children's Hospital in Birmingham, Alabama, with an excellent pediatric neurosurgeon. On the day of his surgery, we brought our entire family into the waiting room, wondering when we would be told where to go next. After an hour of waiting because of an internal administrative error, one of the nurses took my son and told us that we needed to be in his recovery room and to wait there until the surgery was completed. At this point, my wife was becoming highly upset. Although trying to put on a brave exterior, inside I was falling apart as well. I know that had we not done anything, that my child would probably have died within the next five to eight years. His condition was such that the excess of fluid that built up in the spine ultimately would deaden and kill the sensitive nerve cells in his spine. This condition, if left unchecked in my son, would have eventually cause a slow paralysis and finally death. Even though my son had a 1% chance of dying on the table, I knew that as his father, I had done everything possible and ultimately, his life was in Almighty God's hands.

As I sat in his recovery room waiting for the surgeons to return, my wife said "I have got to get out of here. I'm going to the chapel to pray." While she was away, I also was praying to God. "Lord, I have done everything that I can to save the life of my child; he is in the hands of the best surgeon I could find. Preserve the life of my child, let him grow up and live."

At the end of that prayer, my wife came bursting back into the room. She told me while she was in the chapel; there was a large Bible that was open to read. After taking some pages in her hand, she turned and looked at the first open page she could see and read. She said "the first verse I saw was **"He is alive."** I knew that Michael was going to be OK." She was still shaking from that experience and crying when out of the blue; the young surgical intern had our son in his arms. "Doctor, is he going to be fine?" He smiled a wide grin and said "Of course he is, he did great." My son was still groggy because of the anesthesia, but his eyes were clear and he was responsive to our voices.

They quickly got him into the surgery recovery room and then soon after that, they sent him to another room. At that point, my wife wanted to stay with him so I gathered my young daughter and we went home for the remainder of the day. Over the next week, my son recovered and our family was once again together, all healthy and happy.

In December of 1997, I was selected for a new job that required me to travel back and forth to Atlanta at least two times a week. The drive from Birmingham to Atlanta is fairly easy when the interstate highway is clear but after four months of doing this weekly commute, I requested and got permission to relocate to Atlanta. At the time my son's surgery had taken place, we had a medical diagnosis that confirmed of what we thought previously: that my son was autistic and that his condition was that he was going to need additional resources – in follow-on medical attention and speech therapy. We had maxxed out the health care benefits what we could receive in Birmingham area so we had to move to Atlanta for my career and more importantly, for Mike's health and future education. So even though we had moved twice within the past two years, we knew that making this move to Atlanta was the best possible thing for our family.

Once again, in retrospect, I can see the divine hand of God moving us to a better place. We were able to speak with some special-needs school administrators in Gwinnett County on short notice. Once we were convinced that they were able to help us with our needs, we settled on a potential home that we can both afford and would be in the appropriate school district to help our young son.

In June of 1998, we closed on our new home and moved in on the Fourth of July weekend. In the next four weeks, we finally got settled to the point that we really needed to look for a new Catholic parish to join. I typically left that decision to Cindy, because over the past two years, as I had been working hard in my new job, she had really been the spiritual head of our family. After calling several parishes, we settled on St. Oliver Plunkett Catholic Church in Snellville, Georgia – about 25 miles east of Atlanta. St. Oliver's is a medium-size church but was built in a nice residential community which gave it a nice family feel to it. The priests that were assigned to that parish along to the religious order of Our Lady of La Salette, a French Marian order that was based on the apparition of our Blessed Mother in La Salette, France.

The pastor at the time was Father Thomas Carroll, a priest in his late 60s or early 70s but had been a giant within his religious order. Father Tom, as we affectionately knew him as, was known as a builder of churches, having personally built three separate parishes in Georgia alone. A quiet man who was probably only about 5' 6" tall, he shared an open passion for people, for film photography and he was very beloved by his parishioners. As you entered into the church, a life-size figure of the Triumphant and Risen Christ was imposed on the huge brightly colored stained-glass window in back of the altar. The joy of the Resurrection of Jesus Christ is the constant source of our Christian joy and seeing that figure every week above the altar was very comforting to me. As we settled into our new parish, I once again was starting to get the feeling that this was a parish that embraced you. Many of the parishioners were transplants to the Atlanta area. I met more people that used to be from Ohio, the Northeast, the West, or it seemed like every other state beside Georgia!

Assisting Father Tom was Father Cliff who was the youngest of the group in his early 50's and Father Mike who was probably in his late 60's. Because of these three priests, the parish community seemed to have their personal favorites. Father Tom was loved by the seniors in the community as well as the Men's Club. He was a fantastic cook, and his reputation was enhanced by his desire to always be in the kitchen during a large parish event! Try to move Father Tom out of the kitchen was a bad move; he was there to stay, work and direct his flock of co-workers in feeding the hungry! Father Cliff was extremely popular with the youth of the parish; he was extremely athletic and shared their personal passion for Christ. Father Mike was a contemplative and his homilies reflected a very spiritual aspect. Between the three of them, to some extent they resembled a personal representation of the Holy Trinity: Father Tom as God the Father, Father Cliff as Jesus Christ, and Father Mike as the Holy Spirit. They seem to work so well together and during large parish celebrations such as during Holy Week or Christmas Masses, it was very inspirational to see all our priests concelebrating Mass together on the altar during those times.

In addition, this parish had something that I had not seen in a number of years: ordained deacons. Not since my experience at St. Theresa's in the early 70s had I seen a deacon. Saint Oliver's had two deacons: Deacon Bill and Deacon Mike. Deacon Bill had been ordained in 1987 and Deacon Mike had been ordained in 1995. Bill is a giant of a man, easily over 6' 4" tall and Mike stood at about 5' 6". In fact, one time Deacon Bill had grabbed the wrong deacon's stole for Mass and the tail of the deacon stole look like it was just touching his hip!! But both of these men worked in civilian jobs, and it was interesting on the weekends when they preached, how much they talked about their love of God, the love of their respective families and how their faith influenced their working lives.

Over the next year, I look forward to going to Mass with my family and being part of this new parish community. Once again, the voice that started back in 1995 now started to be more firm and resolute.

One Sunday, Father Tom started with probably the most influential homily I had ever heard at that time. He used a series of hats to illustrate his various roles in the parish: a chef's hat for his love of cooking, a Texas Stetson as the role of parish pastor, a kid's Indian headdress for his role as Chief, and then finally a white builder's hardhat with a black cross painted on the front. He spoke about his love for the parish, especially for the children and how we had rapidly used up all of our available space for religious education. What he wanted to do was build a new extension onto the parish building that we give us more space to educate our young people as well is to provide some needed opportunities for us to be able to expand.

All throughout the homily, I was looking at him and feeling that I wanted and needed to be part of that effort. The only thing that he had not done was ask who would join him, because had he had done that; I would've jumped out of my seat and said "I'll give you the money right now." Just as I had done in Columbus, I was prepared not only to open my heart but also my wallet but not necessarily in that order.

At the end of that Mass, I went to him and pressed my new business card into his small hand and told him to give me a call at my office the very next day. I don't know if he was just trying to understand who I was because we had never been formally introduced or the fact that I had really been touched by his homily but he assured me that he would call me. True to form, at 10 o'clock the next day I got a phone call from him. I told him how much I had really appreciated his homily and that I would be extremely honored to help him in his building effort. I asked him if he had a preference that I would be more than happy to give him some shares of stock that I had or to give him a check whichever he preferred.

His response was typical of Father Tom as I would later learn. "Al" he said, "That is a very generous offer and I appreciate it very much. But as much as I would love to have the stock, the Archbishop would prefer to have cash and I would like to do with the Archbishop wants..." I told him "Father, it is my privilege and I will have a check for you by tomorrow evening." The next day, I wrote a personal check and drove to the parish office to give it to him myself. Once again, I think I caught him by surprise, because he had just given that homily only two days earlier. But I knew that if it was important to him, it was important for me to follow through. Eventually, that additional building wing was built and in November of the following year, it was dedicated by a bishop from the La Salette's and it proudly carries today the name of **"The Father Thomas Carroll Religious Education Wing."**

One day after Sunday Mass, Cindy asked me if I was willing to join her in something that the parish had started for that year. During the year 2000, the Catholic Church in the Archdiocese of Atlanta was pursuing a program called **"Renew 2000"**. The purpose of this program was for people in the parish to form small faith groups with the purpose of coming together typically on a Sunday evening to discuss the Scripture references that had been used in Mass that weekend as well is being able to share with others of their faith journey.

Cindy had been asked to join a group and she wanted to do so very much. The typical format was for the group to be able to meet in someone's home and that couple would act as the group's facilitator and typically the size of the group was roughly about four to seven couples. Initially, I would stay home and watch the kids while she went to her group. After the first couple of weeks, she really started to insist that I come with her. She typically felt like the odd person out, and she said that she really liked the format. Besides, I would get the chance to start meeting other people and the parish and that would be a very good thing for me to do.

As we met in the third weekend, we came together as a group and first prayed that our faith would be renewed and enhanced. Then, one of the people would read the Scriptures that had been read in Mass. Then there was a series of open-ended questions that can be used as an icebreaker to start the group thinking about the readings. Typically, a question might be "why did Jesus do what he did in the gospel?" Or "do you think you would have the strength of faith to do the same thing Jesus did?" However, inevitably something would come up such as a personal problem that was affecting one of the members that week and they were somewhat lost on how to deal with it. Somehow, I don't know where it was coming from then but I'm sure it was a prompting of the Holy Spirit, I started to speak not from a position of authority or superior knowledge, but rather trying to first understand what the difficulty was and then it was or anything that I can do to help. Somewhere in this encounter, I started to see things in a very different light. It was through these questions that I felt that I was being tested and prodded. It wasn't like taking a quiz and knowing the difference between a right answer and a wrong one, but rather it was a question of how did my faith motivate me to make a specific decision.

Over time, Cindy started to see a real change in both my desire to stay with the group as well as the depth of some of my answers to the group. Later, she would confess that she knew something was happening because she saw that I was being directed by something else. I started making a real effort to remain with the group; at the final meeting, I thanked the host family for all that they had done for me. Once again, I could feel that there was something working within me and that this was not just something of my own desire. Just as I had been there to help Cindy initially when she was working with her kids at St. Ann's, it was like the situation was reversed for my benefit. I can say with a great deal of confidence, that this was another touchstone moment that had it not happened, I doubt very much that I would be in the position I am today. So I am thankful for both her patience when I was being stubborn and her willingness to allow me to succeed.

Throughout the next year, my career progressed but not with the same intensity as it had previously. I was working in downtown Atlanta and the commute was roughly about 50 miles round-trip. I was also going through some personal issues. At the end of each year, I typically allow myself about one week's worth of vacation after Christmas that is really classified as nothing less than "me time." It's only natural at the end of the year, you look at the entire span of what happened during that year and see some of the things that have gone great, and some of the things that have not gone to great. For about the first six years after grad school, I kept a Word document that highlighted anywhere between six to eight achievements that I needed to get accomplished during that year. Typically it would be something like "earn a 3% pay raise for this year" or "complete three graduate school classes by the end of the year." To some extent, these goals were reasonably attainable and at the end of the year I did feel good that I did some very good things. However, at the end of 1999, the number of goals that I had completed were actually in the minority for the very first time. It wasn't that I wasn't motivated, I typically was very motivated in my professional work, but the level of satisfaction that I was drawing from that work was not really sufficient.

I had a pattern of either working a great deal in my job to the detriment of anything else, or I would go ahead and do some extracurricular academic studies to be able to fill in the gaps of either professional information that I needed, or just a personal desire to be fulfilled. But when it came to my prayer life and especially my religious devotion, attending Mass on Sundays was really about the extent of it. Although one of the immediate benefits that I tried to receive as a result of my mother's death was to reevaluate some of my priorities, I would readily confess that even after two years of my mother's death, I was still reverting back into a typical male mantra of "keep your nose to the grindstone and get the work done." To some extent, I look back on the example of my father working late at night or into the weekend trying to get reports done so that he would be caught up at work. Either I was totally into my work, or totally into my extracurricular activities, but totally out of my faith. St. Augustine in his book **"Confessions"** talks about the restlessness that is in the soul of a man until he comes to rest in the loving heart of God. Maybe since the first time since my mother's death, I was starting to feel that same spiritual restlessness that Saint Augustine was feeling prior to his conversion. He was seeking no less than what we would call **"the God experience"**. He was seeking back then, and we seek for ourselves today a real encounter with the divinity of Almighty God through the human person of Jesus Christ that provides to all of humanity with a sense of meaningful purpose and direction in this life. The divine prompting that was calling him to a new life to do this was simply a small child calling out **"Take up and read; Take up and read."**

Unfortunately, the largest trap in this world is that if we are so wrapped up in our material goods, and then suddenly these goods are destroyed, so are we. If we define ourselves by our jobs and/or in a hierarchical position in a company and once that position is taken away because of a downsizing or layoff, the end result is that we feel utterly shattered. That is why the things of this world cannot give us the ultimate joy that we seek. New cars or houses will not satisfy what we desire inwardly: we desire a divine love that can overwhelm and fill the deep hurts and disappointments that this world gives to us. Therefore, the lesson that our Lord is trying to teach us is that in the loving embrace of the Father of our Lord Jesus Christ, there is nothing else on this world that we should desire, because even if we lose everything in this world, we have not lost but gained everything in the next. That is the ultimate testimony of faith: that truly in Jesus Christ who was born into, lived his earthly life as one of us, knew every single state of the human condition except sin, died for us and then ultimately rose again for our salvation. Our hope is that just as he died for us to rise to eternal life, so by placing our faith in him, we will have the same share in that resurrection.

To some extent, I was also falling as a personal victim to a saying that I heard a few years back that was simply this: **Never love a company too much, because in the end they will never love you as much as you love them.** The bitter reality of this life is that so often we love the things too much that cannot return our love such as our jobs, our professional status, or the trappings that go with them. **However, the things that we take for granted are the very people that we say that we love more than anything else but we don't in reality: our spouses, our children, our faith, and people God sends our way and even Almighty God Himself.** Taken to an extreme, when we love the trappings of this world instead of the people in our lives, we fulfill the very prophecy given by our Lord in the Gospel of St. Matthew-Chapter 16:26

"For what will it profit a man if he gains the whole world and forfeits his soul? Or what will a man give in exchange for his soul?

So as the Christmas holidays concluded, and I had once again this private time at the end of the year for myself, I was trying to evaluate on where I needed to be for the future. In retrospect, that's where the renew group actually was a force in moving me forward to try to do something different. Because it was in those interactions with the other couples, as well as a desire to be prepared each weekend, I was starting to spend more time both reading Scripture as well as just new books besides all of the business journals and professional publications I would typically read during my off time on the weekends. This new personal reading provided me with not only a greater source of knowledge about my faith, but also a source of comfort and strength that I'd probably would not have relied on earlier.

Although our church doesn't have a formal bookstore assigned to it, it did have a small wall-mounted book rack in the back of the church where people could pick up a small book and make an appropriate donation for that book. For what ever reason, I started to notice some of the books that were being displayed and suddenly my spiritual interest was being heightened. I had pulled out some of the various Catholic books for sale and was making a dedicated effort to read them. In the spring of 2000, I had selected and was just starting to read a small book called **"My Daily Eucharist."** This small but powerful book was structured on 365 separate one-page reflections about the Holy Eucharist. It was a good mixture of reflections on various topics: Catholic teachings about the Holy Eucharist, stories about the Saints who had tremendous experiences with the Eucharist as well as various New Testament Scripture verses from the Gospels about the Eucharist. It was the type of book that one could keep on the nightstand, just select any page in the book and then start reading from there. The one thing that I started to both appreciate and come to truly believe as an absolute article of Catholic faith and teaching was that once the bread and wine were consecrated by the priest or bishop, it ceased to be just bread and wine **but it became the body, blood, soul and divinity of our Lord Jesus Christ.** That at the end of the Eucharistic prayer, and then starting with the Proclamation of the Mystery of Faith, we were truly in the presence of our Eucharistic Lord -- Jesus Christ -- true God and true man, the same Jesus Christ that gave himself to died for my sins. The Holy Mass for me started to transition from just a weekly obligation to come to church to instead to be an spiritual eyewitness to the greatest act of love the world has ever seen: **the gift of Jesus Christ - the second person in the Blessed Trinity -- as the perfect sacrifice to his Father for my salvation and to have the Holy Spirit live in me.**

Once I was starting to have this transformation in my faith, I looked forward to going to Mass on Sundays. However, my daughter was not always as cooperative to sit through the typically one hour mass as I was. Christina, who was about eight or nine at the time, had become increasingly more agitated when we went to Mass and my wife was becoming increasingly more frustrated with her. Finally, in desperation, Cindy said to me, "Why don't you just take her alone by yourself and maybe she'll be more attentive with just for you." So over the next three or four weeks, we made it a point to sit right up front, in the first pew on the left-hand side, right in front of the altar. Of course, she wasn't happy about that arrangement but she seemed to be at least a little bit more attentive. Earlier that year, she had just made her first Holy Communion, so at least she was able to receive Communion with me at Mass.

Then what happened next, I will never forget for the rest of my life.

Deacon Bill had been the Deacon of that assigned Mass and he had just gone to the tabernacle to retrieve the sacred vessel with the reserved consecrated hosts. Taking off the top of the vessel and slowly pouring out the hosts to the four individual patens that were on the altar, one of the consecrated hosts had fallen off. It had landed about 6 inches away from his shoe at the time. At first, I thought that he would have noticed that the host had fallen down and that he would pick it up in a moment. But Bill continued to attend to the altar and was oblivious to what had happened. At that moment, I heard a voice in my head that said **"What are you going to do?"**

My next reaction was that as if my body was on auto-pilot. I literally flew out of the pew and scooped up the sacred host with my hands. Probably with my unplanned body movement, I startled some of the Eucharistic ministers that were on the left side of the altar. Of course, Deacon Bill did not know who I was and I must've startled him in the process. But once he saw the consecrated host in my hand, he gently retrieved the host and said softly "Thank you." With that, I returned to my seat, and then took Holy Communion with my daughter. At the end of Mass, he was coming up the right side of the church, I introduced myself and said "Deacon, I'm sorry if I startled you but I didn't want you to step on the consecrated host. I hope I did the right thing." Once again, he smiled and said "Oh no, of course not, you did the right thing. Thank you." I turned with my daughter in hand and walked out. **In retrospect, that's when I knew I had a call to serve.** Our Lord had presented me with a clear situation that required a positive act of faith. If I truly did not believe in the Real Presence of Our Lord in the Holy Eucharist, then what I did was well over the top. But if I did believe that He was present in the Eucharist, then what I had done was a public act of faith because I did not want to see that precious host desecrated by someone possibly stepping on it; even accidentally.

It was at that point, I knew that I was being called to do something more. I'd come to appreciate what these married men who served as deacons were doing in our parish. Inspired by their example of faith in their vocation as well as their service to our community, I wanted to be just like them.

Having served in the US Air Force several years earlier, I felt inner feelings that I had not felt in a number of years. When I was sworn in as a second lieutenant in the United States Air Force, I swore to the Nation that I was willing to die so that others could live. But by seeing both of these humble and enthusiastic men of faith, I knew it at that time that God was calling me to serve my family, my community, and my faith in a new way. I would not have to die just once in the service of my country, but rather I had to die each day to my own self-interests and desires so that I could serve others and their needs instead.

Within two weeks after that Mass, I read in the parish bulletin that the Archdiocese of Atlanta was putting out a formal call for men to join a new five-year diaconate formation process. Having served in the military, I knew that I was probably going to get a very extensive course in Catholicism, but I also now could not reject the voice that had started back in 1994 at my mother's funeral. God was now placing another choice in front of me: **Would I assist Him and the people of God as a servant or what I just go about being more concerned with myself?**

Now the choice was easy, but the process ahead would be filled with moments of both exhilaration and patience. On that Monday morning, I placed a phone call with Father Tom.

"Father Tom, this is Albert Feliu calling. I saw the announcement in the parish bulletin about the new class of deacons being formed. What do I need to do in order to be considered?" The call had been given, the Lord was calling, and my response was clear: **"Yes Lord, your possible servant is listening, what do I need to do now?"**

The Interviewing Year...

The Year 2000 was a very interesting year for me.

At work, I had been involved on my company's Year 2000 Project which involved long hours, travel to distant locations and constant report revisions over the past eighteen months. But during the actual roll over events dates, both on the New Year Eve/Day and on the Leap Year Day – February 29th / March 1st, all went off relatively without a major hitch. By March 2nd, I transitioned into a new position and looked forward to new responsibilities and hopefully a more livable work schedule!

In the late spring of that year, the call went out for the new class of deacon candidates. I had the opportunity to know our two parish deacons better and both of these individuals demonstrated three main characteristics that I was attracted to:

- **They love the people of God;**

- **They were willing to sacrifice themselves through their time and presence for the sake of other people, and most importantly,**

- **They were men of prayer.**

The process that I had to follow for the next few months was relatively straightforward. As St. Paul instructs his communities in his letters "to test everything that is good"; for an individual to feel that they had a call was not sufficient enough by itself. That calling had to be tested and verified by the community. So there must be a great willingness for people who felt called to serve to initially share their personal story with others.

The Archdiocesan selection process for potential deacon candidates was relatively straightforward. First, you had to have a conversation with one of your deacons, who in turn, would recommend you to meet with the pastor. At the conclusion of that second interview, you would receive the approval by your pastor and your name forwarded to the Archdiocese of Atlanta Office of Diaconate Formation personnel. Then, an extensive application would be sent to your home address for both you and your wife to completely fill out. After that application was reviewed, then you would be subjected to a series of interviews, first with an individual conversation with a deacon outside of your parish, then a couple's interview with the same deacon and with his wife along with you and your spouse. Then finally, a small panel board type interview with the Director of Diaconate Formation as well as with other people he designated. The timeline started with the first notice of the call about in March/April during Lent and continued through the final interview process by the end of October-November. At that point, the recommendations from the selection committee would be forwarded to the Archbishop for his final approval and signature. If you were selected, you would receive a final letter of acceptance or rejection being sent on or about Thanksgiving weekend.

At first, this didn't seem to be too much of a burden to me. Having worked in many professional positions, it is not unusual for a person to be subjected to multiple interviews or completing in-depth applications. Each person that you would talk with will have a specific relationship with you. Therefore, it's important that they get some sense of what you are all about. In retrospect, I really appreciated the fact the emphasis that they put on the wives of deacons. When I served in the United States Air Force, although the role of the spouse was primary as your source of emotional and professional support, it was not uncommon for spouses to feel put upon by a spouse of a commander under the "in the support of the unit" perception. This would involve anything from making cookies for the troops at Christmas to being asked to host a dinner party for a visiting person of importance. However, the role of a deacon's wife is very unusual.

First and foremost, a permanent deacon is still a married person. Therefore, his wife makes a demonstrable commitment to the community by making her husband available to serve the community more and having less time for herself with him. When her husband is making a call at the hospital, he cannot be with her or their children at the same time. But she recognizes that this gift of service that he is called to do is also matched by her gift of personal sacrifice. This tremendous gift of self-sacrifice made by all of the wives of married deacons throughout the world is a unique contribution that should be cherished by all of the Roman Catholic Church. Although each of the sacraments have equal validity, the vocation of marriage is a unique responsibility because it is in the mutual self-giving and self-sacrifice of the husband and the wife that confer of the sacrament upon each other. The deacon, priest, or bishop serves as the official witness for the Church but the husband and wife-to-be are the people that confer the actual sacrament of Marriage upon each other. Now with ordination of a deacon, this spousal self-giving is modified that she gave to just her husband is now expanded so that the husband is available to give to a larger family. Her husband becomes a provider of gifts to his parish and the people of God. Therefore, it was absolutely essential for my application to go further, I had to have the full support of my wife Cindy.

When I discussed my desire about possibly becoming a deacon, Cindy was somewhat taken aback by my possible calling. Of course, she had known about my past somewhat erratic attendance at Mass during the time we had been married, and she wanted to learn more about what was driving me. While she had been a youth minister at St. Anne's, she often asked me to help instruct her teenagers on all sorts of topics of our faith: the sacraments, prayer life, and service to the community as well as a number of other different topics. Although she had been the one who went to a Catholic college, she relied on me to serve as a possible substitute instructor or a set of spare hands to assist her in whatever she needed to get done. She had seen me in action and had seen the results of my work. My first formal ministry was to be chief dishwasher at the numerous parish fundraisers that were held in support of the teens when they went to Denver, Colorado, to see the Holy Father during his visit for World Youth Day in 1993. But if that is what she needed me to do for her, then that was fine with me.

Although her greatest gift as a person is that she's always had the ability that people were attracted to her, they could trust her completely, and they could confide in her with their most personal problems. Her ministry was definitely more one-on-one and looking back, I know from personal experience, the number of lives that she positively impacted simply because she was there for others.

My gifts, the way she saw it, was being able to be a good instructor who was prepared, an excellent motivator, and having the ability to work with some special needs kids that needed a slightly different approach.

But she also had seen other sides of me since we left Columbus. One time, when I was coming home from work in the spring of 2000, I was listening to Dr. Laura Schlesinger on the local AM radio in Atlanta when she had her syndicated national radio show on national radio. The caller on that day identified herself as a Catholic and asked a question about her special circumstances that involved a Church teaching. Dr. Laura responded with her answer and the caller immediately told her that Dr. Laura's response was not the Church's teaching. Dr. Laura responded by saying "yes it is" several times before Dr. Laura finally said in a point of exasperation "Honey, I've read the Catholic Church's Catechism and I can tell you exactly what the Church's teaching is". She then proceeded to give the correct answer from the Catechism of the Catholic Church. I was listening to this verbal exchange in my car and thinking "Even I don't even know the answer to this question."

After Dr. Laura had gone on to the next caller, I pulled into my driveway and stayed in my car for a second. At that point, I knew that I was at a critical point. Here I was, a 40-year-old baptized cradle Catholic married male, and even I was unsure on what the answer I could have given is placed in that same situation. That very night, I went to Amazon.com and actually purchased my first copy of the new Catholic Catechism that the Holy Father Pope John Paul II had approved in 1994 and recently had been translated in the authorized English edition. Within a week, I received a copy that I had ordered, and then started to read this book from cover to cover. For many nights, I read chapters of the Catechism at night before bed. I was amazed at the beauty that it presented my faith. To so extent, it was a totally different approach to the Catholic faith that I had learned as a young person growing up. It seemed to flow from one paragraph to the next and drew you in like a conversation with the Lord as he taught His disciples along the dusty roads of Galilee.

How much of this is directly related to my calling, to some extent, I am not sure, but I knew that in my own mind, my personal knowledge of my faith at that time was lacking and if my faith was to mean anything, I needed to start relearning about it. It took me over two months to read that Catechism; however, at the end of that reading, I started to discover for the first time, the real beauty of my faith. The fact that the Catholic Church, from the very beginning, had been the one and true authentic Church founded by Jesus Christ Himself after He was raised from the dead and the descent of the Holy Spirit at Pentecost was truly the strength and cornerstone of our faith. The additional testimonies and writings of the early Church Fathers and first martyrs of the Faith was a personal awakening for me. It was not just memorizing the individual prayers or understanding the rites of the Church that was the source of our faith, although I got a much great appreciation for why they were in the liturgy of the Church in the first place. It became discovering the love of Almighty God, personified through His Son Jesus Christ's acceptance to come among us here on Earth and how the Church keeps its mission alive to bring the Good News to the world through the constant intercession of the Holy Spirit. From that point on, I started to read other books about my faith discovering different facets, and in that personal discovery, I started a new love affair that continues to this day.

I scheduled my first interview with Deacon Bill in about two weeks. I'll talk more about Bill and Mike in the next chapter but needless to say I have a great deal of respect and reverence for both of these individuals.

It was about seven o'clock in the evening when Bill met me in the church office. Although he was not as familiar with me then as he is now, Bill has always had a gentle disposition to anyone he meets. He started the conversation by just trying to learn more about me: where I had gone to school, when I had gotten married, about my family, and what I did for a living. The conversation was easy and unhurried; it was like talking to a good friend about your life and what you could expect as a result of this decision you were considering.

Then he asked the first critical question: **"Tell me about the call you feel."** At that point, it was like turning on the floodgates wide open and I'm sure for the next 15 minutes I spoke almost nonstop. I'd spoken about the time that I felt the Holy Spirit in my heart when my mother had died and how I knew my life was going to be different after that. I spoke about the beautiful spiritual relationship that I had with my previous pastor, Father, now Bishop Boland, who had served as an inspirational role model as well as a personal mentor. I related about the fact that I had felt God's presence even when I was in the midst of my professional career turmoil in Texas and how God had brought me through the trauma of my son's brain surgery that had brought us to Georgia in order that we can get treatment for his autism. Finally, I spoke about how even though I was having some professional success, I knew that there was something more that was out there and that how I had been inspired by his example and that of his brother Michael in our church.

He nodded and would ask a brief follow-on question **"And how does your wife feel about this?"** I replied "I believe Cindy is very supportive or else I wouldn't even be here tonight. To some extent, she is helped in the process by allowing me to assist her in her ministry when she was the youth minister at St. Anne's. The opportunities that she gave me to talk to her kids, for me to witness my faith to them as well is for them to allow me to be in their lives are just continual signs that there is something there and at this isn't just an impulsive action."

Again, he nodded and I could tell that he was taking this all in. What seemed like just a brief conversation ended up being over an hour-long interview. But at the end of that time, I probably told him more about my faith life than I had ever shared with anyone in my life including my own father. However, I felt I could talk to him and therefore, this was a great first start. At this point I had no expectations, but I was glad that, at least, the process was being set in motion.

At the end of the hour, he stood up and shook my hand saying "Let me think about what we have talked about and I'll let you know." I replied "Thank you very much for being with me this evening and I've really enjoyed it."

I left the church that evening both exhilarated and wondering. I didn't know exactly what I was asking for but yet I knew that this had been the right thing to do. For whatever reason, my faith became my own possession, my true ownership, not just something that had been passed down to me from my parents like a family heirloom, but rather something that was my responsibility to enrich or diminish by my actions.

A couple days had passed when I received a phone call from Deacon Bill. "Al, I just want to let you know that I have passed your name to Father

Tom and he would like to speak with you about your possible vocation. Can you make an appointment to meet with him within the next couple of weeks?"

All I remember is saying "Really?" He replied "Yes, I think it's important that you need to speak to him as soon as possible."

"Absolutely, I'll set it up as soon as I can and thank you so much for everything."

I called the parish office and set up the appointment with the pastor. Father Tom had been a priest for over 40 years; he had entered into minor seminary as a teenager, progressed to major seminary and was ordained a priest in his late twenties. But by the time that I had been introduced to him, he had been a parish priest for a number of years and even though he was relatively small in stature, he was a great parish priest -- and I say that with every sense of respect and affection.

He had been recognized as a builder of churches, having built three separate churches in the Archdiocese of Atlanta over the past 15 years, and St. Oliver's had been his crown jewel. He had the respect and esteem of his parishioners and he responded to that respect with a genuine love for all. He looks more like a doting grandfather, a good head of white hair, a small but friendly face with the big glasses but a gentle voice with a burning love for God's people.

As I entered into his office, he looked up from his desk, with his big eyeglasses and blinked. "You're the guy with the stock, aren't you?" He asked, and I replied "Yes Father I am, but you're the guy who wanted the cash!"

He came around his desk and sat down next to me like a father counseling his son. He got himself settled in and looked me in the eye and asked me, "I understand you've spoken to Deacon Bill."

"Yes Father, I have."

"Tell me what you've talked about."

Once again, I spoke about my personal story, not that it was a polished presentation like I would've done in a job interview but more of just a personal sharing between two men -- both fathers and both men of faith. I asked him about his own spiritual journey which he shared with me. Since deacons work very closely with all of the parish priests, I'm sure it was one of his personal desires to get an idea of wanting to know if he could work with me and me with him.

Once again, not paying attention to the time, it was a very personal and fulfilling appointment. As I got the sense that he had no other questions to ask, I thanked him for his time. At that time, he looked at me and said "I don't think there should be any sort of problem, I'll forward your name to the archdiocese tomorrow." He said it with a sense of certainty and fatherly charity, shaking my hand and showing me out to the door.

Within the next month, I received the paperwork from the Archdiocesan office. It was a rather extensive application that had both a request for personal information as well as responses for specific questions.

There was an essay question for the both of us.

For me it was "describe your spiritual journey today 100 words or less. This was my response:

"My spiritual journey began with the birth of my children. As I stood with my wife having two new lives entered into this world, I knew the love of Christ existed in my heart and in my life. I began to see more of the love of God in the lives of my children as they moved forward in their spiritual lives. Just as Christ asked that the children come to him in Matthew's Gospel, I feel God is calling me to serve Him now, especially through the children and the young people of our Church."

Cindy's question was "Describe your spiritual journey and subsequent your marriage in 100 words or less". Her response was:

"Marriage has allowed me to share my spiritual journey with my husband and now my children. I began to share my religion with Christina while I was pregnant and the same with Michael. The Church has truly a guided our family through our lives for the past 10 years. We have moved so many times that the Church has really been our family and we have come to depend on it more and more through the years. The most important and inspiring part of my spiritual journey has been His gift of hope. When my son Michael was diagnosed with autism and even before – it was hope that kept me going today. I am fortunate to have been blessed with Michael because he's shown me and my family and what truly matters in life is being fulfilled and keeping up the humor. I feel rich in my spiritual life and my family life with Albert, Christina and Michael."

With all of the support paperwork finally gathered and submitted, the only thing that was left was to wait. The summer continued and soon became August. But before my birthday on the 9th, I had received a letter from the archdiocese office asking me to schedule an interview with another deacon at a parish close to us. The deacon that I would speak with was Eugene "Gene" Whitmeyer was assigned at Corpus Christi Catholic Church in Stone Mountain, Georgia, roughly about 5 miles away from us. The interview was to be conducted in two weeks.

About a week later, I had left work a little bit early and drove over to Corpus Christi to make sure that I wouldn't get lost trying to arrive at the interview. As I drove into the parking lot, I was amazed by a number of things. Corpus Christi was a very large parish, at that time, having well over 2,000 families. In addition, it was also a very diverse and vibrant parish, serving a number of different nationalities. The pastor, Father Kenny, was still in his office when I knocked on his door.

"Yes, can I help you," he asked. "Yes Father, my name is Albert Feliu and I need your help."

"How can I help you?" He asked. "Well Father, I'm going to be interviewing for possibly becoming a deacon here in the Archdiocese, and I'd like a couple of minutes of your time to get your perspective on some things."

"Really?" he said. "Well come on and have a seat."

Father Kenny had been the pastor at Corpus Christi for a number of years. At one time, Corpus Christi had over four priests and five deacons to minister to this large parish family. Unfortunately now, that number had diminished and he was fully engaged as the pastor. But for the next 45 minutes, he allowed me to ask him several direct and personal questions. Questions such as "What do you expect out of your deacons?" "What are some of the mistakes that deacons make that you would like to make sure I didn't do the same thing?" With every single one of my questions, he was both very polite but personal, I enjoyed the possibility of getting some good feedback and I was interested in understanding where he came from as well. At the end of that time together, I thanked him and said that I look forward to coming back here to meeting with his deacon. He wished me luck and I returned back to my car.

The following week, I had a very good conversation with Deacon Gene as he was known. He had been ordained since 1995 and actually he had been classmates with one of my church's deacons, Deacon Mike. The class of 1995 had been the first four-year diaconate formation classes and when I told him that the new class was five years long, he smiled and said that he was glad he didn't have to have that extra year. The questions he asked me had been prepared and standard; sent in advance and they were several times, he asked me to hold my thought as he was preparing his notes. At the end of the hour, he told me that, if I was selected, that we would have to repeat the process with our spouses together. I told him that would not be a problem and I looked forward to our next conversation together.

Within a week, he called me back and asked if we could come together with our spouses back at Corpus Christi. At this point, Cindy started to slightly change about the process. Although she was so very supportive of this progression, the fact that we now had to meet together, this was taking a slightly different dimension for her. We made arrangements for a baby sitter to mind our two children, and we prepared to go to Corpus Christi. Once again, we met in one of the parish offices and Gene's wife was with him. A gentlewoman of stature, she greeted us warmly and tried to make us feel comfortable right away. Her husband said a short prayer and then started with his questions. Both of them asked prepared questions to myself and Cindy, alternating so that each could have sufficient time to make the appropriate notes for their report. It was a fairly casual and low stress type of interview and at the end of the process; we thanked them for their time and returned home.

Once again, we were pleasantly surprised when we received word that we had been invited to the final interview. The final conference would consist of the man who was to become my director of formation and several deacons. The interview would be held at St. Catherine of Siena Roman Catholic Church in Kennesaw, Georgia, which was approximately 45 miles from where we live. The time was scheduled for approximately 2 o'clock in the afternoon on a Saturday.

At this point, I knew that the possibility of my vocation was now becoming more and more real. Every night, prior to that interview, I was reading once again the Catechism of the Catholic Church, knowing that I didn't want to be caught short on any question I could be asked. I wanted to appear to be knowledgeable and convicted in my faith, and to some extent, I prepared for this interview like I've never prepared for any sort of professional interview before or after.

That Saturday afternoon, dressed in one of my best suits and Cindy looking great, we went into the conference room at St. Catherine's at our assigned time. Prior to that, I saw Deacon Mike in the hallway. Not knowing that he was going to be there, I asked him "Mike, are you going to be in the room with us?"

"Of course, what do you think?" he replied. "Mike, don't you think you need to recuse yourself?" Looking at me, he said, "Al, are you going to lie?" "Of course not, Mike." "Well, if you're not going to lie, then there's should not be a problem of me being in there?"

Mike had a very good habit of talking to you straight from the shoulder. But that is what I had come to appreciate about him. He was the older brother that would keep you on the straight and narrow but he was always still your brother. "Now go in there, and answer the questions."

A voice said "You can now come in please." Holding my wife's hand, we went into the final interview together. The Director of Formation, Deacon Loris Sinanian, introduced himself and the assembled panel in front of us. "Before we start, I'd like for us to pray." He then prayed for the intervention of the Holy Spirit for this process and for all the people present.

"We've read your application and we've received the feedback from your interviews. At this point, we need to ask you some questions and we would like you to respond to those questions completely and honestly."

"Fair enough, what would you like to know?"

"First, can you please let us know how you feel about the death penalty?"

"Okay," I started, "You may not know this but I am a registered Republican and I have served in the Armed Forces of the United States as a commissioned officer in the United States Air Force Security Police. I have been schooled in the basics of both law enforcement and constitutional law. I feel that if a person was properly tried in front of an honest jury, that the jury and judge was presented with evidence that was not tainted or forged, that he was represented by an attorney who gave his best efforts at a legal defense in court but convicted on the charge that is beyond the shadow of a doubt and that all legal appeals have been exhausted, then a person could be put to death without any penalty or jeopardy."

"Are you aware of the Holy Father's recent opinion about capital punishment, that he is against it and that we should work for alternate methods of punishment?"

"No, I was not aware of the Holy Father's opinion, but I will make an effort to read it as soon as I can to understand and see how my opinion differs from his."

"Next question, tell us about your prayer life."

I was caught off-guard by that question but not wanting to stretch the truth, I replied boldly, "I don't know if I have one now but I thought that was one of the gifts you got after ordination..."

With that reply, my loving wife Cindy gave me a look that only a caring, devoted spouse can give that mentally conveyed this message, **"Nice one Al, maybe God will let you be a deacon in heaven because you just blew it here on earth!!"**

Nevertheless, the person who asked the question smiled, and took a slightly different tack by asking this question instead: "Do you pray the Rosary?

I replied, "Yes, I do". He pressed further, "Why?

I answered "My mother died 6 years earlier and of all the things I was offered from her after she died, the only thing I wanted was her crystal glass rosary; the same one she prayed with at Mass when I was a small boy when we attended St. Teresa's Roman Catholic Church. It was the one thing that I have that keeps her close to me. By saying the Rosary when I do, I often think of her and pray she is in heaven."

With that simple answer, he looked at the man who later would be my director of formation and said, "I'm satisfied, next question."

One of the other deacons then asked me a question that really caught me off guard.

"I understand that you have an autistic son. I don't necessarily want you to answer this question now, but I would like you to think about it, are you looking for the diaconate as being a way of not dealing with your son's autism."

At that point, Cindy seemed to take charge and said "I'd like to answer that question if you don't mind."

"I know my son's autism represents a different circumstance to our family that other families would not normally have to deal with but I also know that my husband loves his son and would do anything for him if he could. I believe that my husband's desire to be a deacon would strengthen his family and certainly would not be a circumstance of him running away from his son but rather would allow him to see his son as the embodiment of love."

I looked over at her with both a sense of respect and awe. They were very few things that really got under Cindy's skin throughout this entire process but the fact that someone might think that I would be neglecting my son for something else really rubbed her the wrong way. From that point on, the interview moved at a fairly regular pace, they asked me questions about the Church, my understanding of the teachings of the Catholic Church, as well as some more personal questions. We had been allocated an hour for this interview and at the end of that hour, Deacon Loris thanked us for our participation and that we would be notified within the next four to six weeks of their decision. Turning to go out to the door, I saw Mike sitting down in his chair. He looked up at me and waved goodbye. Once again, I grasped Cindy's hand and we walked out to the car together.

By the time we got to the car, she was visibly upset. "How could they have asked you that question" she said. "What are they expecting out of you, that you don't love your son or our family?" As we got into the car together, I said, "Cindy, don't feel so bad, after I gave that excuse about capital punishment, there is no way that they're going to take me."

"Did you know about what the pope said?" she asked. "No, I really didn't have a clue about that one, but I wouldn't change my answer until at least I saw it. I served in the Armed Forces, I carried bullets on my belt for a living, what more could I have said that was the truth? Well Cindy, I guess this is the end but frankly, I never expected that we would've gone this far."

The reason why I had said that was that recurring guidance for being in formation for the diaconate was that your youngest child had to be 15 years old by the time you entered into formation. Since Christina at that time was only nine, I never really expected that I would get a dispensation because of that. But, I was thankful that I had received all of the support from my parish and regardless of what had happened, I felt that I was still being true to the calling that I had received. The drive home was uneventful; we paid the babysitter for watching our children and then prepared for dinner that evening.

Over the next few weeks, Halloween came and went, and we were preparing to celebrate Thanksgiving. Our lives returned to normal, work, school and church, and I didn't even bother asking Mike about what was said after we had left. At this point, it was in the hands of the Holy Spirit and the selection committee. Whatever the outcome, I was satisfied that I had been privileged to go through the process.

At a sister church, St. John Neumann, they had a men's fellowship group that had a monthly breakfast meeting that was prepared by the Knights of Columbus. A neighbor of mine, Jim Davis, who had also served as one of my references for the diaconate called me at the house on Thursday evening and asked me if I was interested in going to the next breakfast that would be on Saturday morning. The Archbishop of Atlanta, John Francis Donaghue, was personally coming to give his testimony about his life. Jim and I had been friends since I had moved our family into the neighborhood in July of 1998 and he became one of my closest friends. His wife Theresa was also one of Cindy's best friends and we loved their family as well. "Sure Jim, I'd love to go." "Great, it starts at eight o'clock in the morning and I'll meet you there."

The Archbishop gave a very powerful presentation about his life and about his faith. He talked about the numerous times that he had met with converts to Catholicism, how they had fallen in love with the faith that many of us had received as cradle Catholics. It was also the love of that faith that he also had felt the calling early in his life to become a priest and spoke about his family life in Washington, D.C., growing up in a small Catholic parish.

At the end of the presentation, he took several questions from the floor and enjoyed the interaction between the men in the room. When the meeting ended, I walked up to him and introduced myself. I told him that I had applied for coming year's diaconate formation and had not heard anything yet. He responded that was unusual, because he had signed letters himself earlier that week and then surely the letters were in the mail as we spoke.

I thanked Jim for thinking of me being there for this breakfast and then I went home, not thinking about what it just happened.

Going to work on Monday morning and returning back that night, Cindy gave me the mail that had come in that day. One of the letters came from the Archdiocese of Atlanta and I was thinking that this letter was about the Archdiocesan Annual Appeal for that year. I opened the letter quickly, wondering why I'm getting a letter from the Archdiocesan Appeal so early since it had just been announced over the past two weeks in the parish.

The letter, dated December 4, 2000:

"Dear Albert:

It gives me a great deal of pleasure to advise you of your acceptance into the aspirancy phase of the diaconal formation program for the Archdiocese of Atlanta.

This phase of formation focuses on the discernment of your vocation and will concentrate on prayer life, spirituality, the life and ministry of the deacon and a comprehensive review of the Catechism of the Catholic Church.

I am delighted that you have responded to this important call and I would like you to take this opportunity to congratulate you on being selected. You have been through a long and rigorous process thus far. However, aspirancy is just an initial step in the process. Admission to aspirancy does not guarantee a call to orders. Instead, it is the beginning of a five-year process of formation.

Orientation for aspirants has been scheduled for January 27, 2001. Deacon Loris Sinanian, Director of Diaconate Formation will be contacting you with further details concerning this day, as well is provide you with the scheduled dates you will be expected to attend classes.

I look forward to have the opportunity to meet with you personally during this Aspirancy Year,

Assuring you of my prayers and best wishes and kind personal regards, I am

Sincerely yours in Christ,

[Signed]

Most Reverend John F. Donaghue

Archbishop of Atlanta

Copied Rev. Thomas Carroll, MS

Reverend Mr. Loris R. Sinanian

Very Reverend David P. Talley"

"Oh my God, oh my God! I can't believe it, they actually want me!"

I ran up the stairs in my basement and yelled at the top of my lungs **"Cindy, Cindy!"**

She ran to the door of the basement, thinking I was on fire!

"Al. what in the world are you yelling about?!!" she replied.

"Cindy, you are not going to believe this, they've accepted me, they have accepted me!!"

"Who, who?"

"The Archdiocese of Atlanta, they've accepted my application, they want me to come into formation – remember to become a deacon!"

She took the letter from my hand and read it to herself. Looking at me with total surprise, "I guess they really do want you," she said.

"Cindy, is this going be okay with you?" I said.

"Yes Albert, its fine, go ahead."

I asked again.

"Cindy, are you really sure you going to be okay with this? I have to attend classes all day on Saturdays and you'll have the kids by yourself. Are you going to be okay?

"Albert," she replied, "We will be just fine, they want you to become a deacon and so do we."

Walking back down the stairs, I sat in my leather chair at my desk and reread the letter what seemed like at least five times before it finally sunk in. The call that I had received from that day in December back in 1994 when my mother passed away now became a reality. I heard the gentle whispering in the night, I had acted upon the Spirit's prompting by serving my community and my family, and now I was being asked to endure five years of intense study in training to be a servant of God.

There was nothing guaranteed, as it said in a letter, but now things were moving in a direction that I never would have believed that would have taken place had you asked me 10 years ago. But now, as our family prepared to celebrate Christmas that year, I felt like I had already been given a great gift already.

I called Deacons Mike and Bill at their homes that evening. They had already received word but they could not say anything until I got the official letter from the Archdiocese. Both of them greeted me with wide smiles when I saw them at Mass that next weekend.

"We wanted so much to tell you, but we couldn't. But now that you know officially, congratulations!!"

These men who I had just started to know when I joined the parish 18 months earlier, men I had seen on the altar, giving their monthly homilies from their heart and from their faith, now would become my older brothers in formation. They would both serve as spiritual and emotional mentors for me. I would have the privilege of getting to know them and their wives over the next five years and I looked forward to having them being in my life.

The people that had served as my references for the program, some of them being Christian but not Catholics, were equally happy when I told them the news.

Jim Davis, the man who had brought me to that breakfast on that December morning, was extremely happy at the news. Pulling me aside, he said "I know you'll make a great deacon." I was equally overwhelmed by telling him "Jim, you and your family are such a great gift to our family, thank you so much for your love and friendship." Both of us had tears in our eyes as we gave a toast to each other.

So as the year 2000 ended on such a happy note, I looked forward to the end of January, to eventually meet the men that would become the class of 2006 for Diaconate Formation for the Archdiocese of Atlanta. Now, the start of the journey of learning about our faith, the teachings of the Catholic Church, and how deacons filled the various ministries of our church was about to begin.

Deacon Bill and Deacon Mike...

eacons Bill Jindrich and Michael Capozza had been extremely
supportive of my vocation calling ever since I had spoken to each of
them back in 2000. But now with my selection recently confirmed
by the Archdiocese of Atlanta in that acceptance letter in December, these
men would start taking an even greater role in my spiritual development.

In some respects, they were the quintessential "odd couple". Though
Bill is 6' 5" tall, while Mike was probably about 5' 6", they were cut from the
same cloth spiritually. Bill had grown up in Illinois while Mike had grown
up in Massachusetts. Bill worked as a marketing executive in the home craft
industry while Mike had worked in a number of positions, recently as an
assistant store manager for a national supermarket chain. Mike had served
in the United States Air Force in his early 20s while Bill had received an
appointment to an United States Armed Forces service academy but turned
it down so he could be closer to the woman he eventually would marry, his
bride Linda.

But both of these men shared some very powerful values. Both would
readily admit that they had married the love of their lives, and their families
that resulted from that love, they were equally proud of as well. Both of
them felt a call to serve God in a very unique way. Although they had been

ordained about seven years apart, Bill had been ordained in 1987 while Mike had been ordained in 1995, they both acted as if they had been born with their vocations from the start of their lives.

As deacons, they loved to do baptisms! Bill actually ran the Baptism formation program ministry for the parents while Mike just baptized as many babies as their parents could bring to them! They both saw their special ministries in Baptism as a personal expression of love to not only the parents of the baptized children but to the parish as a whole.

Both of them had a unique style in delivering homilies but they shared a deep passion for solid due diligence in their preparation to preaching and a constant quest to uplift the people that they preached to. In some respects, some people like to hear when the deacons preach because often they bring into their homilies, the actions of their lives, especially their married lives and their children. It's one thing to complain about when your own children sometimes disappoint you, it's another thing to hear from a deacon in the ambo when sometimes they are faced with the same circumstances you are.

As a result of my acceptance, one of the conditions that I had to fulfill was that I had to choose a diaconate mentor. This person would serve as my informal supervisor when I was in the parish but also this would be the person that I would learn from a hands-on experience basis all that was required to becoming a deacon. Initially and practically, it was not a question of choosing one or the other, it was a question of being able to learn from both knowing that each man had his own strengths and weaknesses. But, yet with an open mind, I could learn from both of them.

Bill had the quality of gentleness, even in spite of his large frame; however in those great hands of his, they were never clenched in anger but rather always open to those who needed them. Mike had the ability of being able to tell tall tales and laugh with all the men of the parish. Mike always enjoyed a good joke and he would just be willing to sit around with the guys over a cup of coffee after his Sunday Masses were complete and get caught up on what was happening in the parish.

With six masses in the weekly Saturday-Sunday schedule, ideally, each deacon would try to cover three masses. When Mike was going through diaconate formation, Father Tom had him on the altar for all of the masses on Sunday. After Michael got ordained, he still kept up that schedule because he felt that as an ordained deacon, his place was at the altar assisting his priest and the people of God.

Bill had already been ordained for a number of years and he was at a different parish while meeting Mike at the annual deacon's retreat that the Archdiocese held. Bill had been looking to the possibility of going to a new parish after he was compelled to move to a different house because of his wife's medical condition. Seeing that they would be in a new location, Bill started looking for a new parish. While attending the annual diaconate retreat, Bill shared his desire to possibly come to St. Oliver's to help Mike.

Mike responded that he was recently praying that somehow God would send another deacon to lend a hand by relieving him of his heavy parish workload. While Mike did all the advance work on informing the pastor, Father Tom, about Deacon Bill, the Holy Spirit was actively at work. When Deacon Bill called Father Tom to ask his permission about possibly coming to St. Oliver's, Father Tom had already been consulted and after one meeting, he started the process in motion for Deacon Bill to join the St. Oliver's Church staff.

Once together, they served as alternate pressure relief valves for each other. Frequently, they would consult weeks before they were scheduled to preach; partly to see how each of them would approach the homily but more likely to just get caught up and see how each was doing.

When Mike's work schedule shifted that he would have to work at night and, therefore, would not be available for some of his daytime masses, Bill stepped up and would actively serve at all the masses. It was not a question of keeping a running tally or an accounting ledger between the two of them; it was a mutual understanding that they were there to serve the people of God and that between the two of them, they would work out any issues that came between them. In all the time that I had known them, I never saw a tense moment or a cross word between the two of them. Frequently, Mike would sometimes apologize to Bill for something, but his brother Bill would waive that big hand of his and say "Don't worry about it."

When they preached, both of them preached from the ambo – the podium on the altar. Mike's homilies were very deep; he frequently would do preparation work at the Emory University library, and shared with me a very important quote after I was accepted in formation. "Al, I don't care what your library looks like right now," he said," five years from now it's going to be dramatically different. You're going to have more books about the Scriptures then you know what to do with and even then that won't be enough. You're going to have to learn to read deeply and read a lot. Because the more you learn, the more you have got to read. And the more you read, the more you're going to have to make that reading work for the benefit of the people."

He was absolutely right. Two years after I started formation, I gave away 130 business books that I had accumulated during my business career to a new Catholic university in Dawsonville, Georgia, called Southern Catholic. But the home library shelf space that I cleared by the departure of those blocks were replaced by books of commentaries of Scripture, biographies of saints, and various translations of the Bibles that the Catholic Church used.

In their ministries, their presence was equally felt. While Bill ran the baptism and altar servers ministries, Mike ran the ministry of preparing the extraordinary ministers of the Holy Eucharist. Each of them imparted a special reverence for the Holy Eucharist in their respective ministries. When Bill trained the altar servers, he wanted them to know about their special place at the altar, being close to the Eucharist during the Holy Sacrifice of the Mass.

When Mike ran his training class for the Eucharistic ministers, the first thing that he taught all of the assembled people that he was training was about the Absolute Presence of the Eucharistic Lord; especially about the Body, Blood, Soul and Divinity of Jesus Christ present in the Blessed Sacrament of the Altar. There was no doubt in either one of their minds what happened during the Mass: Jesus Christ Himself is truly present under the humble species of consecrated bread and wine to the people of God as their spiritual food and drink. No one can ever say that they did not understand this as an absolute teaching of the Catholic Church after attending either one of their training classes.

With them, they preached with love and passion but they dealt with parishioners with respect and concern. It was these actions that I found myself wanting to emulate someday. They had no favorites among parishioners because they accepted everyone, regardless of their social or economic state, as being fellow brothers and sisters in Christ. And that's what made their ministry so powerful: because they themselves were servants of the people, they sought to identify with all they came in contact with. When Linda, Bill's bride, was identified with multiple sclerosis, it was through legions of parishioners that made time in their busy schedules to take her to her doctor's office for treatments so that Bill could continue being at work and taking care of his family.

Even up to the end of 2005, when Bill finally made the determination that he could retire by the end of first quarter 2006, he sacrificed his own needs for early retirement so that the health care costs of his business' insurance would still be able to cover Linda and all her needs. This was the love that they carried for not only their spouses also it also went to the people of God. And the only reason why they can continue in their ministries was because the work of the Holy Spirit was alive in them by the grace of their ordination.

So as I prepared to start my first year in formation, I felt well-prepared. I had pursued graduate work previously so I was prepared to accomplish the academic class work and homework that needed to be done. I had the support of my pastor and all of the parish priests who looked forward to the possibility of a new deacon sometime in the future. But most of all, I was blessed with the constant positive encouragement of these two men. As we now transitioned to the actual five years of formation class work, I will speak more about these men in circumstances that they probably have forgotten but I will never forget. But most of all, I give thanks to Almighty God for having these men in my life and He would introduce me to other men and women that I would continue to serve with while I was in formation and with God's grace, after ordination.

Year 1 - Aspirancy Year --- 2001...

Time Frame	Activity or Class Scheduled
7:00 am - 8:00 am	Holy Hour (once a month)
8:00 am - 8:50 am	Communion Service Practicum
9:00 am - 10:15 am	Introduction to the Psalms
10:30 am - 11:45 am	Catholic Spirituality
11:50 am - 12:40 pm	Divine Office - Lunch
12:45 pm - 2:00 pm	Catechism of the Roman Catholic Church
2:15 pm - 3:30 pm	Introduction to Diaconate Ministries
3:45 pm – 5:00 pm	Open class period -- personal advisory time

On January 27, 2001, I traveled up to St. Catherine's of Siena Roman Catholic Church in Kennesaw, Georgia, to start my initial academic in-processing to enter into diaconate formation. The car drive was about 45 minutes, with Kennesaw being approximately 25 miles northwest of Atlanta. As I approached the large white church with the matching educational complex, I found myself saying **"This is going to happen, this is really going to happen".**

What made this experience so surreal was back in the previous October, it was at St. Catherine's I had the final panel interview with Cindy where I thought for sure my truthful answers would have tanked me! Upon entering into the church, I noticed that there was a perpetual adoration chapel on the left. During the late 1990s, the Archbishop of Atlanta, Archbishop Donaghue had pursued an aggressive plan to start re-instituting holy hours in his parishes. Some of the parishes actually went further than the initial guidance he provided, instead of sponsoring just monthly holy hours, these select communities had personally committed to having perpetual Eucharistic adoration – 24 hours a day, 365 days a year. St. Catherine's had been one of the first churches to take on this increased spiritual commitment as a faith community and it was comforting to know that our Eucharistic Lord was so close by on that orientation day.

At the end of the hallway, the parish hall had a large meeting room where I heard a number of voices. As I entered into the hall, I suddenly started meeting some of the men and their wives that would become my classmates for the next five years. As you entered into the hallway, you were met by one of the upperclassman who asked you to stand still while he took your picture. Then, you wrote down all your essential information which would later become the yearbook/contact book for that year. In addition, there was the standard book issue for our new academic classes.

After about 20 minutes of this in-processing, a gentleman with a large mane of white hair walked to the center of the room and started to talk. **"Okay, okay -- can I get your attention please? I'd like to get started if you don't mind."**

That man, rather that deacon, was Deacon Loris Sinanian, whose official title would be Director of Formation -- Permanent Diaconate for the Archdiocese of Atlanta. However, that was one of his many titles that he held both formally and informally. Formally, he would be responsible for the direction of all of the classes currently in formation. He would approve the current curriculum, recruiting all of the instructors, and be the repository of our academic transcript information by getting the necessary and detailed feedback from each of our instructors about our performance in classes.

Additionally, he would be the older brother or father figure for the men in formation. He would over time, either cajole us, motivate us or pray with us and over us. He would come in and tell us when we had done good, and when we arrived late for services, he would publicly remind us of our obligations to our fellow brothers-in-formation. He was both Commander-in-Chief and Headmaster of this school for us all. Over the next five years, I would serve under and with him, being able to learn from him as well. But at this time, he was giving the talk and I was there to listen!

On the top of the chapter page, you can see the schedule that we would have for each year of formation, starting in Year 2001. We would meet eighteen times a year, always on a Saturday, twice a month from February through June, we would go on a weekend retreat during the month of July, and then be free for all of the month of August. We would resume class in September and go to December. In addition, we would be responsible for all class work participation and academic homework as well as a great deal of out-of-class reading through out each year. Although we do not have an academic certification as a result of completing this extensive course of study, it was made painfully aware for all of us through the interview process that we have to, not only be capable of doing college-level work, we would be doing a significant amount of that work all through the year.

At this point, it's only natural to start looking around and seeing who else is there with you. We never had been formally been introduced as a group so this was our first meeting together. The youngest one in our group was in his middle 30s and the eldest one in our group was in his early 60s. There were both professionals and laborers, college-educated and high school graduates. We had cradle Catholics as well as converts and we had a unique ethnic mix: we had one Vietnamese refugee who came to this country in his early 20s, an émigré from Guatemala, a person from Columbia, another from Puerto Rico and the rest were all Anglos.

Deacon Loris then started into what would be our program for each day of formation. Once a month, there would be a holy hour from 7:00 to 8:00 a.m. in the morning, which we were required to attend and he would conduct as the presider. From 8:00 to 8:50 a.m., a communion service practicum would be conducted by the senior class as their designated practice in liturgy or the public worship of the Church. Of course, we as underclassmen would be required to attend this service. Classes started from 9:00 to 11:45 a.m. with two separate classes lasting approximately 75 minutes each session with a single ten minute break between them. Lunch would be from 11:45 a.m. to 12:45 p.m. with a recitation of the Evening Divine Office that was applicable for that day. There were three afternoon class sessions from 12:45 p.m. to 5:00 p.m. Of course, there would be assigned homework for all the classes that we would be responsible for completing – on time, of course.

One of the things that Deacon Loris brought out in his briefing was the fact that all of the men that had been accepted into formation would have to go through psychological testing as part of our aspirancy year. We would be assigned on a psychologist that we would have to visit with and talk about our motivations for becoming a deacon as well as other aspects of our personal lives. I didn't see this as being a major hindrance. Psychological screening had been part of my training when I was in the Air Force, and this was a requirement that could not be avoided. Through that year, all of us went through that phase of our training and the results were reported back to the Archdiocese of Atlanta Office of Diaconate Formation.

Finally, Deacon Loris introduced our class to the upperclassman. As I gazed around in the room, there were approximately 70 to 80 men there; the new incoming class as well as the upperclassmen already in formation. Some of these men I recognized when I came in for my final interview. As we were walking down to the conference room for the interview room, they were assembled in various classrooms along the way. As I stood up and said my name, there were a few nods offered and some smiles given too. Then he said something that again caught my attention, **"Okay, classes start next week and we will expect you to be on time."** At the end of the hour, he welcomed us once again to formation.

As the new men and their wives filed out, some of the guys would hug Deacon Loris while some would just shake his hand enthusiastically. The Class of 2002, men to be ordained in the following February next year, would be the senior class that year and you can tell by their demeanor, they were ready for their final year in formation to begin! In some instances, I was ready for the year to begin as well.

The class of 2006 would be unique for the Archdiocese. The Holy See had requested that additional academic training time be extended for the formation of permanent deacons. Therefore, in obedience to the guidance from the Vatican, an additional year was going to be placed on our new class to remain in formation to meet this new direction. All of the classes prior to us would be remaining in their four-year formation process. However, this same requirement was not new to our Archdiocese, because earlier in the 1990's, the class of 1995 had faced the same request: they became the first four-year formation class in reaction to the same guidance from the Vatican. Prior to the Class of 1995, the Archdiocese of Atlanta had a three-year formation program for permanent deacons. However, we were made aware of this difference through the interviewing process many times, so any complaining at this point would be useless. But at this point, the excitement of starting something new was the greater concern.

St. Catherine's was blessed to have a large educational center attached to the church. They had recently gone through a progressive building drive and added several classrooms to the church complex in reaction to a growing church population. The pastor had been extremely generous in allowing the Archdiocese Diaconate Formation program to use his facilities on these Saturdays. So as I went out the parking lot, knowing that in less than a week I would return back for my first class, I made a mental note that we needed to get here early. Doing a quick mental calculus, in order to get to the church by 6:45 a.m. for a 7:00 a.m. show time, I needed to leave my house at 6:00 a.m. which meant I needed to be up at 5:00 a.m. every other Saturday! One those Saturdays when we did not have Holy Hours, I gained a whole hour of sleep. However, as I progressed in formation, I never slept well the night before any of my classes. Maybe it was the dread feeling of oversleeping or maybe it was my military training kicking back in that you had to be at required formations with plenty of time to spare! But as I left the parking lot that afternoon, I glanced down at some of the books that I had just been issued. It was going to be an intense year, but in hindsight, ever year would be an intense year of study, prayer and academic work.

On February 9th, 2001, at 7 a.m., I attended my first holy hour in formation. Since St. Catherine's had perpetual adoration, the monstrance that was used for the Adoration of the Blessed Sacrament for the parish was brought forward into the main church where all of the men and some of the spouses had gathered. Prior to formation, I had rarely attended holy hours.

In fact, the first holy hour that I had attended was at St. Oliver's in the summer of 1999. Eucharistic adoration or "Forty hours of devotion" as it was referred to prior to Vatican II was a common circumstance in most parishes in the United States. But after Vatican II, Eucharistic adoration was used at the parish's discretion and when looking back in my own memory at St. Theresa's, I never remember ever attending a holy hour. Therefore, when St. Oliver's instituted its monthly holy hour of Eucharistic Adoration soon after our family joined, I pledged to go to one to see what it was like.

However, when I arrived that first Friday in the late afternoon, entering into the Day Chapel after signing in at the door, I noticed that the people were just sitting quietly in the pews or kneeling before the exposed

Blessed Sacrament. I slipped into the second pew and I was sitting next to an older lady praying quietly. Within a few minutes, for the life of me, I don't know why, but I became extremely fidgety because in the back of my mind, I was thinking and stressing out **"I don't know what to do, I don't know what to do."** Normally as Catholics, our public worship has a format we follow and pray together. The lady that was sitting next to me was sensitive to the fact that I was uneasy and I will always be thankful for what she said to me that day.

She leaned over and whispered in my ear "Son, what's the matter?"

I replied "Ma'am, I'm sorry but I don't know what to do -- this is my first time here."

She smiled at me and said "Son, it's not what you do; it's just being in God's presence."

"Okay, if you say so. Do I do anything at all?"

She continued "Son, do you have a rosary?"

"Sure, in fact, I have my mom's with me. You see, she passed away about six years ago and I brought it with me today."

"Well, that is beautiful, I'm sure she'd be very proud of you. Why don't you take it out and say the Rosary for her."

So that's what I did, looking at the monstrance as I was saying the prayers, I felt a tremendous presence of God in me and I can feel tears streaming down my face. The gentle woman, who sat next to me gently patted my hands, rosary in hand, and went back to her own private devotion. However, I never forgot that experience because she didn't know me from Adam's house cat but she felt that she could reach out to me in my moment of stress and anxiety. While I was praying the Rosary, I thought about my mom who had passed away from a massive heart attack when I turned 35. At 67, she died way too young and her oldest grandchild had just turned three and the youngest was just six months. She'd always been happy as a grandmother, it gave her such joy to be shopping fool for her grandkids. I remember just repeating to myself "I hope she's in purgatory, and I hope even more she's finally in heaven." And then I felt myself crying, for no strange reason, but I felt all the anxiety and pain from our relationship was flowing out of like water being squeezed out of the full and wet sponge. It was probably nothing more than a total cathartic experience and I felt like the woman who cried her bitter tears at the feet of Christ. Our Lord did not shoo me away, he didn't chase me away, but he took my pain and then, in return, Jesus gave me my vocation instead.

However, during that first holy hour of my formation, there was an organized structure to the Liturgy for a Holy Hour. Deacon Loris came down the main aisle wearing what I would come to know as the humeral veil, brought for bringing in the Blessed Sacrament and began to lead the liturgy. It had been awhile since I had smelt and seen Byzantine incense used in our services. As I would later come to know in my education, the use of incense in liturgy is a very physical presence and a reminder of our prayers being lifted to God. As he incensed the monstrance and then continued into the liturgy, it was just another beautiful expression of Almighty God's presence in my life. He read a passage of the Gospel, gave a short homily, and then lead us in the Divine Praises.

Then he did something that I had never seen before but would come to recognize as the Eucharistic Blessing. He walked to the back of the altar, wrapping his hands with the humeral veil and then lifting the monstrance and creating the Sign of the Cross over the assembly. Of course, as Catholics, we are used to making the sign of the cross with holy water as a reminder of our baptism. But this is the first time to visit Our Lord in this very special way; I had seen a Eucharistic blessing being done.

After singing a hymn, he took the monstrance and led it out of the church where he brought it back into the perpetual adoration chapel.

The communion service was also another part of the Catholic liturgy that I had never seen before. As Catholics, we recognize that the Mass is the summation of two separate and distinct parts: the Liturgy of the Word and the Liturgy of the Eucharist. However, in order for a valid Mass to be conducted, it has to be done by either a Catholic priest or bishop. However, in those instances where a priest is not available, the people of God can still be served by a communion service performed by a deacon. Although a communion service does not and can never replace the Holy Mass, a communion service can be provide a benefit of the Christian people. In short, a communion service has the structure of the Mass LESS the Offertory, the Eucharistic Prayer and the Memorial being said.

The Liturgy of the Word portion of the Mass is the same, however, at the end of the Prayers of the Faithful, the deacon then goes to the tabernacle and retrieves the Blessed Sacrament and places it on the altar. Then at the point of the Mass were the "Our Father" is said, he continues on to the completion of Holy Communion for the faithful and then the final blessing for the people. Again, I had never seen a communion service done but this was a very powerful practical exercise for the seniors as they honed their skills for liturgy.

A major responsibility for the communion service was the fact that the seniors actually delivered the homily after proclaiming the Gospel. Once again, recalling in my military training, this was the best example of what we called a "leadership laboratory". The seniors would be performing as deacons just as we as cadets at the Academy performed as officers within our cadet squadrons.

As the year progressed, you can definitely tell that the seniors put a lot of time and effort into their homilies. Partly, this would probably be the only time that they would be able to do this in their diaconate formation. Secondly, they didn't want to be subjected to the intense evaluative comments that our director of formation would publicly give them after the service was done. But, in retrospect, this communion service exercise was not just an item to be checked off on the way to completing formation that year. In a relatively short time, these men would be ordained to serve the people of God. It was absolutely essential that when they preached the Word of God, that in their preaching, they held fast to the Single Deposit of Faith and the teachings of the Catholic Church as taught by the Magisterium – or the teaching office of the Catholic Church.

At the end of the communion service, Deacon Loris provided some insights in terms of what needed to be corrected for the next communion service, then gave some brief announcements and then sent us to our classes. Since we were a rather large class, we were assigned to a classroom on the far end of the complex. As I entered into the classroom for the first time, the tables were set up so that they looked like a large horseshoe. There was a large podium for the instructor and a crucifix was on the wall over his shoulder. This would be where our process of academic formation would start.

As the men started to come in, another deacon came into the room. His name was Deacon Al Gallagher, a short man with a loud voice, a Santa Claus-like beard, and he would serve as our class deacon for that year. Deacon Al had served as a corporate trainer in his professional work career, but suffered from severe hearing loss and was on permanent disability. However, he had a great love for the diaconate formation program and for that year, he would serve as one of our instructors as well as a valuable source of information. He stood up and started calling the roll.

"Okay, when you hear your name, just reply here." He through the roll call and then went and introduced himself, giving us his personal history.

"Since you are starting your year of Aspirancy, you will need to know what classes you'll be taking this year."

"Okay, you have been exposed to **Holy hours** and **Communion services** by being here today. Your first class will be known as **Introduction to the Psalms**. Each week starting next month, each of you will be assigned two Psalms and then you will be presenting your Psalms and what both psalms should represent to your classmates. We don't have a set format that we want you to follow but we do want you to do good research on the Psalms assigned to you and make the presentation as if you were teaching it to a class in your parish adult education."

"**Catholic Spirituality** will be taught by Father Linus and he will be using his own material. But basically, you'll be learning about Catholic spirituality, its traditions and how that spirituality has been and continues to be expressed throughout the Catholic Church."

He continued.

"After lunch, you'll be introduced to the **Catechism of the Catholic Church** and that will be taught to you by Father Michael. The text that you'll be using is the large green book that you were given last week. That book contains the authentic teachings of the Catholic Church and you will be expected to know it.

Finally, the last class of the day will be known as the **Introduction to Diaconate Ministries**. This is where you'll learn about various ministries that deacons perform as well as to start learning about what exactly a deacon does. I'll be teaching this class with the assistance of some other deacons and this will help you start understanding what you are being called to do."

Concluding, he said:

"We have a time period at the end of the day, in case you need to talk to someone or just need some additional instruction about what took place in class that day. You can either leave or stay at that time but we will be available for each of you in case you need it. Does anyone have any questions? Okay if not, let's go ahead around the table and start introducing yourself to your classmates."

Each man there then started to introduce himself by his name, his parish, whether or not he was married or had kids, and maybe some other personal information such as what he did for a living. Glancing around the room, it was starting to sink in that the same Holy Spirit that called the Apostles to ordain the first seven deacons, recorded in the Acts of the Apostles, was the same Spirit that it called each of these men to go through that year-long process of interviewing and discernment and finally each of us had made it.

"I'll let you know," Deacon Al said, "that there was over 60 men that applied to your class and you are the ones that were selected." That was the first bit of information that let us know how large the potential pool had been. "Unfortunately, there was supposed to be another one with you here today, but he's let us know that he will not be going through formation. So it will be just you men."

"Okay, if it's OK with you, let's go ahead and get started." Academic classes had begun.

The class on the Psalms was done exactly how he had described it. Each of us had assigned up on a schedule to do a presentation both in the spring and in the fall semesters. We would both be assigned to Psalms that either we would seek a connection, or somehow as we did research how the Psalms spoke to us. The importance of this class was to get us familiar with the Psalms because it would be the same Psalms that we did research and would be the Psalms that we would be praying as we did the Divine Office or the Liturgy of the Hours after ordination. The Psalms have a very special quality. The Psalms, as recorded in the Old Testament, were inspired by the Holy Spirit through the lives of the men who recorded it.

For example, Psalm 51 was written by King David in his moment of anguish after he fully acknowledged the great sin that he created by ordering his lieutenant Uriah into battle with the surety of his death so that he could marry Uriah's wife Bathsheba who at the time was pregnant with David's child. When David is confronted by the Prophet Nathan, David's great shame in his sin becomes the words of this Psalm. Psalm 51 is known as one of the great penitential Psalms, frequently recited at services involving the Sacrament of Reconciliation.

At the conclusion of every class, there was always a 15 minute break and it was often looked forward to. The next class would be Catholic Spirituality. As some of the men went out into the hallway or into the cafeteria to grab a cup of coffee, I was sitting at my desk when a tall priest dressed in a Franciscan habit entered into the room. I was gazing very intently upon him and soon he caught my glance.

"I'm sorry, is there something the matter?" He said. "You're a Franciscan aren't you?" I replied. "Yes, I am. I'm Father Linus." "I'm sorry Father, but you are the first Franciscan I've ever met."

With a large smile, he responded "well, I am glad for that because that's who I am." Father Linus was assigned as the Catholic priest for the university students at Kennesaw State University in Kennesaw, Georgia. As he would later tell us in his introduction, he had done a myriad of ministry but really enjoyed being around college students. A tall priest, he had both a very sharp wit and a great sense of humor. You can tell that he enjoyed being around young people and students of all ages and we would enjoy being around him as our instructor. Father Linus had a tremendous love of family, as the year would progress, he would often tell us stories about growing up in his family and his own formation as a Franciscan.

His class was structured informally. He would pick up a topic of Catholic spirituality, lecture on it for about 20 minutes, and then poise us with questions about our own understanding about spirituality. It was a very interactive and lively class and it was extremely difficult for me to constantly remind myself that this wasn't my own personal tutorial; that I had other classmates that had questions that need to be answered as well. But Father Linus was very engaging and you could tell that through his questioning methods as well as his responses that he had a great love of teaching, which was his great gift to us. Unfortunately, Father Linus would only be with us for the first half of first year. Because of some additional commitments, he would not be able to finish the rest of the year with us.

However, we were blessed with a very good replacement. Father Joseph Mendes of the Order of St. Francis de Sale would be recruited to be our replacement instructor. St. Francis de Sale was a French bishop in the late 1800s whose greatest gift to the Catholic Church was his intense spirituality and his personal love of the Gospel. Part of his ministry took place in his written responses to those people that have left the faith and were becoming Protestant in his own diocese. So passionate was his preaching, that people would come from miles around just to hear him preach and then to seek his personal advice on their own spirituality. As a result of this constant pressing for his time, St. Francis wrote a very influential book that remains a powerful book on spiritual direction. That book was called **"The Introduction to the Devout Life."**

However, Father Mendes was not only in this beloved religious order, which one of the many gifts to the faithful was spiritual direction, but also he was a very devout teacher. Father Joe is a small man, probably no taller than 5' 6", but what he lacked in physical stature was more than made up in his strong personal spirituality. He started his class that year with a very profound statement. **"Gentlemen, unless you have had the God experience, you cannot go forward in your vocation."** He then would cram into the 75 minute lecture a virtual treasure of Catholic spirituality and academic teaching. But maybe his greatest gift to us was his patience. Here we were men, advanced in professional careers and in age, trying to learn so much about Catholicism in such a relatively short period of time.

It was his goal to motivate us to try to learn even more, and he was very successful in that endeavor. I gained him as an additional spiritual treasure, I was lucky, for my own sake, to secure him as my spiritual director -- to which I've kept even till this very day.

Our instructor for the Roman Catholic Catechism was a priest by the name of Father Michael. Father Michael was a relatively young priest; he'd gone to seminary but later left to work in the secular world for a period of time.

But as time wore on, he recognized that his vocation was not working in the world but to coming back to the Church, returning back to major seminary and completing his vocation to becoming a priest. He had only been ordained a short time but he was extremely charismatic in his teaching.

He had a very difficult task ahead of him. His job was to teach us through the complete Catechism of the Catholic Church in one year. This very intense document that had well over 2,000 paragraphs of very profound Catholic teaching and this book would be our textbook for this class. However, he had remembered what it was like when he had been a deacon and the one thing that we could constantly comment was that Father Michael was enthusiastic about his young students. He looked like a young Jewish rabbi, and yet, he spoke with the passion of a Catholic evangelist. Father Michael's desire for us to succeed was only matched by our desire not to let him down. A man who enjoyed a good joke, he laughed frequently with us, but also could use that opportunity as a teachable moment. About halfway through the year as we approached our summer break, he gave us a very unique assignment.

"Okay gentlemen, you have an assignment over the summer break. You are to write, one page and one page only, on why Our Blessed Mother Mary is called the "Mother of God." You are to use any appropriate Catholic document, the Catechism of the Church or suitable biblical reference or commentary. Please do not disappoint me with this work."

Most of us were looking around the room, thinking "Okay, is that it?" But Father Michael's assignment was not just an academic exercise, but an opportunity for us to express our knowledge about our faith at that time. He was a very understanding instructor, and as we got to know him better throughout the year, he shared with us some of his own struggles that he had experienced in his life. But you can tell that he truly reveled in his priesthood, he loved being a priest as much as he loved his earthly and heavenly mothers. He would often say that he would drop on the turn of a dime to be able to say Mass and how much he was honored to be at the sides of people as they lay dying in the hospital, to give to them the final sacraments of the Church as well as all the graces that flowed from being in the presence of Almighty God at the final moments of our earthly lives.

It was those moments that we all started to gain a collective appreciation for not only our own roles as future deacons but for that of the priests present in our parishes today. We all seen how the shortage of Catholic priests affected the parishes we were at now. While growing up as a boy, the parish church that I had attended in the 1970's never had less than four priests then and yet the same parish where my mother's funeral Mass in 1994 had been said had only two priests at that time. Therefore, as we grew that year of formation, we grew in a greater love and appreciation for the priesthood. Our priests fulfill a multitude of roles: Minister of Jesus Christ, teacher, counselor, confessor, friend, role model, brother in Christ. Father Michael was all of these roles and then some. As the year continued, our constant comments were "Father Michael, thank you for being here today."

The final class on diaconate ministries was taught by both Deacon Al and Deacon Bob. Both of these men had been ordained for a number of years and were actively working in their parishes. At this point, this class was really as an introduction to the various aspects of being a deacon. Then primary vocation of a deacon **is not** just being seen on the altar every Sunday at Mass, but instead deacons are defined by their ordination as being ministers of charity. Although certainly serving at the weekend Mass and being able to assist the priest in the Eucharistic sacrifice was an important part of our ministry, **it was not simply the sole ministry that we should to aspire to.** Through that year, we are introduced to the liturgical functions of the deacon, the services of a deacon for baptisms, weddings, funerals, as well as visiting the sick, working with the poor, or seeing those in prison. It was all of these ministries and then some that deacons were being called to assist in so that in that silent witness of their ministries, they bring the light of Jesus Christ to so many other people that may not have that opportunity.

Unfortunately, because sometimes when people see you wearing a Roman collar, they automatically think that you are priest and, therefore, when they ask you to hear their confession. You have to gently tell them that you can't because you're only a deacon, they look at you initially with a puzzled face. Of course, Deacon Al always used to remind us to deal with these people by saying, "of course Madame, I can hear your confession, it's just that I can't give you valid absolution." But even with all of the corny jokes aside, all of these men had one mission in mind: to give us a reasonable expectation of what a deacon would and should be prepared to do as part of his ministry and help us question ourselves **"Did we feel called to fulfill that role?"**

For the next five months – from February to June -- the entire formation program met at St. Catherine's. However, in June of 2001, just prior to our departure for summer break, Deacon Loris gathered all of us while we were in the classroom to announce that, starting in September, we would actually be moving to a new facility. The Archdiocese of Atlanta had prepared a new facility that would become to known as the St. Stephen's Center for Diaconate Studies. This new building was located on the campus of Blessed Sacrament Catholic Church in South Atlanta; this location would be our new home for the remainder of our time in formation. We would have larger classrooms as well as our own meeting space so that we did not need to intrude upon the hospitality of St. Catherine's. From a driving standpoint, the commuting distance was about the same for me -- 45 miles, however, it was very exciting to know that we had a place of our own.

The other thing that Deacon Loris would become infamous for would be his summer assignments. Just like any good teacher does not want to leave his students without an assignment to apply their learning they received in the springtime, Deacon Loris constantly used these summer assignments to reinforce what we had learned. While we were in diaconate ministries class, he came in and asked the question **"How many of you men are already either Eucharistic ministers or lectors in your parish?"** A number of the guys raised their hands. "Okay, how many of you are both qualified right now?" Only a couple of hands remained still up. "For those of you who are not both trained and qualified at this time, you need to get trained over the summer break so that when you come back, you are fully trained in both of those ministries. You're going to have to feel comfortable reading the Gospels when you're ordained and the best way to do that is start being a lector right now by doing the first or second reading at Mass. If you're not a Eucharistic minister, you need to be prepared for that ministry as well since you'll be ministers of the cup after ordination. You need to prepare a paper about the training process that you went through and have it for me when you come back in September."

A number of us looked at each other in the same thought flashed through our eyes. "You have got to be crazy, man. Even on top of what we've endured for the first five months, and now this on top of that." But Deacon Loris would not be denied, and he was absolutely correct. The ability of the deacon to perform his core obligations to the people of God was that should be able to proclaim and preach as well as be the minister of charity at the altar. In retrospect, that assignment was one of the first that he would give us that galvanized our sense of vocation. Bit by bit, during that first year, the pieces of the puzzle were starting to set in place, the final mosaic was being sset in place although we were constantly in motion and maybe did not realize it at the time!

But so often as in life, the only way we can fully appreciate the mosaic of our spiritual journey is at some point we have to stop and step back and then take in the mosaic in its fullness. In the spots where the mosaic was not complete, would be the areas that we would focus our attention for the future. But in those areas where the mosaic work complete or at least had some semblance of completion, its beauty was starting to take hold.

As the summer ended and we returned in the fall, the class that started as a collection of individual men started to become a unit. It was through the interactions of our class work as well as the homework that we were assigned, it started that a galvanizing process. As in the military, hard work sometimes is the raw mortar that allows unfamiliar men to bond together in common work and suffering and become a fighting unit. But the suffering that we felt was not just from the academics, the suffering was the fact that our vocation had real implications: the Church was absolutely serious about ensuring that only the best trained men would be able to continue as ordained clergy. The people of God deserved our very best and we had to be prepared every weekend of class to give our very best. Servant leadership at its core is not about our own self-enrichment, but is the enrichment that we can give to others as a result of our service.

Of course, our instructors had a huge positive effect on us during that year. Unfortunately, we also started to lose some men in the process. Two of the men we lost because of economics, they had lost their jobs and had to relocate to another area or had taken a different job that had greater responsibilities that could not be reconciled to their current vocation training. For those of us that remained, it was starting to sink in: **not all of us were going to make it.** However, while I was at the Air Force Academy, we had a saying "Cooperate and graduate." This meant that not doing your very best was not important, but rather in those areas where someone was strong, he had a real obligation to help those that had less strength in that area. Everyone has a superior gift or talent to be shared with the group and it was important for you to start sharing your talent(s) with your classmates as soon as possible. It was during this time that people started to step up to the plate and start being real leaders, servant leaders, among the class. It was leadership, not based on organizational hierarchy, but personal leadership based on your God-given talents and how your talents could be used for the benefit of others.

For example, for those of us that were more technologically sophisticated, we were able to help our other brothers to understand how to use and work their e-mail so we could all communicate better among ourselves so one would be left out of the loop when it came to class assignments or functions that we were required to attend.

For those of us that had extensive backgrounds in Catholicism and religious education, we were able to provide resources to help others that didn't have a similar background because we would all be called to teach our faith to others in the future. When someone had to miss a class for whatever reason, someone else always made sure that they had the appropriate notes and were up to speed by the next time class convened. It was during this process, that I wanted to make myself more available to my classmates and by doing so, I became informally the class representative. I would send out e-mails to my classmates on the Friday night before Saturday classes, reminding them of what they needed to have for the next class, I would be the one to help make coffee and cover for the guys they could not make it in time.

That's how it played itself out during that first year: men came together as individuals but at the end of the first year started to form as close classmates. We were becoming men who valued each other's contribution and talents and in the end, we became brothers in faith and spirit.

Father Michael's Assignment – On Mary, the Mother of God
– Albert L. Feliu / St. Oliver Plunkett

Mary is called the "Mother of God" because she has earned that position by her unique role in being an integral part of the salvation plan for the world, initiated by God after the fall of Adam at the beginning of time.

When God initiated His plan for the salvation of the world, God had to have a unique and sinless vessel to place His Son – At first in the womb of his mother and then to serve as a support for the remainder of His time on earth. Since God, by His very being and infinite goodness and mercy, wanted man to be reconciled to Himself. In order to do that, God had to become man, and in order for God to become man, He had to be born of a woman. The present circumstance facing God was, in fact, all men and women were stained with original sin committed by Adam and Eve in the Garden of Eden at the beginning of the world. Since God, by His very nature abhors and is repulsed by sin, and because of original sin, God cannot be reconciled with man under that prior circumstance. Therefore, the very instrument of His salvation had to be free of all sin so that His Son can flow through her and into the world. That is why the Church has recognized the Mystery of Mary's saving from original sin and celebrates of the Feast of the Immaculate Conception. Because Mary <u>had to be born</u> without original sin to be worthy of receiving the Spirit of God into her womb so that our salvation could be borne of the human Mother and Jesus could be borne of human estate and being both God and man.

Since the beginning, Jesus, along with the Holy Spirit, has been one with the Father. By Mary, by giving birth to our Savior, in fact, becomes the Mother of God because we accept Jesus Christ as coming from the Father. Along with the Father and the Son, Mary conceived Jesus within and by the Holy Spirit. Mary, in fact, became one with God, just as a man clings to a woman to become one, Mary accepted the Holy Spirit to bring forth the Savior of the world. By this action she becomes the Mother of God.

The title of "Mother of God" is reinforced in a number of church teachings. In Genesis 3:15, God the Father reminds those in the garden and specifically the serpent, which is Satan; God reminds this serpent that the foot of a woman will crush his head. We believe that representation is of Mary who holds the Christ-child and her foot is crushing the serpent head. This scene reinforces the supremacy of Jesus over the power of Satan and His ability to bring His kingdom here on earth – Rev 12:1-18.

In addition, this revelation is also reinforced in the John's Book of the Revelation when it is quoted that a woman gives birth in the desert and flees to safety in a place that was built for her. This image also represents Mary and she gave birth to Jesus so that the one that was called the Alpha and the Omega can reclaim the world from the powers of Satan.

Mary, along with the other women, who accompanied Jesus to the Cross at Calvary, is reinforced in her role as Mother of all when Jesus asked John to take care of His mother and for His mother to accept the care of John in this world. This role does not assume that Jesus is abandoning His mother, rather than for the remainder of her time here on earth, she would be well cared for until she could assume a new role in heaven. (John 26:27)

Finally, although not explicitly directed in Scripture, Mary is assumed into heaven, both body and soul, resurrected to act as the Intercessor and Protector of the church. She was present at the birth of Church at Pentecost. She is crowned as Queen of Heaven by receiving a crown of 12 stars and by being placed in a position of honor and privilege. Yet even in that role, Mary assumes a role that leads all sinners to her Son by providing the example of her life to all that believe and that are willing to follow her example. She is highly exalted both heaven and earth yet she still has the role of humility and homage. Because she was so devoted to the mission of God the Father, God the Son provided that she remained in a position of having great influence. The very act of the Rosary, teaches all sinners that she serves as a viable guidepost leading all who wish to know her Son through her and not at her.

Her Immaculate Conception, the acceptance of the invocation of the Holy Spirit at the Annunciation to become the Mother of the Blessed Savior, her steadfast faith throughout the life of Jesus while He was here on earth till the day that she died, and then her glorious assumption into heaven is a powerful example to the role of the acceptance of God's love and fidelity to His word. Because when the Word became flesh, it became flesh through her earthly body, it was provided love throughout His life and beyond, and

He returned that love by allowing her to be preserved both body and soul to reign with him in heaven and to be a position of great admiration and worship through out all time. We venerate Mary because Mary leads us to Jesus and Jesus leads us to eternal salvation and God the Father. We honor Mary as a Mother because we understand the love of a mother for a child, from the cradle to the grave.

Simeon, at the presentation of our Lord in the temple eight days after he was born, saw the glory of God and made the statement that her life would have both great joy and great sorrow (Luke 2:22-35). That sorrow would be so profound that would feel like a sort was piercing her heart, but her joy would be overwhelming, like flooding of God's mercy to the Jews and Gentiles alike. Mary fulfilled her mission here on earth by being a woman of God that she was created today. She held about her faith in God, she fulfilled her mission to protect and bring forth into the world the Savior and when she died, she saw her life's mission was complete. Glory be to Mary, Mother of our Savior, Mother of God.

Year 2 – Freshman Year 2002...

Time Frame	Activity or Class Scheduled
7:00 am - 8:00 am	Holy Hour (once a month)
8:00 am - 8:50 am	Communion Service Practicum
9:00 am - 10:15 am	Church History
10:30 am - 11:45 am	Basic Theology
11:50 am - 12:40 pm	Divine Office - Lunch
12:45 pm - 2:00 pm	Vatican II Documents
2:15 pm - 3:30 pm	Social Justice
3:45 pm – 5:00 pm	The Scriptures - Bible overview

In January of 2002, we took our next step in the formation process by being formally accepted into candidacy for diaconate formation. During the previous year, we had been allowed to attend classes, be evaluated by a psychologist chosen by the Archdiocese, and also be evaluated by all our instructors in our academic progress thus far. The aspirancy year was configured as a mutual shakeout process: our formation instructors and mentors evaluated us and we evaluated them as well as our own vocation call. If someone departed during that year, it was not a sign that they didn't have a valid calling, we regretted every man that left prior to the completion of classes. But in addition, we were having a personal awakening of the possible sacrifices that we needed to be prepared to be make as we progressed in the future and it challenged our ability to see how we were going to meet those sacrifices of service.

We once again gathered at St. Catherine's Church that night but this time under the presence of Archbishop Donaghue, each of us came forward to publicly ask his permission for us to be accepted by the Church and to continue in formation studies. He, in turned, asked for us to continue in our perseverance through our studies, our prayer lives and in our training for future ministry.

Formation would provide us with several formalized occasions, like spiritual milestones, for us to be cognizant of the fact that we were on a journey, a journey that had both a final destination as well as numerous opportunities for spiritual growth and development along the way.

Archbishop Donaghue had embraced the permanent diaconate in his archdiocese and it was my first time that I had seen him since that breakfast back in December of 2000 in Lilburn. This occasion also provided us with the opportunity to meet with some of the spouses and children of our classmates. Since the spectrum of our class was so varied, so were the ages of the children that were there! Everyone from newborn babies to grown children were sitting in the pews of the families and the spouses that night had a special glow of pride for what we had already accomplished in our first year.

The Year 2002 would also be a year of change for me and my parish. Father Tom Carroll, the man who had been both my pastor and my advocate through the formation process in the Year 2000, was stricken with Parkinson's disease. Even though he was an older priest when I first knew him back in 1998, the effect of the Parkinson's was now being readily apparent. His hands would shake slightly and his voice would crack sometimes when he delivered a homily. I noticed that the deacons at the Mass would remain closer to him at the altar than they had previously. The parish family, and especially the parish staff at St. Oliver's, loved Father Tom very much. But unfortunately, he resigned to the fact that he needed to return back to Hartford, Connecticut, where his order had a facility that they could care for him in his remaining years.

In his place, the La Salettes sent us Father James "Jim" Henault, a priest that had been ordained over 20 years and had been a pastor in two separate parishes; one in England and the other in Florida. I made an appointment to talk with Father Jim for two reasons: first, because I was still under his direct guidance as a man in formation and secondly, I would be working very closely with him. We sat in the parish office in a manner similar to when I had met Father Tom two years earlier and I started the conversation with this question **"Father, how do you feel about deacons?"** He replied quite matter-of-factly "I like my deacons very much." After that, we had a great discussion about my progress and what I had learned already. At the end of that conversation, he only had one bit of counsel for me: to continue to persevere in my studies and to learn as much as I could. I asked him for one favor in return, that he would purchase a Sacramentary for my use and as a study resource. To my surprise, he said "Is that all?" I responded, "That's all Father, that's all I need."

Over that next year, I would start to develop a great deal of respect for my new pastor. It was a tough spot for him to be in, taking over for someone that had so much respect and love like Father Tom could not have been easy. It would be like the equivalent of taking over the head coaching position for the Green Bay Packers after Vince Lombardi winning the Super Bowl! But Father Jim had a long-term plan, a vision really, of where he would take the parish in the future and he would need the support of all of the parish family: his fellow priests, his deacons, and the people of the parish. He was a man I could work with and I was blessed to have him in my life.

The St. Stephen's Center in February was still dark as we came back for the first holy hour of that year. Even at seven o'clock in the morning, it was very dim as we parked our cars to begin the second year of academic classes.

Another tradition that we are taking part of was the annual moving of the classrooms. The way the St. Stephen Center was organized, it has two floors of classrooms. Your first year, you are put in the classroom that resembled more of a bunker than a classroom! The next year, however, your class moved to a different classroom that had some windows and access to the outside. Your third year, you moved up to the top floor where you could be closer to the coffee and the occasional baked good treats that that a man's spouse had made for the benefit of all.

So the second year, we moved into a slightly larger classroom and we were thankful for the additional space. The book bags we had gotten for ourselves for our first year had even more books to bring on a consistent basis because of the increased work load.

As we were gathering for the first class of the new year, we also were starting to develop table mates because each table had room for only two men and all their books and I was no exception.

"Hey Al, is anyone sitting here?"

"No, Ken, go ahead and sit down."

And with that simple conversation, I began a friendship been extended for the rest of my formation and, hopefully for the rest of my life. Ken Melvin had been a very successful executive dealing in the health care software industry. However, during our first year of formation, his company downsized and he was left with a buyout package. Although Ken was 18 years older than I was, we quickly became fast friends and for the rest of our time together, we probably acted more like two goofy brothers rather than pious weekend diaconate seminarians! At first glance, Ken probably had the look of the wily professor of the "Back to the Future" movie series. With the silver hair, big glasses and an infectious laugh, Ken and I began a mutual support system. I would lean on him for the extensive knowledge of Catholicism that he possessed and he would lean on me for the support I would provide him as he needed it. But our greatest gift we shared was a great friendship lasting all through formation.

But Ken had a very serious side to him as well. Growing up in the backwater areas of the Appalachian Mountains, Ken was literally a self-made man. And over the many years, he would talk about his childhood growing up as a Catholic, joining the United States military, pursuing his university and post-graduate education, and marrying the love of his life, Linda. However, to the earthly riches that Ken earned and later lost during the tech boom and bust of 2000-2003, he was always passionate about those people that were the least among our society. In later classes, he would share much more of his personal story with us – his work with troubled youth, his love for his daughter and grandchildren and surviving a serious biking accident that nearly cost him his life. As we approached this next year of formation, I would start to see new sides of my friend Ken, and these new revelations would often challenge my own thinking on a number of different issues, especially on the areas of social justice and healthcare for the least of our brothers and sisters. He did not just know about social justice, he and Linda lived it by helping a multitude of people throughout their married lives together.

Our second year of formation also brought about a new change in formal leadership for the class. Deacon Rich, who himself had been ordained a few years earlier, was being brought into our class to serve as the new class deacon/mentor. It was Rich's job to work with us for the remainder of our time in formation. He would watch our performance in class; he would provide insights and answers to questions that we had as well as making sure that all of us were kept on track. This was a tremendous commitment of his own time, giving up 72 full Saturdays over the next four years that he could have spent with his own family and friends. He would essentially remain in formation with us for our time left as well is sometimes serving as a substitute instructor when the assigned teacher had another pressing commitment.

But Deacon Rich brought a great deal of perspective to us throughout our remaining four years in formation. He would share with us some of the challenges as well as joys that he had experienced in his own ministry as well as being able to guide us when we might have difficulties of being in formation. He also understood the tremendous time pressures that we were facing, for he himself worked as a project manager for a large American corporation as well as being active in his own ministry within his church. Therefore, Deacon Rich was much more than just an older brother in Christ; he would be the role model, our confidant, as well as our personal adviser. And as he got to know us as well as we get to know him, he added another level of richness to our formation experience.

Our second year of formation once again started in the month of February. This year, we would have a full complement of five classes in our schedule. Starting the first thing in the morning after holy hours and communion services would be **Catholic Church History**. Then, once again we would have Father Michael as our instructor but now in **Basic Theology**. The afternoon sessions would become more difficult then the morning sessions. **The Study of Vatican II Documents**, **Our Introduction into Social Justice**, and finally **An Overview of the Scriptures** would complete our academic class year. As we approached annual book issue this year, we all collectively groaned that our book bags would become a little bit heavier this year.

Deacon Stephen would be our instructor for Catholic Church history. A former naval aviator and now an independent business consultant, Deacon Steve had taken the study of the Catholic Church history very seriously even after he had completed his own formation. Although he enjoyed being around us, you can definitely tell that he enjoyed teaching Church History the more. Every Saturday morning, the very first class of the day, he would come in, set down his notes on the podium and say in a very authoritative voice, "Okay gentlemen, settle down because we have a lot of material to cover today and not enough time to do it in." By the time his 75 minutes were completed, we'd always have that expectation that we didn't even get through all of the material he prepared. Of course, we were never ever disappointed. This meant, that we probably would have more reading to do for the next class, and so drinking from a fire hose began again the next time this class came together.

Of course, any time you teach any sort of comprehensive history, especially about the Catholic Church, you're going to be challenged. With so many facets of our faith to uncover, or discover for the first time and learn, it was not just a question of going from A to Z, but rather a challenge to understand how is that our faith has developed and is sustained over time. The Catholic Church is the only institution in the entire world that has been a continuous organization for over 2,000 years. Charged by Jesus Christ Himself "to teach everything that I've taught you", the Catholic Church has been faithful to that mission then and remains faithful to that mission today. As Deacon Steve would constantly remind us, any organization built by mortal man would have failed a long time ago, but it was through the active intervention of the Holy Spirit that allowed the Catholic Church to thrive and flourish even during times of great human persecution.

With Father Michael back as an instructor for Basic Theology, we knew that we were going to be in for a great teaching session. Having gone and survived the study of the Catholic Catechism, Father Michael was even better the second time around. Now he had known us for a year, his demeanor to us was more like that of an older brother that wanted to make sure his younger brothers truly understood what they were being asked to do. I cannot honestly say that I had never met a priest that had more enthusiasm for his priesthood than Father Michael.

During our second year, our director of formation added a day of reflection for the entire family, in addition to our regular formation classes. Our first day of reflection was held at a Life Teen retreat facility in Tiger,

Georgia. Roughly about two hours ride north outside of the Atlanta perimeter, this facility was clearly out into the countryside. On this facility was a small Catholic chapel that had been affectionately named the "St. Stephen Chapel." In all our days of reflection, typically before lunch, we had a Mass celebrated for all of us. During our first time, Father Michael came out just to celebrate Mass with us even though clearly this Mass request was a great imposition of his time even for a Saturday – two hours car drive to Tiger, two hours visiting with us and saying Mass on site, and then the two hours drive back to Atlanta.

As we gathered in a chapel that was probably constructed in the late 1800s, with the bare wooden floors and the wooden rafters exposed, Father Michael, in his homily, talked about the fact that the Mass, every Mass that is celebrated throughout the world, brings all of its participants literally to the gates of heaven.

In the presence of our Eucharistic Lord, we, even as unworthy sinners, are brought into the very presence of Almighty God. Father Michael did not just say the Mass, he prayed the Mass, and at the end as we were walking up to him and thanking him for the gift of his time and of his words, he would always have a broad smile and say "You know, I would always take care of you guys." And for that next year, even in light of his own personal health issues, he always made it to class to make good on his commitment for us.

Our study of Vatican II documents probably drove home the point to the extent that we needed to be prepared for her classes. Our instructor for this class, Kersti was an enthusiastic Catholic educator whose background was in teaching high school students and in Adult Education Ministry. She burned with a tremendous love for the Lord as well as a desire to have a special opportunity, as a layperson, to prepare the future servants of the people of God. Kersti also could be a rather tough taskmaster, with high academic standards for her charges. She took no prisoners and we knew it. But she was always prepared for us and we appreciated her commitment of time and energy for that. This class involved a great deal; of deep reading and you could not read these documents like the newspaper. It was intense and soul-filled reading that was required. It was a bit intimidating because some of us had not seen a thick textbook since high school or college and now we got it five times over because each class was an intense academic and spiritual exercise.

On studying the documents of Vatican II was not just a mere academic exercise, most of the men in the class with the exception of a very few of them, grew up in the Church as a result of Vatican II. There were very few of us that had actually heard a Mass said in Latin, could memorize and even repeat the responses of the people in the Mass, or other similar events. We'd grown up with a Mass being said in our own native tongue, with the inclusion of the Responsorial Psalm, the sign of peace, and taking communion in our hands instead on our tongues at the altar railing. But the greater issue that we needed to be well-versed was why the holy conclave had taken place in the first place; why the Catholic Church needed to be open to the outside world and rededicate to its mission of proclaiming the Gospel of Jesus Christ to all.

In studying the documents of Vatican II, we became even more motivated because it was a result of Vatican II that permanent deacons were brought back into the Catholic Church! We were able to fulfill our calling because Our Church saw the needs of our vocation as married men to being able to fulfill that same calling of preaching of the Gospel: by our actions and our words to the workplace, and to our neighbors where a priest could not have the time or ability to come to.

Our instructor for social justice was Deacon Tom. Tom was also a very strict instructor, but his strictness came not just in his assignments, but in his desire to make sure that we, as future deacons, understood that our future ministry had to be grounded in social justice. As our Lord reminds us in the Gospel, "the poor you will have with you always", Deacon Tom challenged us to not only read about issues of social justice but to find those circumstances in our community where social justice needed to be brought into the light of the community's attention and something being done about it. It was not a question of just donating a few dollars for another special collection after Mass and feel good about it, but rather it was a question of how do we live our own lives so that we are open to understanding the plight of the poor as well and is being the messenger to the larger community on what needs are to be done.

The poor are not just those who are without economic resources, the poor could also be those who have the trappings of great material possessions but have the stark emptiness of their own spirituality. Catholic Deacons would be the eyes, the ears, the arms and the feet of social justice. To see the poor in our midst and to stay silent was like ignoring the plight the person being attacked in the story of the Good Samaritan. Certainly we could do something, even if it meant bringing it to the greater awareness of the community. During that entire year, we had extremely lively discussions about many different facets of Catholic social teaching: preferential option for the poor, health care for the needy, and distribution of resources for all.

The highlight of that year on social justice was his introduction to us all was a religious sister that had done a great deal of work in South America, working with the poorest of the poor. He had served as a member of her Board of Directors for her foundation but also had made his own trips down to visit and work with the people she cared for. It was this combination of both the academic work but also the human element that started our training to becoming more relevant and more personal.

Our Lord worked and loved the poor throughout his entire time on Earth and our response to the poor is the active ministry of the Roman Catholic Church here on earth. The Church, in its infinite love for the poor, gave her deacons to be their advocates and their ministers. But at the end of that year, even with the increased workload that he demanded, Deacon Tom succeeded in making sure that all of us, without a doubt, understood what was required of us. There is a saying that I once heard from Hubert Humphrey, the former Vice President of the United States under President Lyndon Johnson. The quote, which I'm going to try to paraphrase as best I can, is simply this: **"The greatness of a society is determined by how that society treats those in the dawn of life, the twilight of life, and the fringe of life."**

These three references go to the unborn and the small children, the elderly, and all in our society that possess special needs. Having a young son who is autistic, knowing that whatever physical limitations he currently has, he will have to overcome by formal education and training that he will receive in public school, but these experiences pale in comparison to the love that he embodies to those that he meets and care about him. To him, the love of God is not just a theological abstract; it is a living part of his life. Special needs people, who society sometimes shuns because of our own desire for self-fulfillment, are living fonts of love and gratitude. The divine gift of love we say we all want, lives in the hearts of people such as these. The song of "Looking for love in all the wrong places" rings true. Open your heart to these people and you would be amazed how much it returned in its place.

For those of my classmates that would later go on to mission trips either to Haiti or Jamaica, they would come in contact with the same people that we studied about. These people that had been rejected by society for their physical or emotional deformities would be embraced by those Catholic charities and by religious orders whose sole function was to serve the least of these brothers – **in the faces of the poor and suffering, the rejected and outcast, they discovered the loving face of Jesus Christ in their midst.** When my brothers in formation returned from these mission trips and spoken about how they encountered a living and loving Christ in all that they had come in contact with, the words that Deacon Tom spoke about would ring true that much more. Social justice that year was not just an academic exercise, but a patient awakening process that would remain for us and with us for the rest of our lives.

Our final class in an Overview of the Holy Scripture that year was taught by Rusty Mawn, a retired IBM human resources executive, and a devout Catholic layman. Rusty had sent all of his children through Catholic high school and he openly would joke about the fact that he had multiple copies of a T-shirt that said "My money and my child go to a Catholic high school!" Once I asked them if he ever felt that he himself had the call to become a deacon, but he patiently smiled and said "no", he just enjoyed teaching them. Rusty also had a very large task, to do a survey class of the entire Sacred Scripture. For the first five months of class, he took us through an extensive drill of the Old Testament, showing us salvation history as it was presented in Holy Scripture. Always a man who enjoyed a good story, Rusty knew when to push hard and never let up. Giving us a simple mid-term exam question **"Show the history of salvation revealed in the Old Testament. Use all appropriate biblical examples and timelines. Do not omit anything and you can start writing now."** That was 75 minutes of the most intensive writing we had ever done. But just like all our instructors that year, he demanded that we be well-prepared for class and for those of us that were not as prepared as he thought we should be, he made us recognize that he did not suffer fools lightly.

All of our instructors that year had to teach us very important topics. Upon reflection, that was the year that we truly had to be broken down in order to be made better. The military frequently uses this type of training with new recruits because they're so much to learn in a short amount of time. Of course, for us that are on the receiving end of this training, is the equivalent of drinking from a large fire hose. If you are lucky, you can hang in there for a little bit at a time before you either blow up or learn to drink differently-quickly! But this was part of the formation process; it was both leadership laboratory and learning from your mistakes - rapidly! The desire for us to learn was evident but it was also matched by the desire of our teachers to know that we understood what was being taught that year.

Of course, as we ventured into the summer break, we knew that we would also have extra homework to do. Deacon Loris, true to form, came into one of our classes just prior to our summer departure with a big smile on his face. "You didn't think that you would get away without something to do over the summer, did you?"

I leaned over to Ken and murmured to him, "Just what I thought it was safe to get back into the water, here comes the shark." Of course, Deacon Loris looked at me and said "Albert, you have something to share with us?" "No sir," I replied, "Not at all, just let me know what the assignment is and I'll get it done."

"Okay, since you asked" he continued with a smile on his face, "you will take part in watching a ministry being performed by a deacon in your church. You will take part in the training, and you will write a report that will be due to me when you return on what took place, how the people received the training, and what you got out of it."

"You can choose whatever ministry your deacon does in the parish, but you will see how that training is done."

In looking back, the use of the summer assignments was the application phase for our preparation for future ministries. That summer, with the permission of my diaconate mentor Deacon Bill, I was able to watch the training our new parents received prior to their children being baptized through our parish Baptismal ministry. One of the great direct benefits of the growth of the Catholic Church, especially in the Southeastern US, was a great number of children that were being born and baptized into the Catholic faith. In our church, there was a required formation process for parents to go through that consisted of four hours of instruction gone over two separate weekends prior to the baptism of their children.

Deacon Bill led the ministry being assisted by two laypeople so then each instructor essentially taught four times a year. But each time they taught the class, they would encounter some parents that might have been away from the Church for a number of years. I know in my own circumstance, that I did not go take my faith seriously as an adult until my own children were born and we were preparing for their own baptisms. It was at that moment, I knew that it was not about me and Cindy after they were born. Just like it was not all about me alone after we got married, but it was the acceptance of the great grace of children but also having the responsibility for them to grow in the Catholic faith.

That summer provided me with a great opportunity to learn. Deacon Bill's class was very low-key and relaxed. As we worked through the textbook in four separate one-hour sessions, you began to hear the stories from the parents about their own faith journey and the aspirations that they have for their children. Sometimes, the parents got very introspective when they completed the spiritual journey section of the class. For those who had been away from the faith, looking into the eyes of their children served as the quiet reminder of their faith renewal. Once again, the responsibility of your future office became readily apparent. The people enjoyed hearing from the deacons because they shared the common responsibilities of parenthood and being Catholic. This was also a touchstone moment for me, because soon after my own ordination four years later, I became the deacon in charge of our Baptismal formation ministry!

Having conducted two classes already since being ordained, I've come to love the people as well as their children in a very special way. Each child, regardless of their circumstances, is precious in the eyes of their parents and of Our God. It is the responsibility of our community to be that enhanced social and spiritual support net that embraces all Christian Catholic parents and helps them in their desire to grow in their own faith.

This year also took our class through a series of turns. We continue to lose a couple more men that year, and when they made their decisions known to us, it was painful for us to hear. We're becoming that tight band of brothers; any potential personal barriers that were brought into formation were being chipped away at. Talents that could be used for the benefit of one person before were being brought and being shared with all. To some extent, it was the exact opposite of working in corporate America where the singular personal motivation is always looking out for "number one" and seeing where we can make career points, even if it's to the detriment of other people, as long as its to my own personal benefit.

Formation for us was the building of a community of brothers who shared a common desire: **to love God and serve His Church**. As our class continue to progress through that year, some of the men struggled and strained with the additional academic workload. All of us were employed in full-time work in the secular world as well is trying to maintain a very rigorous academic schedule and then an active prayer life as well. Twenty to thirty hours of personal time a week of study was not uncommon for that second year of formation; on top of normal work and family life commitments.

This was the cross of our formation that we were prepared to accept and the weight of that cross was made more evident during the second academic year. But also this was the time where charity was expressed from the heart. When needs were made known because someone lost a job, someone else would make a phone call and try to find out if a possible opening was available. When someone was sick or not in class that day, he could count on either multiple e-mails or phone calls being made to his home to see what was the matter and how can we help. Self-interest was replaced by silent but constant common concern and in that process of breaking people down was now being replaced by a process of we were lifting each other up instead.

As we returned in September, doubt was being replaced by confidence. Our instructors were focusing less on straight lecture for class and began relying on us more to be prepared and to being responsible for presenting our positions on various issues and teachings. Spirited debate became part of our norm as opposed to just simply listening and taking lots of class notes. But through it all, our instructors continued to focus on why we were there: **to be prepared to serve the people of God.**

In December, at the very last day of classes, a final Mass would typically be said at the end of the day instead of having the communion service in the morning. This Mass was a Mass of Thanksgiving for the graduating seniors but we all were giving thanks that another year had been completed. The Mass on that day, we celebrated the feast day of the Annunciation of Mary, the day that the Blessed Virgin was greeted by the Archangel Gabriel and told of God's grace in her. Would she be prepared to bring forth the Son of God for the salvation of Israel and for the entire world? Mary simply said "Yes" and with that yes, salvation was able to come into the world and God would dwell among his people as a man in the human and divine person of Jesus Christ. Sitting with my family that evening, the Deacon of the Mass who was Deacon Rich reminded us in his homily that we needed to be able to say yes as well to what God was calling us to do – each and every day.

Having survived the toughest year yet in our formation, I gave thanks to Almighty God for his many blessings we were prepared to celebrate that day. But we still have three years left to finish and the Year of 2003 would become a pivotal year for me and the Class of 2006.

Year 3 – Sophomore Year - 2003...

Time Frame	Activity or Class Scheduled
7:00 am - 8:00 am	Holy Hour (once a month)
8:00 am - 8:50 am	Communion Service Practicum
9:00 am - 10:15 am	Church Fathers
10:30 am - 11:45 am	Moral Theology
11:50 am - 12:40 pm	Divine Office - Lunch
12:45 pm - 2:00 pm	Prayers of the Church - Workshop
2:15 pm - 3:30 pm	Spirituality
3:45 pm – 5:00 pm	Sacred Scriptures - The Prophets

The Year 2003 would become a pivotal year for our class in formation. The public scandal that the Roman Catholic Church faced because of the misguided actions of the few priests who abused the people under their care was under the constant barrage of television news and in the print media. As we gathered once again to start our classes in February, we would sometimes talk about what had been revealed that week in the news or on television.

But even through the previous year and up to that point, not a single one of us would have even considered leaving our diaconate formation. Just as we have learned in Church History in our second year, the Catholic Church has been facing external persecutions and internal strife throughout our 2,000 years as a Church. We did not condone what had happened, because as more and more details became apparent, each and every one of us as fathers of children could understand how the abused victims could feel towards the Church now as spiritually injured adults. However, this negative attention we were subjected to made our resolve that much stronger as we grew closer as a class.

The best change that we got that year was that our classroom that moved to the top side of the building and we would also take a greater part in the Communion services. Up to this time, we had just served as readers of Sacred Scripture in either the first or second reading of the Communion service. However, this year, we would be functioning as acolytes for the Communion service which also meant that we were to assist the seniors in the preparation of the Communion service itself. In addition, we were also granted the privilege of wearing our white albs during the service we assisted at. Each of us was allowed to purchase our own albs as long as the alb was liturgically correct and was the correct fit for our body shapes.

Over Christmas of 2002, I contacted a store in Birmingham, Alabama, that would get for me a beautiful hooded alb based on the simplicity of St. Francis. When I finally received the alb at my home, I did a quick test fit and then looked at myself in the mirror. "It's now starting to come together" I said to myself. In the meanwhile, my wife and my daughter came in from the garage and saw me in my new alb. My young teenage daughter Christina, never missing an opportunity to make a point or a joke at my expense, sweetly smiled at me and said "Dad, you look like Friar Tuck!!" then she giggled and ran away to watch some TV. In response, Cindy gently placed her hand on my forearm, and then patted my sleeve and said "Al, you look like an angel. Of course, it's the angel that they place on top of the Christmas tree in Rockefeller Center." My daughter heard that comment and laughed even louder! So much for my family respect, but even in their gentle comments, they too started noticing that a change had been taking place in me.

Our sophomore year was significant because as we approached the summer break this year, we would officially be half way through our formation process. In addition, in October of that year, we would be formally accepted into the Church as both readers and acolytes. We could take a more significant role in the public liturgy and this step brought us closer to ordination, over 117 weeks away. The Church would bestow official recognition on our status above and beyond what we had experienced in January of the previous year. But also, Mother Church would also demand even greater fidelity and perseverance for the remainder of our formation.

Our classroom schedule would also be extensive. This year, we would be studying **the Early Church Fathers, Moral Theology, Prayers of the Church** which would be a workshop-directed class, **Catholic Spirituality II and Sacred Scripture with an emphasis on the Prophets**. At the start of formation, we were told specifically that if we were involved in other ministries besides being a reader or Eucharistic minister, that we were to depart from those ministries as quickly as possible. Now the full workload of formation was made readily apparent. Our spare time to study and prepare was at a premium as well is dealing with the requirements and needs of our secular work lives. Formation was now a full-time job, above and beyond what we did for a paying work in our family lives. Formation became a delicate balancing act with God as the head, then the needs of our family, the needs of our job, and then diaconate formation. In actuality, it was like a giant plate that was being balanced on the tip of a wooden reed. As long as the correct amount of attention was being paid to the plate to keep it spinning, its chance of tipping over was minimal. However, any lapse of personal attention would cause the plate to possibly tip over and crash on our heads.

Our instructor for Church Fathers would be Deacon Rich, our Class Deacon. As we examined over 400 years of early Catholic teaching by the early Fathers of the Church, we gained an even greater appreciation that our faith was not based on a repetition, but rather on Sacred Scripture and the Sacred Tradition combining together to form the Single Deposit of Faith. That Deposit was given to the Church and was protected even as the Church was growing in the early years under the persecution of Rome and under the constant guidance of the Holy Spirit. It was our responsibility to pick a topic such as the **"Real Presence of Christ in the Eucharist"** and to do specific and deep research on how the teachings of the Church Fathers reinforced that specific teaching. This sort of practicum exercise had a real specific purpose. As we would be challenged in ordained ministry to be able to teach the Catholic faith, we had to have a strong foundation on where the teachings of the Church came from and how the Church consistently throughout its history reinforced that teaching and applied it.

Once again, the richness of our class was brought forth during these exercises. Some of the men had very extensive teaching backgrounds either through RCIA or Adult Education and were extremely polished in their presentations on their respective topics. This class was not going to be just another exercise to pass. But the class also had actual ramifications that would remain with us for the rest of our ordained ministry. Deacon Rich consistently commented how he appreciated the seriousness that we approached this class and he would start treating us less as just students and more as future brothers in service to the people of God.

Moral Theology was taught to us by Father Kevin. Father Kevin was a young priest of Irish heritage whose specialty in seminary was Sacred Scripture. However, he had been part of the teaching staff for the permanent diaconate for a number of years and enjoyed the interaction between the men and himself. As a young priest assigned to the Archdiocese of Atlanta, he would frequently punctuate the lessons being taught with his own experiences ministering to the people of God. **Even St. Augustine said "to hate sin, but to love the sinner."**

So all through that year, Father Kevin constantly reminded us that we had to meet the people of God where they are to begin with. Therefore, as men of charity and faith, it was our obligation to understand that people will always have issues but it is our primary job to be examples of Christ's love to them. Of course, he always enjoyed a good joke and had a fine-tuned sense of satire which he lavished on us throughout the year. For example, he would ask us all a question and one of my brothers would try to give him what we thought was a very good response. Father Kevin would then nod and say quickly "No, I don't think so, but nice try!!" But even with his tough love, we always enjoyed this class.

Prayers of the Church were a workshop class that again required us to do a great deal of personal and academic research. The structure of this class was very simple: we were to take a prayer that the Catholic Church used extensively and then make a presentation on how that prayer was either developed, used, or the history of that prayer. I was lucky because that year, the new Mysteries of Light for the Rosary was introduced by Pope John Paul II. Having a love for the Rosary based on my mother's example, I seized on the opportunity to relate how each of the new ministries directly related to a deacon's experience. For example:

1. **the baptism of Christ in the Jordan River would be related to our sacramental responsibility to baptize the people of God as ordained deacons;**

2. **the wedding feast day Cana would be related to our experience as being married men with wives and children;**

3. **the Sermon on the Mount would be related to our future ministry of preaching and teaching the Catholic faith to the people of God;**

4. **the Transfiguration of Christ could be related to the**

transformation process that formation would have on each one of us, especially coming into the Presence of the Lord during holy hours or the Mass;

5. Finally, the celebration of the Eucharist would be related to our service at the altar, being ministers of the chalice, and bringing the Holy Eucharist to the sick and the dying.

All of my classmates brought a unique instance to their presentations in this class and also provided us with another opportunity to start honing our skills that we would later use in homilies next year.

Once again, Kersti would favor us as our instructor for Catholic Spirituality. She personally would have a great deal of change in her life: during the last year, she got married in Atlanta and went to Rome for her honeymoon with her new husband Joe to have their marriage blessed by the Holy Father, Pope John Paul II. But in 2003, she and her husband would be looking forward to adopting a child in the future. They would be successful in that effort, eventually adopting a child from China and bringing her home to Atlanta. That year, she really wanted us to deepen our understanding of Catholic spirituality above and beyond what Father Linus and Father Joseph had taught us in our first year. Once again, she proved herself to be a tough instructor, tough because she had high expectations for her future deacons that she was willing to give her time to train. Of course, she can hold her own against our complaining of the workload because she taught in Catholic high school and heard a lot worse for her students! But it was good to see her and to have her as an instructor once again.

For Sacred Scriptures, we were blessed to have Father Tim as our instructor. A tremendously talented priest, Father Tim was also a canon lawyer as well as having an expertise in Sacred Scripture. He could read Greek and Hebrew as well as having a mastery of Latin. Although he had served as a pastor of a parish previously, he really enjoyed teaching the deacons and gave us the first semblance of professional respect as future brothers in clergy. But that respect also came at a price, because he knew the importance of the time that we had together, that we had to make every bit of academic class time count because there was so much that we had to accomplish that year.

As Holy Week was beginning, on the home front, I was being asked to be part of each liturgy from Holy Thursday to Easter Sunday. Although I was a spare set of hands, if needed, my primary responsibility was to start learning because as Catholic Christian people celebrated the three days from Holy Thursday to the Easter vigil as the foundation of our faith, there was so much that I needed to learn and to be prepared for.

Father Jim was also being a spiritual father to me. He would ask me how classes were going, if there was anything that he needed to help me with, and being extremely supportive.

During the Easter Day services of 2003, I was starting to become more sensitive to what was happening during the services. During the Easter Day masses, we were running concurrent services between the parish hall and in the church. The courtyard that was normally deserted during Mass was filled with over 300 people that tried to get in either the church or the hall with no luck at either place. Some people were coming over to me and asking "Was I still at Mass even though I was not inside the hall or the church?" I responded to them that as long as they could hear the liturgy and respond to the prayers, they were at Mass. But it was also frustrating to see people who drove in the parking lot, saw that the parking lot was filled, and then drove away without even making an effort on their part to try to stay. Even on this greatest day of the Christian calendar, people were still seeking their own comfort instead of coming to be in the comfort of Almighty God.

When it came time for communion, I asked for a ciborium to take out to the people in the courtyard. Father Jim smiled at me and then placed the sacred vessel in my hand. To each person as I gave the Body of Christ, I started feeling on unmistakable sense of joy, pure joy, as I fulfilled my duty that day. The calling that I had responded to was now taking shape into the ministry that I would be privileged to continue in after ordination. Even after being up for the Easter Vigil the previous night and then returning very early for the sunrise service the very next day, at the end of Holy Week that year, I was both exhilarated and exhausted.

Also in the late spring, there was an addition to the parish staff. Deacon Rafael Cintron and his lovely bride Nilsa were joining the parish staff to assist us in building up a Hispanic outreach ministry. Rafael had been ordained in 1989 and was previously at St. John Neumann before he transferred over to St. Oliver's. Rafael and I quickly became good friends. As I learned more about him, he shared with me that he had always felt he would be a deacon to both communities, the Anglo and Hispanic, and he worked very hard to make that happen. Although I speak very little Spanish, I always look forward to the opportunities that I could serve with him. He had tremendous respect for my vocation call and I would frequently offer any support that he could use as he needed. Over the years, we would serve together during Holy Week and especially at the Feast Day of Our Lady of Guadalupe in December of each year.

Each year, our director of formation sent out a request for information on how we were performing in the parishes. Father Jim was always kind enough to let me know that he had received that information and he had responded to it. Deacon Bill had been selected as my formal diaconate mentor because officially, I could only have one but I still stayed close to Deacon Mike as well. Both were pleased at my level of progress to date, and both were kind enough to share on those items that they felt I needed additional preparation for. But if as if there weren't enough opportunities to succeed at the parish level, the Archdiocese of Atlanta certainly gave us opportunities in order to increase our faith as a complete local church.

The Archdiocese, typically in June of each year, sponsors a Eucharistic Congress on the Saturday prior to the Feast Day of Corpus Christi. Well over 20,000 Catholics from the Archdiocese of Atlanta as well as neighboring dioceses come to hear speakers of interest talk about various aspects of the Eucharist.

First of all, we are extremely privileged that we can have these annual Congresses at the Georgia International Convention Center in College Park, Georgia. This center has a huge exhibition space that gets readily converted into a large cathedral. The large exhibition room itself is probably the equivalent of four football fields under one specific roof. In one word: enormous.

The front part of the convention floor room is converted into a cathedral: complete with the chair for the Archbishop, two deacons chairs as well as a large altar that is elevated for the benefit of the people. In addition, closed-circuit TV cameras as well as large projection screens are set up so that everyone, regardless of where you are seated, has a beautiful view of what is happening up front. At the Mass on Saturday afternoon, which is the Vigil Mass for the Feast Day of Corpus Christi, there will probably be no less than 20,000 people assembled for Mass.

The spectrum of presenters to the people assembled that day is usually quite impressive. They are chosen because they have either a very special gift or they have a special message that they wish to share with the community. In the year 2003, we were extremely gifted to have a very special guest speaker.

The Eucharistic Congress has a very formal program for the day. Here is an outside procession that takes place at the start, then an inside procession of the people moving to the main convention room where the people of God participate and that takes well over an hour to complete. Then the monstrance is brought back into the general hall where there is a complete one Hour Holy Hour. However, the Eucharist is then transferred into a small chapel where people can start coming in to worship and silently pray some more. In some instances, some people spend over an hour more in private adoration of the Blessed Sacrament above and beyond the mass adoration that happened earlier in the morning.

After the Eucharistic Adoration is completed in the main hall, then there are several educational tracks that are presented for the people's enrichment in different parts of the Convention center. For example, there is a life teen track for teenagers, there is a young children's track, there is a Spanish track where all the presenters speak in Spanish, there was begun a Vietnamese track, and then finally, there was a general audience track.

During 2003, the upcoming movie of "the Passion" or "The Passion of the Christ" as we came to know it as, made by Hollywood actor/director and devout Catholic Mel Gibson was getting a tremendous amount of national press. One of the featured speakers for that year's Eucharistic Congress was James Caviezel, the 33 year-old actor that would be portraying Jesus Christ in this movie.

When it came time for Jim to speak in the latter part of the afternoon about playing Christ in the Passion, the audience was first given an extended trailer of what the upcoming movie would be like. We heard the stories about the whipping scenes in the movie from the popular media, but we were unprepared for what we saw that afternoon. The selected scenes in that trainer confirmed what we had heard about; the audience was silent as we sat and looked on the screens above. It was nothing less then powerful and at the end of the movie trailer, the lights slowly came up, the audience was quiet from what it had seen, and he began to speak.

Jim talked about his childhood and his career in Hollywood, how he had been a struggling actor but how his Catholic faith had persevered, even in Hollywood. He continued about how he got his first major movie role, praying the rosary before he went up the door of the home where his meeting was, on giving a beautiful rosary that had been his wife's to a person he thought was a maid. But instead, it was the wife of the director of the movie he was auditioning for and how she had graciously received his unplanned gift. While he thinking that he had blown the opportunity to be in the movie, the director's wife was overwhelmed with gratitude for his hasty gift.

Ultimately, he did get that part in that movie and his career in Hollywood was well on its way.

Then he talked about how he was contacted by Mel Gibson to play our Savior in this upcoming movie. The two things that he spoke about that really caught Mel Gibson off-guard initially was the fact that his initials were "JC" and at the time that they were filming; he was 33 years old – some of the same attributes Our Lord was at the time he finished his earthly ministry.

The role of playing Christ during the Passion had not been easy to perform. While on location in Italy, he spoke about how he had been exposed to the constant cold and wind as well as being positioned precariously close to the cliff on the edge of town where the film shoot had taken place. While being on the cross for those long hours of film shoots, his body was racked with pain and fatigue along with the extensive makeup he had to wear for the role. It would have been so easy to walk away from that, but he, like Our Lord, did not. He stayed until the job was done. But in light of all of that personal suffering, God's grace came through that filming; despite all the press prior to its opening, this movie was destined for becoming a major impact on our American society. Months later, as the movie opened up on Ash Wednesday of 2004, there were countless tales of people that have been drawn to Christ as a direct result of seeing the movie.

Finally, he spoke of his tremendous love for the Blessed Mother. He spoke of the times when his faith had not been as strong as it should have been but he also spoke about the times that he could feel her presence in his life. At that point of the presentation, I reflected back in my own current circumstances, being part of a parish that was being supported by an order of Catholic priests who came into being because the Blessed Mother presented herself to two small children asking them to turn their lives to God. Glancing out into the audience that afternoon, who could deny the power of Mary – our Universal Mother – was it not a mother's love that could move us all to come together with ourselves, was it not her love that caused us to gather all of her children together who soon worship her son, our Blessed Savior, through participating in the Holy Mass?

At the end of the day, the Vigil Mass for Corpus Christi was celebrated. Thousands of people stayed for the Mass, hundreds of priests and deacons assisting the bishops, numerous laypeople who read with passion and solemnity their respective readings in Spanish and other languages with the Gospel being proclaimed in English. People skilled at sign language performed so that all could be included at the celebration of the Mass that day. The prayers of the faithful were also multilingual, reflecting the rich diversity that is the Archdiocese of Atlanta.

During the consecration of the bread and wine into the Precious Body and Blood of our Lord Jesus Christ, I glanced out to thousands of people who were on their knees, in the presence of our Eucharistic Lord. Who could deny the saving power of the Mass, the precious gift that our own Lord had given to his disciples on Holy Thursday, as a way for Him to be able to remain with His Church until He came again in glory? With each sentence of the Eucharistic prayer being said, you truly came to believe that you were in the presence of Christ himself. But as Catholics, that was the purpose of this day – to proclaim and celebrate the real and total Presence of our Lord Jesus Christ in the Eucharist.

Finally, when Holy Communion was being distributed to the people, I was allowed to bring communion to a section in the back. Once again, my vocation as a Eucharistic minister was being realized. It was a total joy to do this for the people of God. The young, the old, the married and single, the rich and the poor – all of these people extending their cupped hands in a unified gesture to receive our Lord in Communion.

The Mass concluded, the final blessings given with the choir starting to sing, we processed out, the people of God started in spontaneous applause for the clergy as they exited. That day had been a great day and as I returned home that night, I was both excited and exhausted. It'd been a long day, when

I got up at 5:00 am to get my spiritual director, Father Joseph Mendes that morning, he said Mass for the nuns at the convent at 6:00 a.m. and then we departed to be down at the Convention Center by 7:45 a.m. By the time we got home that evening, it was close to 9:00 p.m. However, once again, God had granted me a great grace of service that day.

Summer vacation came and went in that year and, of course, with summer came the annual summer assignment. This year, however, it was different. We had to interview our pastor about our progress and how he envisioned utilizing our talents and ministry after ordination. This was a rather dramatic shift for what we had previously experienced because now we're focusing on what we would be doing in the future as opposed to just learning about something and reporting back. The proverbial light at the end of the tunnel was just starting to gleam but at least it was there for us to see.

In the autumn of that year, also provided us with another milestone to be completed. We would be formally accepted as readers and acolytes within the Archdiocese of Atlanta. On October 8, 2003 at 7:30 p.m., a tri-lingual Mass was celebrated at Our Lady of Vietnam in South Atlanta. A beautiful community of over 700 families, our brother Joseph acted as the liaison for this great occasion. His pastor and entire church community welcomed the opportunity to receive us as well as the Archbishop on this great occasion. This also would be the first time that we would wear our albs together as a class.

The ceremony within the Mass was both dignified and uplifting. After once again being formally introduced to the Archbishop, we would kneel in front of him to receive a copy of Sacred Scripture as well as to receive the chalice as symbols of our devotion to learning and practicing our faith as well as being ministers of the cup to the people of God at the altar. As each one of us knelt before him, the common thought ran through all of our heads at the end of that Mass: the next time that we will do this will be at Ordination and at that time he would lay his hands on our heads as the official affirmation of our call to serve as deacons.

Joseph and the entire parish community of Our Lady of Vietnam came through for all of us with a very lively and festive reception at the end of that mass. The women were dressed in the traditional garb of Vietnamese culture, and the men all wore suits and ties. The reverence that they held for the Archbishop was signified by them either bowing, kneeling before him or kissing his ring. For our class, they gave us nothing less than a great welcome and a tremendous feast that we long remembered after that date. As we approached the end of this year, we looked forward to officially serving at the altar when we returned back to our parishes. Christmas would be celebrated in less than 11 weeks, and our third year of formation would be ending in eight weeks. Now time was starting to slip away as we rapidly prepared the final assignments for our classes.

But for me, the end of that year would result in a great personal loss.

I was at work on the morning of November 19, 2003, when I ran into a fellow parishioner they used to work for the company that I work for. Len had been a former employee with the company but had been in a serious car accident and was medically retired as a result. Being excited that I met him at work, I said "Len, what are you doing here?" He said, "I'm here for a meeting of the Pioneers." Then he added "Have you heard the news yet?"

"What news are you talking about?"

He said "You haven't heard, Deacon Mike is dead."

"Dead, what do you mean, dead?"

"He died last night -- he was responding to an accident that it just happened in front of him, and he was hit by a passing car."

At that point, I was stunned senseless. The man who had been my mentor and friend for over three years was now suddenly gone? I was just standing there when Len said, "I was just stunned too when I heard the news."

"Okay Len, I got to go. Thank you for letting me know."

I went back to my cubicle and called the church. They had confirmed what Len had told me and at that point I was just speechless. My boss at the time, Jim, who was a retired Army lieutenant colonel and a Lutheran, had known about my diaconate vocation when he hired me. When I explained to him what happened, he told me to leave immediately and not to worry about work. After a 45 minute drive, I arrive at St. Oliver's and went immediately inside the church. There were several people kneeling in the pews and I joined them.

On this huge stained-glass window right in back of the altar, there is a large figure of Christ's triumphant rise to His Father, as He is ascending into heaven. I looked at that figure and I suddenly started crying. My friend, my confidant, my brother in Christ had been responding to the scene of an accident that had just taken place. As he pulled over on the opposite lane of traffic, he was attempting to cross the street after dark when he was hit by a vehicle head-on. His act of self-sacrifice in death would define him as he lived in life: with the last full measure, he gave his life to the people of God, in this case, to people he had never met before in his earthly life.

As I was meditating about this fact, a woman took a beautiful arrangement of flowers and placed it on the deacon's chair to the right of the presider's chair. That was one of the two deacons chairs that he had sat in when he assisted at Mass and now my friend was gone. At that point, I sobbed uncontrollably and one of my brothers from the Men's Club came over to share in my grief. Deacon Bill came in from the church office and saw me crying. "You know about Mike then?" he said. "Yes I do, Bill. What can I do for you?"

"At this point, we're making the final preparations for his funeral. We would appreciate your help on that day."

"For Mike, anything, anything at all."

The masses that Sunday were a bit difficult to get through. The flowers on the deacon's chair were a constant reminder of his loss to us. The traditional parish Thanksgiving dinner was canceled on that Sunday afternoon out of respect and the food donated for the dinner that would be used for Mike's reception that would take place after the funeral Mass on Monday.

My brothers in formation heard about the news about Mike and were either calling me or e-mailing me with messages of encouragement and support. They were no strangers about Mike either. For two and a half years, I had told them about his personal encouragement to me and his constant concern for my formation process, but I was thankful for their support that week.

Mike's vigil service that Sunday night was heavily attended by our parish community. As the casket was brought in and then the casket lid opened, it was hard for me to take in his death was a reality. He was dressed in a white hooded alb with the new white stole that he had worn for Easter Masses that spring. In his hands held a Benedictine rosary with the Cross of St. Benedict given by a fellow parishioner. My brother in formation, Ken Melvin, who had driven from his home to attend the vigil, had his own personal connection to Mike. Because during the second part of the interviewing process – when we had to meet with a deacon and his wife in a parish other than our own -- Deacon Mike had been his interviewer for that part of the process. Afterwards, he threw his arms around my shoulders and gave me one of those warm brotherly hugs that he would've given to a member of his own family. "You holding up okay?" he asked. "I don't know Ken." I replied. "You just hang in there; he would've wanted you to be strong for him."

Mike's entire family was present along with the entire parish community. There is a saying that the wealth of a man is not contained in the riches of his life but how many people attend his funeral in death. Using that standard, Mike had been a very, very rich man. He had touched a great number of people in his public ministry and his loss was starting to be felt throughout St. Oliver's.

At the end of the two-hour vigil, I was one of the last people to be with him. Even to the end, I would not leave the man who had been my "wing man" over the past three years. I would stay with him for as long as I could because I know that if the situation had been reversed, he would be there for me.

The funeral Mass on Monday morning was packed; every space that could be filled was and people were coming out into the hallway as well. The Archbishop of Atlanta, several priests, as well as Mike's classmates in the diaconate formation as well as many ordained deacons came to his funeral. As I was standing in the back, I was wondering if Mike himself knew how many people he touched in his life. Father Peter, a young Polish priest who had been transferred to our parish, gave the homily. Always known for enthusiastic preaching, Father Peter reminded us of the tremendous love that Mike had, not only for the people that he knew but for those people that he did not know that night. "Of all the homilies Deacon Mike gave throughout his ministry, the final actions of his life was the greatest homily of all", he said.

The archbishop celebrated the funeral Mass which would be customary for the death of any clergy in his diocese. However, his presence as the chief shepherd of the flock of the people of God for Atlanta was especially poignant because he himself was a fellow servant to the people of God.

As the casket was being brought out of church, the deacons assembled formed a double line on both sides when the casket passed by for the last time. At that point, I could not hold back the tears that came finally came out. My friend was gone, and I had not had the chance to say a proper goodbye to him.

The last mass that I served with Mike had been the Veterans' Day Mass two weeks earlier. We have a traditional ceremony at St. Oliver's after communion where a poem is read that talks about the service of people that have been in the military. At the end of this poem, all of the veterans that have served are individually called and asked to stand. Mike and I were serving together at the 11:15 a.m. Mass when both our names were called. Mike had also served in the United States Air Force in Massachusetts and I had served with the Air Force in California, Michigan and England. The fact that a deacon and a deacon candidate had both served in the US military was not lost on our larger parish family that day. After that mass, we both were enjoying some donuts and coffee when in traditional fashion, he drained his cup, tossed it in the trash, and then said "Okay, I'll see you next week!" as he left in the back of the hall. It was always implied, we'll be together each week, get caught up on what happened and be with the people afterwards.

Of course, I didn't see him the following week because we were scheduled for separate masses that Sunday and that Mass on Veteran's Day weekend was the last time I saw him alive. The next time my friend and I were together was at his funeral vigil service.

Deacon Bill saw me after Mass and was sympathetic to my grief. However, to his credit, he told me that I needed to learn from this experience because this would not be the only time I would experience death, especially after Ordination. Our deacons typically, when asked by the pastor or the family of the deceased, will do a funeral vigil service the night before the funeral Mass. Therefore, it was important for me to know that I would have to deal with death and I should be prepared to be a comfort and a source of support to the parish family. Bill, to his credit, would not know how prophetic those words would be in my own life as I came to the end of my formation.

The parish reception was held immediately after Mass because Mike had requested his remains be cremated and therefore there would be no immediate burial at the cemetery. The reception held in the hall was filled to capacity and it seemed that each table had its own collective memory of what

Michael had done either for them or with them. My wife Cindy was a great comfort to me during this time. I personally had not felt grief this profound since the death of my mother and I was having difficulty personally dealing with it. To that end, Cindy just gently reminded me that all the great lessons that Mike taught me, that I should be prepared for the future.

But even in the midst of great tragedy, God works all things for good. As luck would have it, a retired deacon was sitting at the same table as the Archbishop. When the Archbishop asked him if he knew him, the senior deacon said no. He had been retired for a number of years and looked forward to being able to sing in the choir with his lovely bride of many years. Then the Archbishop asked him a question, "Would you be willing to help the parish out for a little time as they worked through this temporary situation?" The deacon responded that he could, and very shortly afterwards he joined the parish staff as well. That deacon was Thomas Mackin and Tom has been a vital part of our liturgies ever since. Although happy in retirement, Tom was willing to come out of that retirement to help our community. As I would later learn, Tom had been a classmate with Deacon Bill while they went through diaconate formation together. So once again, they were together again serving as deacons in the same parish. As I would later get to know Tom and Eileen, his lovely bride of many, many years, along with being parents of four daughters, that the love that they shared for each other and for our parish was a very beautiful and powerful gift.

So in the midst of this tragedy, Almighty God in His infinite mercies, had made excellent provision for our parish. We now had three ordained deacons while I was still in formation and we were looking to expand our outreach into the Hispanic community.

As I returned back for the last two classes in December, my classmates were especially supportive of me. They'd known of my personal respect and love for Mike, and they offered me whatever support they could. Ken and I had known Mike the best and his loss in our lives was both personal and heartfelt. Deacon Loris also made an effort to pull me aside to offer his support as well as to educate the other men in formation about Mike's contribution while he had been in formation after the communion service that morning. Mike had been part of the first class that Deacon Loris had been Director of Diaconate Formation for. He recalled Mike had some difficulty while in formation, that the academic workload had not come easy to him, Mike had struggled greatly with the increased work load. But he had persevered to the end because he wanted to serve the people of God and that is where he felt he was called. All of us, he said, could learn well by that lesson and to remember that personal sacrifice made for the benefit of others is the greatest attribute of a Christian.

So the Year 2003 ended with the celebration of Christmas and a reflection that God's promise for a Savior for all of mankind had been fulfilled. In time, our parish family returned to normal. But for myself, there would not be a single Sunday that I would not think of my brother Deacon Michael. I was the recipient of his friendship, his real love for me and my family. In turn, I had also received his good guidance and his challenge to grow as a Catholic man and as a deacon in training. I was just blessed to have him in my life for the time that I did.

Almighty and Eternal God, grant to him – my brother and your servant Michael, eternal rest and peace to his soul. Amen.

Summer Retreats 2001-2005 and Spiritual direction...

Summer retreats from 2001 through 2005

Retreat Year	Weekend Retreat Masters and Retreat Topics
2001	Father Thomas Valenti "Be Still and Know I am God"
2002	Fr. Chris Williamson - "A Systematic Theology of Conversion"
2003	Fr. Chris Williamson - "Grace - Not a Girl's Name"
2004	Fr. Tim Gadziala "Hope has a Face"
2005	Fr. Larry Richards - "Yes Lord, Your Servant is Listening"

During every summer in July, all of the men in diaconate formation were required to make a weekend retreat. As Director of Formation, Deacon Loris was responsible for organizing these retreats. Like birds that return to the same spot each year, every year we had our retreat at Saint Bernard's Abbey, the Benedictine monastery in Culman, Alabama. Culman is approximately 65 miles north of Birmingham so the one thing that we can count on every year was as long as the sun was shining; Culman was going to be hot!

However, the retreat facility itself on the monastery grounds was situated right next to the school's gym and the entire facility was always within walking distance. The Ave Maria Grotto served as a local tourist attraction and destination of pilgrimage. In addition, the worldwide headquarters of Eternal Word Television Network or EWTN was also nearby in Irondale, AL. So even in the middle of the Bible belt, Catholicism was proudly represented.

As you can tell by the schedule at the top of the chapter, each year a different retreat master brought in a specific message that we needed to focus on for that weekend. In retrospect, in the year 2001, the topic of "Be still and know that I am God" was extremely important. For the past six months, we had not only been immersed into formation, but many of us welcomed the break from the nightly reading assignments/short answer essays/or other assignments are instructors gave to us during that time. If you don't plan for it, you can enter into a tendency of working so hard to get stuff done, that the spirituality that you are seeking becomes more and more difficult to reach. The Benedictines had a great motto that was posted prominently in their cafeteria. The English translation of this model from Latin is simply this "prayer and work." Both of these critical elements are crucial for the development of a successful Christian life. Needless to say, we will always be engaged in all things that we call work – our secular work to provide for families, our physical training to keep our bodies reasonably fit, our leisure activities that may involve some work in order to become better – but sometimes the prayer aspect gets lost in translation or more often probably just gets lost. What these weekends provide for us is not only a form of relaxation; it provides us with a spiritual work that gives us a different sort of reward, the reward of peace, tranquility, and a closer proximity to God.

Personally, I had never been on a Catholic weekend retreat before. If the opportunity had presented itself previously, I simply don't remember it.

However, Benedictine monastery at Culman would serve as an ideal spiritual vacation respite. It seemed that during the other times that I took vacation time in the spring, I gave those weeks to the diaconate as being the only times that I can focus on my large writing assignments without having it being disruptive to my family life. Typically, Cindy would be at work and the kids would be at school during the day, so this provided me plenty of time to be able to do research in my writing undisturbed. However, when I went away for the first time I told Cindy what a great experience it was for me, she took a slightly different direction. Cindy and the kids, however, had a different view of their own needs to get alone with the Lord and starting in August 2001, every time I went to Culman, they sought the beaches of Tybee Island, outside of Savannah, Georgia, as their yearly respite / retreat. All in all, it was a small price to pay. I never protested because frankly, I'm not a beach person. The close as I get to the beach is where the pool stops, so if that's what they needed to be spiritually recharged, I was all for it.

Of course, as we arrived at the monastery for the first time, we were overwhelmed by its simplicity and beauty. The Benedictine monks that we would soon come to know in our annual visits were extremely receptive to us being there. We were no ordinary visitors that were there just to simply walk the grounds, buy tickets to walk in the Grotto and then purchase some religious items in the gift shop at the conclusion of our visit. We were there for more, to find a peaceful place so that our hearts could rest, the fears about our vocation set aside and to be able to start building up the inner strength that we would need to get us through the remainder of the year.

The monastery church that had been constructed over the years was made out of the local limestone and had tremendous acoustics. Built like a classic Jerusalem cross, each part of the cross had a specific meaning. As you entered into the church from the west wing, you walked in and saw a beautiful stone altar at the very center that was elevated slightly off of the floor. To the left of the altar in the north wing, you would see a beautiful large tabernacle

143

with an iron figure of the crucified Christ hanging on the cross. Looking over the altar and into the east wing was the segregated cloister with the wooden rows where the monks had their assigned seating; you needed to look back at the crucifix that had been suspended over the altar.

As you looked at the altar from the west, you saw the crucified Jesus with his mother and St. John at his feet. But looking at the same crucifix from the cloister in the east wing, you saw the figure of Christ triumphant at the Last Judgment. Therefore, on one crucifix, you saw two sides of Jesus: the human side that died for our sins, and the divine side that would judge us on the Final Day. On the right of the altar in the south wing, were the confessionals for the Sacrament of Penance/Reconciliation were located and also some additional seating for the church. As I said before, the acoustics in that building was unbelievable. Several times, we would be singing without the benefit of any background music and yet the sound of over 100 men singing such songs as "Holy, Holy, Holy" or "Here I am Lord" were tremendous spiritual experiences onto themselves.

The abbot and the individual monks would be extremely generous to us in so many different ways. Early in our retreats, we were invited to join the monks in their daily prayers; not just to join them outside of the cloister, but to actually join them in the cloister, chanting and praying. The abbot, on occasion, would remain after prayers and ask us how our stay was progressing. I cannot remember more considerate nor hospitable hosts than these gentle and holy monks.

Near the grotto, was the cemetery where the monks were buried at the end of their earthly pilgrimage. Late in the evening one summer night, I was out walking around with my brother in formation Ken where we stood at the edge of the fence that would lead us into the cemetery. For about fifty yards, on both sides of the road are within a densely wooded area were the fourteen Stations of the Cross are displayed. The trees formed a natural and thick canopy over the large pictures that signify each of the stations. But at the end of the wooded area and in the open, being lit by the rays of a full moon was a large white crucifix where our Lord was hung on it. Even at night, the Glory of the Cross would not be silent or be hidden in the dark. As you walked past the Crucifix, you can see the grave markers arranged in a semi circle around each other where the previous monks had died and were buried. Yet, even as they rested in their faith in Jesus Christ, this holy place was at peace.

To some extent, this was an ideal place to meditate on what we were trying to undertake. In marriage, each person – the husband and wife – are to be mutually submissive to each other. Each day, the husband "dies" of his own self so that his wife and later his children can live. Therefore, as many of us work to support our families, we know that there are more important needs that must be set ahead of our own in order for our families to thrive. Our wives, on the other hand, also "die" because their constant thoughts for the welfare of their spouses and families are set above their own welfare and desires. The greatest challenge that we face in marriage may not be the lack of money, but rather the lack of courage to be able to die daily to our inner self so that others can live.

In a larger sense, the vocation of the diaconate is a life of service to others. Not just the needs of our immediate family, but the needs of a larger family, the body of Christ will sometimes take a higher place. Therefore, if we cannot even die to our wives for their benefit and the benefit of our families, how can we die for the benefit of people that we may not even know personally? These monks, the servants of God who have gone back to their rest in the Creator that made them, served as a constant and silent reminder of what vocation is: the conscious decision to follow the path not drawn by ourselves, but what was planted in our hearts by God the Father. Even Christ Himself was faith to the plan His Father devised. Christ embraced that divine plan and proclaimed it as His Own. So each and every one of us must with the remaining time we have left.

All of my brothers in formation, regardless of their age, education, and outward social standing, were willing to set that personal self-interest be pushed aside to become servants. In the image of Christ being the Ultimate Servant, they were willing to give of themselves, their God-given talents and whatever lifespan on this earth they have left, so that the people of God could be drawn closer to Christ in their ministries and through their examples of their lives. But just as any battery cannot constantly give energy without being occasionally renewed and recharged; we would come to love Culman as being that place of spiritual refreshment and vocational renewal.

Of course, as we arrived into the dormitory for the first time, our director of formation once again served as both the welcoming committee and the boot camp sergeant. "Gentlemen, I expect you to be on your best behavior so please be respectful of the facilities while you are here." Of course, the sound levels in the hallway always increased, as one by one, our classmates arrived, safe and sound, and we would greet each other with loud hellos, warm handshakes and affectionate hugs.

During our time in Culman, the conference facility itself went through a transformation process. Initially, it'd been a dormitory that they had converted into a retreat place, but on the inside, it kept the appearance of a high school dormitory. However over the years, they actually completed a very extensive renovation of the property so that our last two years at the retreat house were spent in a very nice facility. The conference room that we celebrated Mass as well as had the four of five conferences of the weekend had been totally redone. New furniture had been brought in the place that had gone through nothing less than a total physical makeover. The bedrooms, especially the beds, had also been replaced, however; there was one very clear distraction that had been removed: there were no telephones in the rooms at all.

Naturally, many of the men carried cell phones with them to keep contact with their loved ones back home. However, the intentional exclusion of the phones in the room had a specific message: sometimes, you have to get rid of some things in order to grow closer to God. Initially, the phones and later the Internet, would invade our lives while we were outside of the monastery. But on the inside, we had to make a definite effort to put something aside and the phone/Internet were natural targets. Of course, if someone was needed, a cell phone could always be made available so that a communication with the wife or child would not be unnecessarily delayed. However, it was amazing to think that we could actually live without an entire weekend, constantly checking up on the work at the office or making phone calls home.

The following schedule was usually used for our annual retreats.

Friday evening
Dinner on your own
6:30 PM – Evening Prayer
7:30 PM – Conference #1

Saturday – All Day
7:00 AM – Office of Readings & Morning Prayer
8:00 AM – Breakfast in the Cafeteria
9:30 AM – Conference #2
11:00 AM – Mass in the Retreat Center
12:15 PM – Lunch
1:00 – 2:45 PM -- Sacrament of Reconciliation at the Church
3:00 PM – Conference #3
5:30 PM – Supper
7:00 PM – Evening Prayer
8:00 PM – Holy Hour & Conference #4 in the Church

Sunday morning
7:00 AM – Office of Readings & Morning Prayer
8:00 AM – Breakfast in the Dining Hall
10:30 AM – Mass & Conference #5

As you can see in the schedule, it was also important that we had elements of both private and public prayer. Using the example of the cemetery, that place provided us a very secluded place for private prayer and meditation. However, as the year progressed, each of us developed our own special place that we could go to for private prayer and meditation with the Lord. Of course, inside the church, we gathered together for the Liturgy of the Hours. This communal prayer provided us with a constant reminder of what our Lord himself commanded us to be in constant prayer for the sake of His Church. But there were also times for us to simply sit or kneel in the presence of the Blessed Sacrament at any time of the day or night. It had a single lone spotlight that always shown on the tabernacle, providing it with a wonderful glow of subdued lighting.

In addition, the monks made generous use of incense with the sweet smell of Byzantine resin being used in their liturgy. For us as Catholics, incense has a very special place in our liturgies – it symbolizes our individual prayers being offered in rising back to the Father who received them with the Son who intercedes for us at the Father's right hand and the Holy Spirit that continually urges us to live lives of sanctity and holiness while we are on our earthly pilgrimage. Yes, Culman offered us all of these benefits and for a short 48 hours, it was indeed a very welcome respite in a very busy and selfish world.

We rarely ever knew who would be a retreat master prior to the actual start of the retreat. However, each one of the summer retreats in the five years of formation reflected on a very strong point. However, each priest that served as a retreat master made a special effort to ensure that his conferences offered us both hope and insights. The challenge of having a successful retreat is not in the power of the speaker, because even in the weakest of public speakers, the Holy Spirit gives them the grace to preach God's truth, but we must be willing to be open to what is being said. Therefore, the summer retreats allowed us to be able to both learn and experience God's love and sense of purpose in our lives in a very special way.

I remember with great detail that during the holy hour on Saturday evening, the retreat master Father Thomas was talking specifically to the seniors about the importance of being adequately prepared for preaching after ordination. He spoke about too many times where the celebrant or the Deacon had not been prepared and they tried to "wing it." **Father Tom then looked into the audience declaring how the people of God deserved our very best.** If we were not ready to preach that day, then don't try to bluff your way out of it. Even as a young formation student, that message resonated then and still does today. At that time, it would be years before I started learning the great art and craft of preaching, but that message of being prepared to preach, was foremost on my mind when I did start to learn homiletics. The people of God did deserve my very best, and therefore it was absolutely essential that I kept that attitude in front of me when I started to learn, and as I continually learn, even after ordination.

I do know this, that I was in that chapel that night because through many years prior, I had listened to various homilies given by priests that I respected and their homilies as well as their ministries changed the course of my life. They do not change me by beating me up with a spiritual hammer, or parading my weaknesses in front of myself and others with the use of shame, but they changed my heart by challenging me to become a better man, a better father, and a better brother in Christ Jesus. For an ordinary guy, being on retreat for an entire weekend would have seemed like a tremendous sacrifice, if I was not worthy of it being done in the first place. But as we progressed in our formation, there was no other place that I would've wanted to have been, other than being with my family, and being with my brothers at beautiful stone church in the middle of northern Alabama. It was in that church over the years that my vocation was presented to me, where I reaccepted it for the next year and it was perfected in the process. In fact, at the end of our last summer retreat, we glanced back over the familiar view of the campus and I was silently recalling all of the things that happened to me over the years in Culman.

The monastery, the abbot and monks, as well and is the local community, provided us with a safe comfort zone that we could use to be rejuvenated and then pushed forward. Culman was quite indeed a literal island of oasis in peace that was focused on Christ in a world that still remains focused on itself.

Spiritual direction

Spiritual direction was something that was thrust upon us very early on. At some point prior to our collective departure for the first summer break, our director of formation told us that we needed to have a spiritual director. Not knowing what spiritual direction was, I asked "How do you get one?" He replied that he would be giving us a book called **"Seeking Spiritual Direction"** and this would help us find a person suitable as a spiritual director. However, there were specific restrictions that we had to follow.

First, the spiritual director had to be a priest – a fellow Deacon or a religious person would not be acceptable as an individual director. The reason why was that we had to make ourselves available to be able to receive the sacrament of reconciliation and only a priest or bishop would be able to do that for us. In addition, it was highly suggested that we do not have our pastor serve as both spiritual director and pastor at the same time. Because this same person would be responsible for reporting back on our progress, the idea that the spiritual director had to have some level of independence was the reason for this requirement.

Secondly, we had to meet with our spiritual director at least once a quarter but ideally once a month at the beginning. The idea of getting into regular habits was absolutely essential for our first year.

Finally, we had to keep an actual written log of the dates that we had met with our spiritual director and submit it on a quarterly basis. What was actually discussed at spiritual direction meetings, was totally up to us and none of his concern, but we had to properly document that we had met with our spiritual director on a regular basis.

During the first retreat, I read the book "Seeking Spiritual Direction", and was quietly asking myself "what is so different about this from mentoring? Spiritual direction is really a form of spiritual mentoring." With a more educated explanation, I started to look for a good spiritual director.

From my adult life, I was blessed to have several men that served as a great mentor for me in my personal and professional life. I come to look to these men as being like proxy fathers and older brothers. So as I continued in my search for a spiritual director, there were three attributes that I felt that I needed to have.

- **The first attribute was that of personal chemistry, because in actuality, spiritual direction involves a lot of sharing of your personal experiences and development. Even under the seal of sacramental confession, I wanted to know that this was a person I could trust all the past experiences that I would be make known to him.**

- **Secondly, the next attribute was the availability of time. Of course, all of us are struggling with the issue of too many things and not enough time to do them in. So I would make a dedicated effort not to be over committing on their time, but I wanted to make sure that they would have enough time for me as well.**

- **Finally, I was looking for someone that could really challenge me to grow. The best men that I've worked for were the ones they knew how to challenge me, to stretch me and my talents so that at the end of a project or an assignment, I could look back and see some real development that had taken place.**

As I mentioned in the previous chapters, Father Joseph Mendes had served as my second spirituality instructor after the departure of Father Linus. Father Mendes also was relatively close by, living only about 10 miles from where I lived in town. Not knowing whether he would be available to take on any additional spiritual directees, I made the request in faith to him. He said that he would be willing to take me on as a directee and I have been with him ever since. Those early days of spiritual direction were, at first, mutual sessions of both growing in knowledge of my faith as well as dealing with my stubbornness and conceit.

The formation academic assignments seem to be too large, the timeframe always seem too short, and my sense of pride was too big. However, over time, my spiritual director challenged to first trust in God's mercy. Throughout most of my adult life, I probably could have counted on both hands how many times I sought the sacrament of reconciliation of my own free will. In fact, prior to the start of the process, I made the equivalent of the general confession with one of my parish priests and found that result extremely liberating. However, over time, I looked forward to our monthly meetings with the full intention of receiving the sacrament of reconciliation at the end of our session. It seemed to be in natural conclusion that in order to move forward for the next day, we had to be accountable for what we had done in the past as well as seeking God's mercy. My confessor and director acts in the image of Christ: not one to throw the first stone, but rather the first one to extend his hand and to help you up after you have fallen down because of sin. I once asked my spiritual director why frequent confession was so important. He answered with a very profound statement, **"Albert, it is far easier to clean a soul with a small amount of sin than to try to clean it at the very end with so much to confess."** Frequent confession provides us with the ability to be accountable but also for us to grow in sanctity. As human beings, we make mistakes, we do stupid things, but if we seek the Lord's forgiveness, then over time, we stop doing the same stupid things that got us there in the first place. The confessional provides Catholics with a spiritual emergency-room, we enter into it as wounded people, and we emerge as people that are spiritually healed and filled with God's strength.

The part of being an effective servant that I struggled with the most was understanding whose will were retrying to accomplish: my own or the Lord's. I initially sought to complete my academic assignments not from a position of just trying to learn and apply the teachings but to seek the highest grade or the best comments by the instructor. Therefore, when I threw myself into my academic studies, I was looking at seeing how high in the pecking order I could go. What my spiritual director challenged me to accomplish was seeing these classes as being like with the Lord when He taught the apostles throughout their travels in Galilee and Israel. Jesus had not set up any sort of GPA requirement for the apostles to need to have at the completion of His earthly ministry, but he did require their absolute attention to understand the teachings of His Father, and to have the faith in Him so that they would be able to be effective messengers for the kingdom of God.

Over time, I began to change from the large grain of wheat that is placed in the grist mill prior to being ground into the fine dust which the bread is then made up of. The crushing of my pride had to be accomplished before the good results could be produced. Adding to that, he gave me a constant emphasis on the importance of prayer, prayer that was both structured and unstructured. Over time, I found myself giving way to seeking the Lord's advice and strength through prayer as opposed to demonstrating my overall confidence in my studies.

Father Mendes also was extremely kind to always review any sort of material that I produced, especially if I was asked to give a class presentation or some sort of instruction at my parish. Early in my formation, I found myself drawn to the young people in our Life Teen Mass and parish community. I'd started at St. Ann's assisting my wife as a youth minister volunteer, and I found their enthusiasm to be extremely contagious. Our kids were on fire for God, but they also wanted to be instructed about our faith. So as opportunities developed for me to give informal and formal classes about various aspects of the faith, I looked to my spiritual director to be able to review my material, to make sure that it was free from any sort of potential error as well as insights in terms of how best to present the material. His hands-on mentorship became a staple of our relationship as I found myself learning from them, I wondered what it would have been like for the apostles to learn at the feet of Our Lord all those years.

Finally, during those instances when I sought the sacrament of reconciliation, I did not find the voice of a wrathful God, reminding me of how many commandments I had broken since the last time I went to confession. In fact, I found the gentle voice of Christ himself who was instead prodding me and constantly reminding me that I was the product of a loving God who created me to do good and to love Him and His people. So to seek God's forgiveness was not just a rote exercise of prayer and absolution, but rather a living encounter with a forgiving God who sought to wipe away my sins and make me worthy to stand in His Presence by His grace.

Filled with His sanctifying grace as I departed from those days, he gave me the strength to move forward instead of looking backwards. That was a true value of spiritual direction: the ability to walk with sometimes an older or in some instances a younger brother in Christ, knowing that we both have feet of clay but also seeing that God had created all of us to be together with Him, not only in those Fridays afternoons in a parish rectory but hopefully at the end of our lives to with Him forever in heaven.

Year 4 – Junior Year 2004...

Time Frame	Activity or Class Scheduled
7:00 am - 8:00 am	Holy Hour (once a month)
8:00 am - 8:50 am	Communion Service Practicum
9:00 am - 10:15 am	Methodology - Apologetics
10:30 am - 11:45 am	Canon Law I
11:50 am - 12:40 pm	Divine Office - Lunch
12:45 pm - 2:00 pm	New Testament - Pauline Letters
2:15 pm - 3:30 pm	Christology
3:45 pm – 5:00 pm	Proclaiming and Preaching

The Year 2004 found us moving once again into a new room and into a new academic year. Because of the timing and the transitioning between the four-year program and a five-year program, the class of 2004 that had been ordained in February of that year left a two-year gap of student leadership in our formation program. So, the class of 2006 would have the privilege of being the highest class in formation for two years instead of just the one. With the class of 2010 coming in February of the next year, it was only at that time where there were five full classes of men in diaconate formation.

The morning communion services took on a slightly different aspect for that year. The newly ordained men of the Class of 2004 were invited to come back to the St. Stephen's Center and they were the ones who proclaimed the Gospel and delivered the homilies to the men in formation. Once again, we would serve as acolytes for one full year before we were finally allowed to resume our places of leading the communion services. As you can see by the schedule above, the final class of our days was our first introduction to formal preaching and proclaiming of the Gospel. But needless to say, we were chomping at the bit to start preaching, even if it was to our fellow brothers in formation!

Our days were started with a class on **Apologetics**. We were privileged to have Deacon Scott who had been ordained two years earlier as our instructor. Apologetics is the way that aspects of the Catholic faith was presented to either those people that had fallen away from the Church or people that had never been Catholic. My own spiritual director's order, the Order of St. Francis De Sale, was based on this French bishop's ability to present the Catholic faith to many who had fallen away from the faith in France in the middle 1800s. Apologetics was not the equivalent of verbal war, using Bible verses like rifle bullets, firing at one another in a rapid-fire response and retaliatory manner, but rather as our Lord taught while He was among us. Presenting the Faith to those who sought the Truth and being able to answer their questions as they tried to comprehend what was being taught is how Christ taught us all.

Once again, we were graced with Father Tim who taught us **Canon Law**. We had Father Tim as an instructor of Scripture and the Prophets, but with this class, we were now seeing a different side of him. Trained as a Canon lawyer in Rome, he was serving in the Archdiocese Tribunal, where people applied for annulments and other dispensations of the Church. Already presenting his credentials as a scholar, Father Tim motivated us and demanded an even higher standard of performance than he had previously.

Since in many parishes, deacons actually serve as caseworkers, this is where the rubber started meeting the road, where we were coming out of the strict application of academics only and now into meeting the needs of the people in active ministry. Although many non-Catholics have their own opinions about what exactly an annulment is, a degree of annulment was not something that was entered into lightly. A person that had been granted an annulment could be free to once again to being married in the Church and to once again receive all the benefits of the Sacraments. Therefore, when a person started the process to get an annulment in the Church, this was not a paperwork drill, but actually dealing with a matter of the soul.

For **Pauline Letters,** once again we are graced to have Father Kevin as our instructor. Although he'd gotten a year older, he still look like a teenager in his Roman collar. In fact, we'd gotten so used to his love of a good joke, and he'd like to laugh a lot at our expense, we gave him in new nickname "Father Seinfeld." But Father Kevin was in his element in this class, because his expertise had been in Sacred Scripture while he had been in seminary. Therefore, the Letters of Paul as he explained to us took on an even more richer and significant meaning for us. His explanation of how St. Paul exhorted his communities to grow in holiness served as a rich precursor of what we would eventually do in when we were preaching at Mass on Saturdays or Sundays.

Reading St. Paul's letters to the various communities, dealing with the issues that each community faced, to some extent is much like the same issues we face today. Each community is unique, each community has both challenges as well as things that it is proud of, and all are seeking to grow in holiness and sanctity. Father Kevin would frequently pepper his own experiences of ministering to an incredibly diverse congregation that came to the Cathedral: everywhere from young families to single people, to older folks as well as all people of color. Here, he made the Church real by forcing us to consider what we had to do to serve the people of God.

Christology was taught to us by Father Fahy, a priest from the Order of the Passionists, who had an extensive career in the Archdiocese of Atlanta and was presently serving in the Hispanic community of Atlanta. Father Fahy was an older priest who had a rich depth of experience of his priestly ministry as well as ministering to the people of God. Using books taught by a fellow seminarian who became a great instructor himself, Father Ray Brown, Father Fahy took us through the liturgical year starting in Advent, through Christmas, then Lent, the Easter season and then through Ordinary Time in seeing how Jesus Christ was presented in the Gospel. His greatest gift was his patience for us because Christology by its very nature is a mystery: Jesus Christ is both truly divine and truly human -- true God and true man. This material is not easily understood and needs both prayer and patience in order to be mastered.

He frequently wrote articles for the Georgia Bulletin, the Archdiocese of Atlanta local newspaper, on various topics that dealt with the personhood and ministry of Jesus Christ. Always warm and receptive to the man that he taught, Father Fahy also was a priest. Frequently, because of our schedule in formation, it was sometimes difficult for us to be able to make it to the sacrament of reconciliation on Saturdays. It was not uncommon that at the end of class and during the 15 minute break, some men would lineup so that they can have their confessions heard by Father prior to the end of the day. A small gesture of generosity, but a font of God's grace was Father Fahey's presence for us.

Finally, our final class of the day would be our **Introduction to Preaching** and that would be taught by our own director of formation, Deacon Loris. Of course, we had heard him preaching at various holy hours and special occasions throughout the years, but now it was his turn to place a special mark on each and everyone of us. It was not just that the Church needed for us to be highly qualified, but it was his desire to produce deacons that could set the people of God on fire for Jesus Christ.

He recognized that each and everyone of us would not be carbon copies of the other, but he wanted to start the process of us being able to use the gifts that God had given us. For some of us, the Lord would prod us to examine our own experiences as married men to be able to translate the teachings of the Gospel into experiences that our congregations would relate to. For others, he given us great gifts of scholarship to be able to teach our faith to others as teachers to the faithful. To others still, He give us great gifts of empathy so that we understood where our people were coming from in order that we could lead them to Jesus Christ.

When I first started writing my first homilies, I went to my spiritual director, Father Mendes, and asked his advice on what made a great homily. Reflecting over a little bit of time, he said simply this **"Albert, you have two great responsibilities. You must feed them and give them hope. If you have not done those two things, you may have written something very nice, but you have not brought them Jesus Christ. Therefore, even our Lord told St. Peter to feed my sheep. So you must feed the people of God as well is give them the hope in Jesus Christ."**

That was probably the best lesson I have ever learned in formation. Going back in my mind over the many years, I have been privileged to hear Catholic priests in ordinary Sundays give homilies that it changed my life. Father Tom's homily when I first came to St. Oliver's literally changed my life and God willing, at some point, I would have the opportunity to have the Holy Spirit worked through me to better some soul sitting in the pew on a given Sunday. After much prayer, I took that advice to heart and started viewing these opportunities, even though they were just practice, as real spiritual gifts. I was an experienced public speaker, having been a state champion for public speaking even back in high school, gained further training while I had been in the Air Force, and was used to speaking to a large number of people in my business career. But preparing for a homily was a totally different experience. It was not something that you would go and try to 'wing it".

But rather, the homily served as the spiritual glue that held together the Liturgies of the Word with the Eucharist. For together, the two liturgies made up the spiritual power that is the Mass, the greatest prayer that the Catholic Church can offer for its own salvation and that of the whole world. Therefore, any homily given to the people of God is important, because a great homily is not just based on the size of the audience receiving it but rather the homily must attempt to speak to every single person that is listening and responding to it.

Our academic workload continued to increase in this fourth year, but on balance, we could start seeing more of the application effect versus just the academic learning. Many of my classmates had been actively involved in various ministries of the Church, specifically in teaching and leading liturgies. So at this point in our formation, those ministries that we had embarked upon as laypeople were being viewed in a different circumstance, now that we grew closer to ordination.

After being accepted as acolytes and readers back in October of last year, many of us were being allowed to wear our albs at weekly Sunday Mass and participate in a greater extent in our churches liturgies. Over time, we could see that our parishioners that once knew us as laypeople were now starting to evaluate us in a different light. It would not be uncommon that people sought us out for advice and counsel or for prayer requests, where as in earlier years, they might not have been so forthcoming. At St. Oliver's, I was being utilized in a greater capacity, being asked to participate in sacramental preparation, specifically for Confirmation, and to assist in Holy Hours for our Life Teens. Our teenagers had always been a vibrant part of our parish community and I welcome the opportunity to be of service for them in whatever they needed.

One of the fondest memories I have was being asked to do a holy hour for them on a weekend off-site retreat in Conyers, Georgia during the season of Lent. I asked two other men from our Men's Club to join me because we would be transporting the Blessed Sacrament as well as the monstrance out to the retreat location. With my pastor's permission, I graciously accepted their invitation to be with them and in early March during the season of Lent, I was allowed to do my first Holy Hour for the benefit of our teens. They had created a multi-tiered table complete with burning candles on which the monstrance would be set on.

The topic of the retreat was called "Being free from the chains of sin" and they relied heavily on material from the movie "The Passion of the Christ". In a large room, dark by the lack of direct light, was this table that took on an appearance of the burning bush in the Old Testament, our Eucharistic Lord came and spoke to the hearts of all the children that were there. I gave a brief reflection on how the movie "The Passion" had affected me personally, on how when I saw the movie, walking out at the end, hoping that I would run into a Catholic priest so that he could immediately hear my confession.

The final scene where the Blessed Mother is looking directly out into the audience holding the battered remains of her Son still causes me to be ashamed of my sin. In fact, one of my classmates, Mike, who had seen the movie twice said that at the end of the second time, he openly wept at the end of the movie. The source of his grief and sadness was this thought: "Because of my sins, my sins and my actions did this to your Son, and you still wish to be my Mother still?"

At the end of the evening, as we were getting to ready to leave, I was looking for the head of our life teen ministry to thank her for the invitation to be there that evening. She graciously accepted my thanks and said instead "Thank you for being here tonight, it really meant a great deal to the kids for you to be here." It was through these opportunities that were rapidly coming to me during this year; that I saw my vocation start to crystallize as never before.

The Holy Spirit now was molding my direction and my motivation and the fruits of that movement were then our children were demonstrating a greater love and appreciation for our faith than even I had possessed back when I was their age. In the world now that suffers from the blight of terrorism and economic uncertainty, the faith that these young teenagers have gives me pause for great hope for a more vibrant Church that will be a light to the world and our teens to be there for each other.

With the passing of Holy Week and the Easter season once again brought us to the Eucharistic Congress back in the yearly scope of the Archdiocese. In 2004, it was an even greater privilege to attend the Congress. The men of the Class of 2006 would be granted a great privilege: we would be the ones that carried the canopy over the Blessed Sacrament while it was being processed outside in front of the people of God.

Once again, I would be the chauffeur to my spiritual director who really did not want to drive that early in the morning. However, the drive down to the Congress as well as the time together gave us the precious opportunity to have each other's undivided attention and the opportunity to just talk. Once Mass was completed at the convent at seven in the morning, we departed quickly down through the metro Atlanta area to the Georgia International Convention Center for the start of the Eucharistic Congress.

Some of my classmates had already arrived by the time I got there and were putting the canopy together. The outside procession would start at 8:30 a.m. so it was extremely important that everything was set in place and ready to go by that time.

This year's Congress also was a special event because this was the first time that I had seen Bishop Boland since our family had left Columbus nine years earlier.

At about an hour before the start of the procession, Bishop Boland came in to dress in his vestments. My spiritual director and I were standing together when he came over and I introduced him to the bishop. Father

Mendes did something that is rarely done by most Catholics today, he gently kissed the bishop's ring and said "Good morning, Your Grace."

I was just too excited at seeing him so I just gently hugged him and said "Thank you for everything." Sensing my excitement, he gave me one of those wide Irish smiles that I hadn't seen in awhile. Bishop Boland asked about Cindy and the kids, how would they doing, how old they were, and everything else. I told him that I regretted that they were not here this morning, but we look forward to seeing him on Ordination Day – some 600 days in the future. He said for me to send him an invitation as soon as I knew the day.

Then the outside procession started. Holding the canopy with my classmates, the Blessed Sacrament in the center being held by the presiding minister, with incense and lit candles surrounding us, and two seminarians alternating the ringing of the small bells used at Mass especially at the consecration, the Eucharistic Lord, the King of Glory, humbled under consecrated bread, was held in front of the people of God and the people responded by falling to their knees in silent adoration.

After the outside procession was completed, we brought the canopy inside and then took our places before the deacons as we processed in to the main hall. For a distance no less than a quarter-mile, we walked into the large convention hall floor. Lining our route at the final 200 yards was a full dress ceremonial guard of the Knights of Columbus with sabers drawn and their eyes fixed ahead of them.

We bowed together out at the altar base, ascended the stairs and then I sat down with one of my classmates, Jim. The choir sang with great intensity, the choir music profound and filling the hall with musical joy. For some strange reason, tears were streaming down my face and Jim asked me what was wrong. "Nothing is wrong Jim" I said, "I'm just so happy to be here." He smiled at me, winking and said "Me too."

To some extent, that holy hour was a mere precursor to what heaven will be like. We will all, God willing, enter into a banquet hall that is beyond our human comprehension, people of all colors, nationalities, united under one faith to feast at the Table of the Lamb. This earthly day was filled with music from a choir that singing like the angels from heaven and once the monstrance was brought in once again to the great hall, all of the people of God fell down in humble adoration.

Bishop Boland gave the homely for that holy hour. He talked about the significance of presence, how he had been asked to attend the wedding of one of his nieces, and how people have traveled throughout the world to be together for this special event. The importance of presence was that we all shared a common belief that this event was extremely important for us to attend. So much greater, was the importance of knowing that Christ was present in the Eucharist, and that it was his desire for him to be with us as we desired to be with him.

At the end of that holy hour, Bishop Boland remained with his fellow bishops on the altar and the monstrance was processed out at the end of the service. I was so thankful for his presence to me on that day. He had been instrumental in my formation because of his graciousness as a pastor and a priest. He had fired up in me a love for my faith when I had been lazy in attending to that faith. He had been at the side of the bed of my wife when she was sick in the hospital and she had seen his ordination when he was made a bishop. So his presence was important in my life and it manifested in my desire to know that I had a vocation to serve the same people he had: the people of God.

The timing of our last summer class is always right after the Congress, and hoping upon hope, we thought this might be the year that we just might not have the dreaded summer assignment. Unfortunately, this was not meant to be. But his most assignments later turned out, this summer assignment had a very unique opportunity. Our summer assignment was to interview our diaconate mentor. We were to ask him specific questions about his ministry, his balance between his work and his family obligations, and about his years after being ordained.

However, as Deacon Bill started making his verbal list ministries and he was involved with, I rapidly made it count and he was involved in 18 separate ministries in our parish. Now I was concerned, is even I was starting to think that I was being overcommitted while I was in formation, so is this what I had to expect after ordination.

Now he assured me, that all of these ministries don't have the same demands of his time. For example, as being a minister for the Stations of the Cross, is only done during Lent and not throughout the year. However, Bill's total personality was a man totally focused on being of service. He commented that earlier in his ordained life, he and Linda did active ministry together and that was a great possibility for them to be able to combine their time together as well is to be of service to the people of God.

However, Linda's health had started to become a concern in those opportunities became fewer and fewer. However, on those rare times, especially during Holy Week, where Linda could be a reader during the Liturgy of the Word and Bill could serve at the altar, you can see their love transcended their church responsibilities. In addition, even his grandchildren were being schooled for lives of service. Bill's granddaughter served as an altar server which he was the head of that ministry, and there were a couple of times where I served at Mass together with them both. It was those sorts of opportunities, it made me appreciate what this man did that much more as well is to start prepare me for what I needed to do and now the not so distant future.

At the conclusion of Holy Week, I was approached by Father Peter who is also serving as an additional coach for me in homiletics. As we were going over one of my assignments, we were talking about the recent announcement that my pastor had made about a parish trip going to Argentina. Previously in November of 2003, he invited the pastor of a large church in Argentina to come up to our parish for a week. At the conclusion that visit, Father Jim signed a declaration of mutual support with this pastor, Father Alfredo, on the altar at the 11:15 a.m. Mass. The purpose of this declaration was twofold: it formally bound our two parishes into a mutual support framework of both prayer and communication and would provide both of our communities with a way to become closer. Father Alfredo's parish was in a community that was approximately 650 miles northwest of Buenos Aires, in a part of that country that probably resembled northern New Mexico.

There was over 4,500 miles that separated between our two communities but we shared two great traditions: we are both vibrant Catholic communities, and we were supported by this great Marian order. The La Salettes started in France as a religious order but presently it was around the world and they had been in South America for well over 100 years. However, in their constant mission of evangelization of the Gospel, they found themselves having to meet the people where they presently are so they were often compelled to not only preach, but to build as well. They built chapels so that the people in the countryside and who could not have the ability to come into the city to worship would have a place to attend Mass. They would visit the sick and the needy as often as they could, as well as say the Mass on a monthly basis instead of the weekly obligation we had in the United States.

Father Alfredo was an extremely charismatic individual who spoke English with a slight accent. Father Peter who had learned Spanish through immersion training, developed a very high-level fluency rather quickly. Earlier that year, Peter had been appointed as the mission director that would lead a parish mission from St. Oliver's to visit our Sister Parish in Argentina. The cost of the trip would be approximately $1,500 which was the going rate for a round-trip ticket from Atlanta to Buenos Aires plus the cost of a transfer flight to Cordoba. We would be staying at the rectory in town so our lodging was taking care of. When the announcement had been put out, initially I was torn.

When we started back in 2001, we're told as part of our formation, that our class would be making a mission trip either to Jamaica or to Haiti visiting with a Catholic mission that serviced the poor and the outcast. It was during that time, we were making preparations to go on that trip. However, Peter was persistent in asking. It was a longer time commitment than what our guys had made in the past; this parish mission trip would be about thirteen days in duration versus the five days that our guys typically went on. However, after much prayer, and seeking my wife's permission as well as my boss's okay about the time away from work, I elected to go to Argentina instead.

Early in July, after the celebration of the Fourth, the parish mission met twice to consolidate the clothing that we would be bringing to Argentina. At all the masses a month earlier, Father Jim announced for a generous outpouring of our parish: if anyone in the parish had some gently used winter clothing that they were willing to donate, we would be willing to transport those clothes to our Sister Parish for their personal use. Of course, if you remember your geography lessons, that when the Northern Hemisphere is in summer, the Southern Hemisphere is in winter. Therefore, we faced a challenge packing for this trip as well: we would be leaving Atlanta in the middle of summer but arriving in Buenos Aires in the middle of their winter! But as we approached our date of departure, we collected over 1,000 pounds of clothing that we dividing up between two mission teams leaving Atlanta the next week.

I was paired with a fellow parishioner named Rosemary who had originally been born in Peru but spoke excellent Spanish. In addition, completing our team was a young man by the name of Courtney who had actually been to Bolivia on a mission trip six years earlier as a young teenager. We gathered at Hartsfield International Airport and met the other members of our team and working our way through the enhanced airport security that had been instituted after the 9/11 attacks, we finally got through to our departure gate. The weather, however, was not being very cooperative that day. Atlanta had been subject to what is called "popcorn thunderstorms" where a brief but intense thunderstorm was making its way through the area. Since we would be flying to Miami first, and then making our connection to South America from there, it was absolutely essential that we leave on time or we would be possibly delayed.

Unfortunately, nature won out over our schedule that day. We ended up being delayed by about three hours. When we were finally able to leave Atlanta, we had to divert off of our flight plan to avoid the numerous thunderhead storms that were plaguing the entire eastern seaboard that night. However, one of the most awesome spectacles I had ever seen was being played out before my eyes. As we were flying well over 30,000 feet south to Miami that night, occasionally the entire sky lit up as if it was day as we can see thunderstorms well over 100 miles away to the left and right of us. As nature was delivering its fury on the ground, that same nature was providing us with one of the most fascinating and brilliant light shows I had ever experienced. As we prepared to land in Miami after that short flight, we're hoping on hope that our Atlanta delay would not push us out of the window for making our connecting flight to Argentina.

There was only one daily flight out of Miami to Buenos Aires, Argentina, and that flight typically departed at approximately 8:30 in the evening. Unfortunately, by the time we arrived in Miami it was 10:30 in the evening and even though the airline had delayed their departure in anticipation for us, by the time we arrived in Miami, our flight was already gone. The customer service representative at Delta offered us a certificate for a reduced lodging rate at a local hotel near the airport but we would be staying in Miami that evening to catch that same flight on the next day. As we gathered our belongings and made our way to the hotel's transportation, we were all thinking the same thing "Is this going to be a precursor for the next two weeks?" But after getting in to the hotel and notifying the pastor of our current circumstances, we just settled in to get a decent night of rest. Our other mission members had taken a slightly different route: flying from Atlanta into Miami and then flying to Santiago, Chile, before arriving in to Cordoba, Argentina. Luckily, they were able to make their connection flight and would be arriving ahead of us in Argentina. But for now the best thing we can do was just rest and then be prepared tomorrow.

We awoke to a beautiful day, and spent the remainder of the day lounging around, eating a very late lunch, and then making our way back to the airport for that evening's departure. We checked in with plenty of time to spare, thinking that the difficulty we had that night, would be the greatest thing that we would encounter, however, we were wrong. In addition to being told the wrong gate for departure when we checked in, we had to immediately leave for the new gate. By the time we had traveled about a quarter of mile through the Miami airport with all of our carry-on luggage, we found that our new plane was being delayed because of new mechanical difficulties. After waiting over two hours to finally get it fixed, we're finally departing for South America. Even though we were traveling at night so hopefully we can get some sleep in, we were still traveling in coach and the plane that night was fully packed!

So in between dealing with tight seats in a fully packed plane, we started on our adventure to South America. I had brought a knotted rosary with me and seeing that the amount of time ahead of me, I started just praying the Rosary. I thought of my mother, and started wondering about her. Although my father was still alive and had been supportive of my vocation, my mother never knew in her life here on earth about what was happening to her son. I prayed that she was in heaven and hopefully was made fully aware about my progress thus far. I thought about my family, especially my young daughter and son who were seeing their dad change. My daughter was funny, generally she liked the idea of me being a deacon, but she also wanted to know if I still thought she was important in my life as well. Of course, as much as I tried to reassure her, she always needed something extra. My son Michael's progress had been extremely encouraging, but Michael's greatest gift was the fact that he was the embodiment of God's pure love. Michael always has a big smile available when I need it, and as he was growing up, his hugs were starting to get as big as mine. But he would soon notice that his dad was not around when he got up in the morning. So he would constantly asked Cindy "Where's Daddy?" So Cindy would have to constantly tell him that Daddy went away but would be back very soon.

Because of the unique nature of the trip, I received permission from my director of formation to use this trip in lieu of the trip that he had organized for the men in the program. The purpose of the formation mission trip was not just a "press the flesh and then leave" type of trip, but rather it was an immersion to seeing how we must serve the poorest of the poor, recalling what Christ himself speaks about in Saint Matthew's Gospel about how people encountered him on earth prior to the great judgment scene. For as long as we did these things -- feed the hungry, give water to the thirsty, take care of the sick, visit the prisoners -- as long as we did to the least of our brothers and sisters, we did it for Him.

Every fall, after a trip had taken place, and the men return back to the classroom, we would be given a brief report about what they had experienced. Each man, regardless of his own previous experiences, came back with a great burning of conversion and encountering the Holy Spirit. I did not know what to expect in my own trip, but I did know that these were my brothers and sisters in Christ and therefore my allegiance was not to the country of origin, but rather my future allegiance would be as a citizen in the kingdom of God.

We landed in Argentina at 8:30 in the morning the following day. I had never been to South America, before but this airport was both modern and large. Rosemary warned us to stay close to her throughout the process and both Courtney and I readily complied. As we approached customs, we brought out our passports and patiently waited in line. The customs officer noted the amount of luggage that we had and asked why. Rosemary patiently told him we were on a mission trip and then he glanced up at the T-shirt that I was wearing. It had a small white cross on a black background and then he looked at me and asked in Spanish, "Good morning Father, how are you?" Rosemary looked at me with the look of surprise and I winked back at her. Finally, he completed his inspection and welcomed us to Argentina.

After gathering all our luggage, we went out to the front of the airport in search of a taxi, in order to make our connecting flight, we had to travel to another airport that was across the town and we had to complete their trip within the next 90 minutes. The taxi captains that ran that part of the airport spoke very good English and we were able to make a connection with a large taxi relatively quickly. Although I had not had the chance to convert some of my money into the local currency, the taxi captain that handled us was more than happy to take US dollars.

Driving in Argentina is a quite an experience! Of course, they have a very good road system in this city, but the driving takes on an almost NASCAR-type quality. After sleeping all night on the plane, this taxi driver kept our attention almost constantly. Rosemary spoke in rapid-fire Spanish but the driver was thoroughly amused that he had three Americans in his cab! Finally, entering into the next airport, we paid the taxi driver and took out all of our luggage. A porter that was waiting for another fare seized the opportunity to take our luggage to the appropriate gate where once again we waited in line to process in.

Unfortunately, our travel arrangements failed to notify this airline that our excess luggage was actually in support of a religious mission. Thus, we generated about a hundred extra dollars in additional baggage handling costs and unfortunately the customer service reps could not accommodate our pleas to waive the fees. Rosemary looked at me, and I told her that we can take care of this right now. Taking out my credit card, I paid the excess fees. Father Jim was very good about being kind to reimburse expenses, and this was one of those instances where I don't think he would've complained too much.

Finally, we received our transfer tickets and waiting in the airport for a plane. Buenos Aires, as a city, was really quite cosmopolitan, complete with large parks in beautiful modern buildings. The airport was large and open and as we had a chance to look at some of the local merchandise, I was amazed at its beauty as well as its affordability. I made a mental note that I would buy some items for my family when I returned back. But for right now, just looking to get some food and an open chair would have been perfect.

Finally, they were calling for boarding of our connecting flight, and we entered into the Boeing 737 for the short one-hour flight. The airline that we're using was the equivalent of America's Southwest airlines. They were extremely efficient in turning around the plane and making us feel welcome. We landed in Cordova and met up with our mission party. The other members of our mission, had already landed the day before and stayed overnight in the La Salette seminary house. Father Alfredo had driven down the night before with his parish's van that resembled the vehicles used at the airport to transport customers from the airport to the Rent-A-Car businesses. However, after loading all of the excess luggage as well as ourselves, we started to make the seven hour plus drive to Las Termas.

The terrain that we are entering into starting to resemble the American Southwest, complete with cactus near the roadside and plenty of dust and sand. The main road that we are traveling on would be seen as primitive by American standards because it was a single two-lane paved highway with every sort of vehicle from bicycles to extended tractor-trailers traveling on this single road. We also had the opportunity to meet with two of Father Alfredo's closest companions: Pancho, who is going to be ordained a priest within the month, and a religious sister. Although they spoke very limited

English, Rosemary served as our translator and soon was breaking out in laughter and stories about our trip. My good friend Mark whom I had known through the St. Oliver's Men's Club also came on this trip and I look forward to Mark's company. Mark was also married with a small daughter Sophie who frequently came to the children's Mass on Sunday morning. Mark was a professional engineer by training, but was a man who is also looking to grow in his faith.

Finally, we came home to the rectory which we would be staying for the next two weeks. Even though it was midnight, our new hosts had prepared a light dinner to welcome us to Argentina. We would also be trained in the finer art of dining in Argentina. Too often in America, family dinners are rushed because we have other things to do: watch a movie, get on the Internet, or just do our own thing. However, during our two-week stay in Argentina, we rediscovered the great privilege of spending time in each other's company meant. Meals were served and conversation and fellowship was even more important. All too often, especially at dinner, which was served from 8:30 to nine o'clock at night, and often would sometimes last until midnight. Father Alfredo and his brother priests were consummate hosts, always asking if the accommodations were fine or if there was anything else that they can do for us.

The very next day, we started out on the first day of the mission. We were not there to build anything physical such as a church or school, but rather, we were there to learn about the circumstances that our brothers and sisters in Christ dealt with on a daily basis. But it was also more important start building relationships. As an American, we are blessed with so much material wealth, it is no wonder that we are the envy of the world. However, even with all that material wealth, that prosperity has little significance being stockpiled for some future use that may never come to pass. However, even under meager circumstances, Father Alfredo was reaching out to the poorest of the poor, feeding them in makeshift kitchens and cinderblock chapels.

But the God-given dignity that we saw in the eyes of the people, as well as learning the stories of their circumstances gave me significant pause for reflection. We met teenage girls that served as mothers in proxy for children whose own mothers were unable to take care of them. We saw older women who took care of entire faith communities by leading them in daily prayer as well as keeping the small concrete chapels so clean so that the people in the country could attend Mass in dignity. We met with men after working in the fields and doing all sorts of manual labor who volunteered their efforts to various small building projects within their communities.

The idea of feast days was also portrayed differently. Throughout the Catholic Church Liturgical Year, we celebrate specific feast days in thanksgiving for those Saints that given their lives in the service of the Lord. Frequently, in America, we would note that special day and then move on to what needed to be done. However, what was ordinary in Argentina was that the people actually celebrated their patron saint's feast day with a fiesta or large party where the community came together to be in each other's company. Even being among the poorest of the poor, we were welcomed as fellow brothers and sisters in Christ. And with hearts wide open, they shared from their small bounty and made us feel welcome. Mass would be celebrated in the chapel, and then in the courtyards outside, a primitive sound system would be set up, barbecues would be fired up and dancing and music prevailed. The people pressed forward to try to talk to us or at least shake our hands. The wealth that these people possessed was not that of material goods, but that of Gospel virtues: Charity, kindness, and love of neighbor combined with the love of God.

During another visit to a school, Father Alfredo performed over 25 baptisms on children ranging from newborns to approximately 8 years old. In his parish community on Saturdays, he would be baptizing anywhere between 30 to 50 children each time. So hungry were his parishioners to receive the sacraments, he would be stretched to the very limits of time and strength.

But throughout it all, he loved being a priest: a living example of Christ in the world today. He preached with the intensity of Juan Peron but he loved his parish with the heart of Jesus Christ. Before Mass, he could be found leaning against the side of a building with a parishioner, probably hearing their confession because that would be the only time they would be able to receive the sacrament of reconciliation. After Mass, he would be with the people, getting caught up on the status of family and friends, trying to make sure of certain details were being performed, and dispensing blessings as the people requested them. In watching all of this, I understood why I needed to be there. As training to be a servant of Christ, I saw Father Alfredo's example of meeting the people where they are. Even with what seems very little in the eyes of the world, Alfredo was transforming their Catholic faith into hope and joy.

Father Alfredo had plans to help these people in other ways as well. His parish ran a small high school that would be able to train young men during the times when they were not being utilized in the field to better their educational possibilities for the future. He wanted to open more kitchens to be able to feed more of the poor, especially the children and the widows. One woman, whose sister had died of breast cancer left five children without a parent. So this woman, her sister, took it upon herself to raise not only her own five children but her sisters as well in a single room shack that was probably no bigger than 15 x 20 feet with an outdoor bathroom and kitchen. Alfredo wanted to do more, and was able to get enough contributions to build her a small cinderblock shack instead. The cost was relatively minimal by American standards -- probably about $1,500, but of course this represented a small fortune by Argentinean standards.

All during the next two weeks, we saw examples of how the Catholic Church was for filling its mission to evangelize the world – one soul at a time. Although my Spanish is not extensive, it was good enough for me to be able to converse with some of the people. For many of them, this was the first time that they had ever seen an American. Over the next two weeks, we probably visited no less than seven chapels the Father Alfredo had either built or had renovated to serve his ever-increasing flock.

About two days prior to our leaving, he brought together his own parish council to meet us and to exchange with his team what we have learned by being in Argentina. It was a grace-filled meeting and I was so thankful that I had been able to make this trip. However, on the final night that we were in the rectory, Father Alfredo received a call about a parishioner's death that had happened that morning. Because of the lack of American-style funeral homes in South America, when a person dies, there is very little time available. The body is typically washed in clean, a simple pine casket is secured, and the body is placed in the casket.

Father Alfredo came with his prayer book and holy water and conducted a simple vigil service. The family continues to stay with the body all that night and then very early in the morning, the body was transported to the church for a funeral Mass. Then, the body is brought to the graveside were typically is left in an aboveground grave for a year. Then, the grave is reopened, the bones recovered in place and placed in a smaller box where the remains are finally interred. The small home that night was filled with friends and neighbors that spilled out into the street. As Father Alfredo blessed the body with the water he had brought, I looked at my friend Mark. Mark and I had really bonded together as close friends and fellow Catholics. Mark returned my glance with a nod, and in my best Spanish, I turned to the widow and expressed my condolences on her loss. Leaving from that home that night, once again, I was getting a clear indication of what my future would be like. In my own parish, the deacons do the vigil service for the benefit of the families. To some extent, I was seeing my future vocation being made apparent.

The next morning, we started the seven hour plus journey back to Cordova. After many affectionate hugs for all they had done with and for us, we left Las Termas as changed people. Even though we had encountered people in desperate circumstances, we had encountered people of great faith. Every night, Mass was celebrated in the main church and it was packed. At the end of Mass, some people prayed silently before some of the various icons that were throughout the church as well as asking a personal blessing from the presiding priest. All around me, people of faith were living that faith, trusting in God's fidelity and mercy. Their frame of reference was totally different than my own but I knew that I had to change as well. Once again, I took out my rosary and started praying. I had been given a great gift over the past two weeks, and I spent the rest of my time reflecting on what I needed to change for myself.

Arriving in Cordova late that afternoon, we were welcomed with cold drinks and warm dinner. The one luxury that I took advantage of was access to the Internet and after trolling through the 500 e-mails that I had received over the past two weeks, I was able to send out a couple of e-mails to my brothers in formation as well as my family. The seminary house that we stayed in was large and spacious with an American-style dormitory area complete with bunk beds. Our final night in Argentina was coming to an end.

The next morning, our transportation to the airport came. The taxi driver was very kind in making sure that he kept his speed under 60 miles an hour. Arriving at the airport, we gave him a generous tip that he was thankful for. The priest that accompanied us was prepared to say goodbye when we begged him for general absolution for our final trip home. He graciously gave us the absolution and then he hugged us all one final time. The flight back to Buenos Aires was uneventful but quick. Once again, we had to make another long ride back to the international airport but did this on a large passenger bus instead of a very small taxi.

We entered into the airport with plenty of time, once again making through customs with no disruptions, and then prepared to wait at the gate for a flight. Rosemary surprised us with a generous gift: a fully inflatable neck pillow for the flight home. On the way down, she'd noticed that I had fallen asleep with my head forward sometimes to the point of coming out of my seat! However, as we entered into the airplane for the flight home, I drew a very uncomfortable seat because of my size and ended up falling asleep in the same position once again. She would later comment that I looked like a big ox with this great yoke wrapped around my neck!

The flight back to Miami was very smooth, and once again we arrived at morning that had been through some thunderstorms the previous night. Traveling to the new gate we were looking forward to coming home and be with our families. Finally, our flight departed back to Atlanta with the full sun and clear skies. We arrived back at the airport to find our family and friends waiting for us at baggage claim. Rosemary's husband Bill and daughter Michelle were there to meet us and we finally gathered ourselves through baggage claim out to their van.

Finally arriving at home, my family came out to greet us. I made a special effort to hug my children slightly longer then most, and my son reciprocated with a very tight hug on my neck. It'd been 13 long days and Cindy told me he had missed his dad very much. My daughter was excited to hear about my trials and, of course, to bring their presents out for my luggage.

My wife in a quiet moment asked me a pointed question, "So Al, what exactly did you learn on this trip?" I didn't know what she expected as my response but I did tell her, **"Well honey, for as long as I live, I will never complain about my life ever again."** I don't think that was the answer she was looking for, but she was rather taken aback that that was my final answer. As I later would tell her, I met so many different and loving people that my chance for conversion was just understanding all of the great gifts that I had received throughout my life. I had always given my personal testimony as being the following:

I'm a rich man already. I have a loving wife, two children that still love and miss me when I'm gone, I had a yellow Labrador that loved

me unconditionally and I have the paw prints on my chest to prove it. Although whatever earthly wealth I am able to accumulate, my greatest wealth I already had received: the love of my family and friends, the faith that was given to me by my parents, my health to be able to provide for my family, my future vocation and the love of my God. What else more did I need?

Mark had made it dedicated effort to take a tremendous amount of pictures while we were in Argentina. A month after we returned, he made a slideshow complete with music and gave it to each one of us as a present. Having a chance to see the pictures for the first time, as well is getting some other developed film that I had taken, I shared what I had learned with my brothers in formation. The two other men spoke of similar experiences when they went on their mission trips, and now we can see how our vocation was rapidly coming into focus: our main gift were to be men of charity and possessing God's love to be given to our brothers and sisters in Christ.

As always in the life of our formation process, fall followed the summer and with this year coming to an end rapidly coming on the horizon, the idea that we are entering into our final year of formation was becoming a reality. With the final academic papers submitted and our final grades given by our instructors, the fourth year of formation came to a close. The attitude of "cooperate and graduate" was continuing to pay dividends for us all. For some of us, we were already talking about ministries that we wanted to be a part of. While for some of us, our pastors were chomping at the bit to see us finally ordained. As my first full year without Mike came to an end, I often wondered about what he would've thought had he the opportunity to see me now. Would he be proud of me, or would he still have things for me to work on? As I prepared for my final year of formation, I was still struggling with questions of my own worthiness as well as my sense of preparedness.

But one fact of comfort was this, my God did not bring me this far only to abandon me. He still had even greater graces to bestow but that would be done in His time, and not in mine.

Year 5 – Senior Year 2005...

Time Frame	Activity or Class Scheduled
7:00 am - 8:00 am	Holy Hour (once a month)
8:00 am - 8:50 am	Communion Service Practicum
9:00 am - 10:15 am	Canon Law II and Liturgy
10:30 am - 11:45 am	Homiletics
11:50 am - 12:40 pm	Divine Office - Lunch
12:45 pm - 2:00 pm	Scripture and Gospels
2:15 pm - 3:30 pm	Social Justice
3:45 pm – 5:00 pm	Diaconate Practicum

February 2005 was a welcome month in all of our lives. Since the class of 2004 had been ordained in February of that year, there was no diaconate ordination this year. However, our class, one year from today, would be ordained as the first five-year formation class being complete. So now, we were finally in charge or so we thought. The communion services routine was now brought back to its original premise: the seniors would be responsible for the planning of the service, proclaiming the Gospel, and giving a practice homily to our brothers-in-formation.

Since I was the class representative, I had the responsibility of developing our final communion service schedule. Unfortunately, we lost one of our classmates at the end of our junior year. He had decided that he was being called to doing missionary type work and at being a parish deacon was incompatible to the new calling he now felt. Although we hate to see him go, we all understood his reasons for going and in several months, when he returned after a missionary trip, we could see that he made the right choice. He loved working with the poor, and he was at a stage in his life that his occupation, family circumstances and point of his career would allow him to incorporate this new vocation into his life.

For the rest of us, we still faced a competitively challenging schedule. Our pastors were starting to utilize us more in a variety of different roles so that we really were now starting to balance for major obligations all at once: our secular jobs, our academic workloads in formation, our obligations within our parish, as well as our family lives. Once again, the sense of balance that we all saw in juggling all of these obligations was being a precarious act but with God's grace, we were hanging tough!!

Deacon Loris also had his hands filled because now he had five complete classes of men going through a five-year formation process. Here was a man who was always working for God. In order to view his position, you have to see him like a head coach for a Big 10 college athletic program:

- **Not only does he have to coach the players under his care now;**

- **He is actively recruiting throughout the Archdiocese, talking to people as well as talking to pastors and to individuals who feel they have a vocation;**

- **He has to schedule the men who responded to the annual call for the diaconate with their initial interview schedule and monitor their paperwork flow;**

- He **has to schedule the annual retreat and mission trips for the men in formation;**

- Finally, **he had to recruit new instructors for the classes when old instructors themselves receive new assignments or were unable to continue their present teaching assignment.**

During all of this action, he still has local parish obligations that he has to fulfill as well. Over the past five years, my attitude toward my director of formation changed considerably: it went from being the formal and stiff drill sergeant instructor that I met in prior to my first year of formation to more of a counselor and spiritual director and finally as a mentor and role model. I had not always taken his suggestions kindly, but in retrospect, I knew they were given for my ultimate benefit. He made a special effort to be available to the seniors, especially, because now he knew both our strengths and our weaknesses. Deacon Loris wanted to make sure that we would be ready for ordination.

An important part of our readiness would be our ability to preach and now homiletics took on an even greater dimension. Even though our fellow brothers-in-formation were essentially a very friendly and captive audience for us, they still represented the people of God. Therefore, we were compelled to give them our best efforts when we had the opportunity to preach to them during our schedule communion service. Typically, we scheduled ourselves based on our place in the alphabet, and as luck would have it, I had the opportunity to preach on the feast day of St. Joseph – March 19th, 2005. Recalling how St. Joseph had been such a positive influence in my life, it seemed like a welcome bookend to my diaconate formation – I had written about him in my very first year, and now I was able to preach about him in my senior year. During the week prior, I spent two nights after work going through the complete liturgy rehearsal by practicing at St. Oliver's. I wanted to give my brothers my very best effort and the only way that I was going to be able to do that was to consistently practice so that it seemed flawless.

As that morning approach, I seemed a little bit nervous than usual. As always, Deacon Loris was in the back, counting heads, taking attendance and just being present. I pulled him aside and asked for his blessing prior to the start of my service and he willingly complied. As we started down the aisle toward the altar, myself and my acolyte from the Class of 2007, a feeling of comfort and ease came over me.

When it came time to preach the Gospel, I had selected the scripture passage that dealt with Jesus being lost in the Temple and Mary and Joseph frantically searching for Him. There was something about that Scripture that had spoken to me when I was preparing my homily, because in times of my life, I had been lost and my God had been constantly searching for me.

Proclaiming the Gospel that morning was a beautiful experience and as I later closed the Book of Gospels to prepare to deliver my first homily to my brothers in formation, I said a small prayer of thanksgiving before I actually started. Below is my homily that I gave that morning.

> **Today we celebrate a very special day in Our Church: the Feast Day of St Joseph.**
>
> **As recorded in the Holy Scripture, St. Joseph has a very pronounced presence at the very beginning of the Gospels in both Luke and Matthew. Physically, St Joseph has often been seen in two different lights: Sometimes he is the same age as Mary and they look like a typical young couple. In others, he is seen as being significantly older than Mary, looking more like a doting older brother then her husband.**
>
> **From a perspective of faith, the greatest difference is that nowhere throughout the New Testament is a recorded comment directly attributable to St. Joseph. He**

says absolutely nothing but in the power of his actions, we see a man possessing great faith.

Moreover, we see that faith being severely tested throughout his life.

This Gospel reading is also one of the liturgical readings for the Feast Day of the Holy Family where the familiar situation is that Jesus somehow got separated from his family and is reported as lost. Mary and Joseph seek to find him; looking for three days, looking, and worrying the entire time – "Where is our son?" They discover their son is in the Holy Temple back in Jerusalem.

His parents encounter a young Jesus who is clearly advanced beyond his tender years. Jesus, as a young teenager, Himself is teaching the elders, he is so well-versed in Scripture that He holds them spellbound with his answers. Of course, with most of us being fathers ourselves, St. Joseph, in his mercy, is not recorded with any written testimony of his own words during this episode.

But I can assure you; had we had a similar situation, at least he would have understood from our position all of the strife and panic He caused in our family for making that choice - of staying back and teaching in the Temple. Yet Mary, sees the answer her son responds with for his unique circumstance; it explains perfectly where and why he was in the Temple: He was teaching in His Father's house, his Father being Yahweh, the God of Abraham, of Isaac, of Jacob.

Joseph's foster son was already starting his mission already as a great teacher even as a young teenager, yet Joseph was himself was an adult who was just a humble carpenter of advanced years. Joseph was a worker with his hands, not a great and learned rabbi.

But we do know that he did then what dads do all day and every day, he worked hard and provided for his family. Joseph was a man of service to his family, his community, his faith, and his God.

With St. Joseph, there is a tremendous appeal because he defines himself as a man in three different and distinct areas:

First, St. Joseph is a devoted father to his foster Son.

Although initially, he reacted like any normal man when he finds out that his son is lost, he goes looking for him and does not stop until he is found. His training of Jesus, both in carpentry and in his personal development, represented the firm commitment to raise this boy as best he could with the faith that he had and with all the personal devotion that he can muster.

Second, St. Joseph really loves his wife. I believe that he showed his love to Mary in a number of ways. He probably held her hand, placed his arm across her shoulders, and looked lovingly into her eyes as they spent their quiet time together.

Third and finally, St. Joseph represents the ideal that every man who elects to become a father has to develop a sense of patience.

How else could one survive in a period of such stark reality -- Romans had conquered Judea and was an occupying force. So many people lived on the fringes of poverty and dire straits, and even the very Temple where they worshiped had banners of false gods nailed into the very pillars that supported it.

St. Joseph was the embodiment of a decent man, who sought to help others when he could, protect and feed his family, and be true to the very values that he grew up with. All men, regardless of their present occupation, can learn a great deal from looking at the life of St. Joseph and seeing how he measures up to that ideal.

It would be easy to say that St. Joseph represents the Hollywood version of "the strong, silent type" of a male figure. However, St. Joseph was a man -- maybe even a flawed man -- because so much was directed to him that he had no control over. However, in that flawed perception of having no control, St. Joseph emerges as a strong figure that other men can model their lives around.

He knows that his God is looking out for him because God entrusted him with the greatest thing that God can give anyone -- he gives St. Joseph care of his Son, his only begotten Son, until he is ready to start His public ministry.

As men who are married, we need to love our wives, our families, and Our God. It is not a question of having one over the other, rather it is a question of how we balance all these commitments and not having them suffer in the process. St. Joseph continues to be a source of strength in our lives and in the life of the Catholic Church that he has been designated as a Universal Protector.

It is through his example of living with the greatest uncertainty we come to know there is only one certainty: That believing in His Foster Son and living the true faith He inspires us to live will grant us an eternity of happiness and joy. We will soon be invited not to the meager table of just a human carpenter, but of that of His foster Son who was also trained as a Carpenter but became the Great Sheppard of the entire world. We enter the threshold of this altar to encounter and receive the source of never-ending and boundless love.

Jesus Christ gave his life, so that all the people of the world who have been lost to the tyranny of sin may find their way home. Happy are we, because of God's love for us, that God found St. Joseph worthy to be the protector of His Son and His mother until Christ gave himself in the Holy Eucharist for all our salvation. For our faith in Christ will lead us from our present distress and our families can flourish and prosper.

So today we rejoice with the entire Catholic Church for the God's gift of St Joseph, a man of great faith who continues with constant and never ending intercessions of a humble carpenter from Nazareth who followed the desire of His God for our sakes. The Saint we give thanks today for - St Joseph. Amen.

Continuing with the prayers of the faithful, I made a special point to include the names of those people that had been so helpful in my formation, especially Deacon Mike and Father Tom who had also died in 2003; deceased but never forgotten in my mind. After retrieving the Blessed Sacrament from the tabernacle and preparing to say the "Our Father", I looked out in the faces of my classmates and my brothers-in-formation. It was an overwhelming experience to say the least. It was one thing to be praying with them, but it was quite another thing to be leading them in prayer. As they lined up to receive Holy Communion, my classmates gave me silent signs of approval. It was either in a smile, a wink of the eye, or slight touch of the forearm as they left.

As I prepared to give the final blessing, I inadvertently messed up the wording of the blessing, and that was my only thing that I did incorrectly. However, my mistake was readily made apparent by my director of formation but this time, not given in harshness, but in love. My classmates were more generous when I returned back to class. They all stood up and clapped with some of them saying that I looked so natural on the altar. So, all in all, my one-shot in liturgy practicum had gone well.

Our schedule for that year was full as always, Father Tim was our instructor in **Canon Law** for the first five months, and then we had Deacon Bill as our instructor for the second year of **Homiletics**. Father Tim would later return that day for a class in **Scripture and the Gospels**. Once again we would benefit from his intense academic background, especially in Greek for which all of the New Testament was originally written in. We also had another full year of **Social Justice** training with the emphasis on encountering various people who had done Social Justice Ministry as well as deepening our understanding of social justice teachings of the Catholic Church.

During the second part of the year, we were thankful for Father Victor who taught us the **Basics of Liturgy and the role of deacons in the liturgy of the Catholic Church**. Father Victor was truly a special gift to us – his father had been a Catholic deacon as well. So Father Vic was especially motivated to ensure that we, as future deacons, could perform our liturgical functions that uplifted the people of God. A very special treat for us was as we were practicing some liturgical responsibilities, he brought in some of the vestments that his father had worn when he was ordained in which Father Vic used when he was a deacon as well. It provided us with significant pause for thought that day, his father had gone to be with the Lord and it was the gift of his own son that was teaching us to be better deacons. We are truly blessed for all this assistance, professionally and personally, because Father Vic was sending me emails with help and guidance for me especially when my father was dying. Father Vic was answering the e-mails that I was sending from my text pager with constant words of encouragement and prayer, bolstering my strength so that I could be there for the friends of my father at his funeral. Father Vic's gifts of charity and kindness did not go unrecognized.

Our instructor this year for Social Justice would be Simone, a just-married and newly minted graduate student with expertise in social and economic development. Although she had been counseled by Kersti before she accepted the position to teach us men in formation, she rapidly adjusted to teaching us. However, with the aid of a sharp wit, a wealth of personal know-how, and the fact that she had the power of the grade book in her hand, she rapidly tamed us and got us into shape. Finally, we had a full semester of **Diaconate Practicum** which was taught by a number of different deacons on various things that we need to be prepared to do: baptized children, perform marriage ceremonies, conducting funeral services, and ministering to the sick and dying. This is where our formation took a dramatic dose of reality: we would be the ones responsible for assisting the people of God at very powerful spiritual moments of their lives. At this point, the mantle of transitioning from student to worker-in-the-field was taking place.

We also had signs that are ordination was not a pipe dream but something to be looking forward to! We were in the process of ordering the actual invitations to our ordination as well is meeting with a company that would make a unique ordination stole for our class. The vestments that we would wear at the actual ordination was already purchased by the Archdiocese, however, we would be responsible for providing our own stoles, albs, and cinctures that we would wear on Ordination Day. We started a very informal but very visible countdown checklist on the right side of the whiteboard the instructor used for class. Our instructors, from time to time, would inadvertently wipe off the countdown or would just comment that **"only by the grace of God this is going to happen"**, we would be ordained as deacons!" But even if their outward demeanor was sarcastic, each one of our instructors embraced the solemn trust that they had been given, by using their talents they were preparing the future of the Church and they took that obligation very seriously.

Once again, the Eucharistic Congress in June would arrive for the Archdiocese in Atlanta. And once again, the seniors in formation were asked to play a very specific role in the Congress: we were asked to provide four men that we would carry the canopy over the monstrance used for the Congress. Myself and three of my brothers were selected for this blessed opportunity. This would be our last Congress as men-in-formation and that point was not lost on any of us.

In addition, the Archdiocese of Atlanta had gone through a leadership change earlier in the spring. Archbishop John Francis Donaghue who had been our archbishop throughout our entire time in formation to date had reached the age of 75 and submitted his retirement request to the Holy Father. In December of 1994, Pope John Paul II accepted that request and named Archbishop-designate Wilton Daniel Gregory, the former bishop of Belleville, Illinois, as the new Archbishop for Atlanta, Georgia. Bishop Gregory had previously served as the President of the US Conference of Catholic Bishops for the previous three years. His presidency from the start had been consumed as the allegations of abuse from Catholic clergy had been played out in the press and the courts throughout his tenure. We were privileged to have him as a new Archbishop and we look forward to working with him. Our class would have a very special status with him, because God willing, we would be his first class of ordained deacons. A truly graceful man, Archbishop Gregory celebrated the 10th Eucharistic Congress as a celebration of the 50th anniversary of his predecessor's priestly ordination.

As we gathered inside just prior to the procession, my classmates and I once again were amazed by the turnout of the people of God. Literally, thousands of people would show up to celebrate their love and reverence for the Blessed Sacrament and our Eucharistic Lord. Once again, the program was robust but also it would be a full day indeed. My spiritual director, Father

Mendes, had dual responsibilities on that day: to show up in support of the people of God and to hear confessions. He would literally process at the end of the holy hour with his fellow priests, take off his alb in the dressing room and then walked down to the end of the concourse that had been set up as a mass confessional. Leaning forward because his hearing was starting to fail slightly, he would hear confessions continually, only taking a break for a small lunch and then returning back to the concourse to hear more confessions. Occasionally, he would ask for a small bottle of water to be brought to him but then he would motion for the next person to approach and please sit down. Watching him from a distance, I was always filled with a great respect for his devotion to his priesthood. He'd been given a great gift at his priestly ordination: in the name of his Lord, the power to forgive the sins of God's people and to grant absolution in His name. He embraced his vocation with passion and fidelity. Often, on the way home I would mention how I had seen him provide relief to people that were obviously in spiritual pain. In response, he would gently smile and say "God had given me a great gift to be shared."

The final Mass is always a thrilling event. Thousands of Catholics gathered together on the floor, hundreds of clergy surrounding the Archbishop and his invited brother bishops on the altar and our Eucharistic Lord brought in the presence of the people of God during the Eucharistic prayer. How can anyone deny the power of the Catholic Church in this world? Our annual Eucharistic Congress was starting to become a pinnacle event during the year and each time it simply got better and better. Then once again, we had our final summer retreat to look forward to in the following month.

As we returned to Culman for our final summer retreat, we made a dedicated point to look for a very special person. Brother Andre, who was one of the senior monks also served as the head of the retreat center. Although he is a relatively small man just over 5' and over 60 years old, he was a beautiful man of God. Always checking in with us to confirm our arrangements, Brother Andre served as a touchstone for us all. For every year that we traveled to Culman, Brother André was always there. When we prayed with the monks, he was the one that set the prayer books so that we can follow along. When we came to the church for confession, he was the man who always make sure that priests were available for us. He was just a consummate servant and through the years, we had grown to love him as a wonderful gift that we have been given through our five years of formation. My best memory of him would be him leading us in to the cloister during prayer in the church. He would silently lead us to our respective places and then gently verify we were on the right page before we would start. But while we were all in prayer, he was totally absorbed with what he was being called to do – to be a man of prayer.

Recently, he had been assisted by Brother Brendan, a younger monk who lent a hand with in the running of the retreat center. Between the two of them, our final summer weekend at Culman was a beautiful experience. So often, our retreats were not just an individual interaction with God, they were close bonding experiences with the people that were important to us. And these two Benedictine monks were truly living out their vocation to serve others: On behalf of the monastery and the abbot, they opened their arms to us in welcome to their home, they were always looking out for our physical and spiritual needs, and their collective example of work and prayer would be an inspiration that we needed to carry forward to our own ordinations that we would be receiving in less than 30 weeks.

As we returned back to class in the fall, our academic workloads had decreased significantly. Most of the written assignments had been completed in the early part of the year, and now our training was focused on more practical issues. The final exercise in our Scripture class was to develop a full hour teaching lesson based on a Scripture passage of our own choice. This lesson proved very prophetic for me because I was able to use that same lesson for a confirmation class that I had been asked to be a part of in the fall. Once again, lessons learned previously were being used to be the foundation of future teachings and in gratitude, I started letting each of my instructors now how much their efforts were already starting to pay off.

As we approached the months of November and December, our future was starting to be revealed. Our ordination stoles had been completed and delivered to us on the final day of class. Our ordination invitations had been printed and delivered to us by Stuart, one of our brothers in formation. Our days in formation were rapidly coming to an end and at the final day of class, December 10, 2005, we gathered together in class and drinking non-alcoholic champagne toasted each other on finally finishing all of our academic work!

Starting in February of 2001, we had completed 90 full Saturdays of classes, took part in five weekend retreats as well as did countless hours in parish work, mission trips and active hands-on-ministry. Deacon Loris was starting to beam with the look of both proud father and enthusiastic older brother. Our Deacon mentor, Deacon Rich also took part in the celebration. The constant refrain of **"I'd never thought I'd see the day"** was constantly being said, mostly in affection. Rich had been through formation himself, although only for four years instead of five, but he also looked forward to having his Saturdays back to be able to spend with his lovely bride of many years instead of 16 of his knucklehead brothers in formation!

As we were finally getting ready to depart for that final time, I slipped away and went back into every single classroom that we've taken a class in. With every room that I entered into, I remembered specific memories that had taken place: the instructors that had formed us, and my brothers who had encouraged me. As I made my way top side to rejoin my brothers, most were starting to make their way out the door to drive home. Collecting all of my books, I made my way back to the car. As I prepared to drive away, I found my brother Ken in the parking lot, I looked forward to seeing him in our pre-ordination retreat that was going to be held four weeks from now.

However, the joy I felt that day would soon be replaced by the reality of life because within the next four weeks, I would have to deal with death on two separate instances: the death of my father Leopold, and the death of my classmate Victor.

In the epilogue, I talk about in much more deeper detail about my father's death. However, at this point I'd like to focus on my brother Victor.

Victor had come into diaconate formation as an immigrant from Columbia and as a married man whose bride still remained in Colombia while he was in America. A large man, Victor, was probably over 350 pounds at the start of formation, who worked very hard for both his family and his parish. He had come to the United States, like most people, looking for a better opportunity for his family and soon joined his brothers that were already in the United States.

Victor had a very limited English vocabulary, and often struggled in our academic classes. In retrospect, if the situation was reversed, that is if our classes were taught in Spanish with my limited knowledge, I would know exactly how he felt. Our instructors were very accommodating, trying to find the appropriate text written in Spanish as well as allowing Victor to complete his assignments in Spanish and then either translating those assignments themselves, or giving them to an another trusted priest who was bi-lingual to read and evaluate the test. However, Victor had endured both economic and personal challenges.

In our freshman year, his wife was savagely gunned down in the streets of Columbia, she was caught in the crossfire of a drug deal that had gone bad. For the next two years, Victor made every attempt to get his daughter out of Colombia to join him in the United States. Every once in a while, we would ask Victor what the status was of his daughter's exit. Unfortunately, between dealing with government officials, and meeting all of the residency requirements, as well is just the difficulty in communications, her departure seemed like it was never going to happen. But finally, at the end of two years, he was successful in getting her out of Colombia and she joined him in North Georgia. All of this additional stress was taking its toll out on him and combined with having high blood pressure, this was certainly not helping matters either. We knew that he was on some sort of medication for his high blood pressure, but because of the high cost of the medicine, we didn't know if he was taking it on a regular basis. His face, over time, became redder and he subsequently gained additional weight that was taking its toll on his knees as well. But he remained in formation, and was very active in his parish community of St. Lawrence, working with his fellow brothers and sisters that had emigrated from South and Central America as well as Mexico. He was a pillar in that faith community, teaching classes, holding retreats, and leading prayer groups.

In early January, we received an e-mail from one of our brother classmates telling us that Victor had a massive heart attack while visiting friends in Texas and had died. We were stunned, if there was anyone who wished to serve the people of God more than any of us, it was our brother Victor. After a rapid series of e-mails, we learned that his vigil would be in Lawrenceville, Georgia, and his funeral Mass will be held at St. Lawrence Catholic Church. How appropriate was that fact: St. Lawrence had been brutally martyred because of his tremendous love of the poor in the City of Rome during the early Church persecutions. Our brother Victor who had loved the poor among him would have his final Mass celebrated at a church named after a revered deacon and saint in the Catholic Church.

All of our classmates gathered together that morning as we vested together in the choir room prior to Mass. Many of our priest instructors made the journey to be with our brother Victor, and that fact was not lost on his family or his local church community. As we processed in and reverenced the altar, we were all overcome by our tremendous sense of loss. The Mass was said primarily in Spanish but it was simply our honor to be with our brother Victor. With my limited Spanish, I understood the priest who gave the homily about Victor's love of teaching, his eagerness to help lead prayer services and his work with the poor. At the conclusion of the Mass, we formed our own line from the church door to the hearse as we said our final goodbyes to our brother. He had requested to be cremated so this would be our final time that we would see him in this life. Once again, I was to overcome by the circumstances and tears came flooding out of my face. Just a week earlier, I had buried my own father in Winter Park, Florida, and now I was seeing my brother Victor one last time. One of my classmates came over to bolster me and at the conclusion of the service we went back to the choir room.

My annual men's club day of reflection was taking place as we spoke, and I made plans to join them for the remainder of the day. The following day, however, I was preparing to depart on my pre-ordination retreat – five full days of prayer and reflection that was required under Catholic Canon Law prior to ordination. However, after all that had happened, I knew that I needed this quiet time to start my own grieving process, mostly for my dad, to remember the gifts of my mother but also for my brother Victor.

I had the 9:30 and 11:15 a.m. Masses that Sunday morning. At the end of the normal parish announcements, I spoke to my parish community from my heart:

> **My brothers and sisters, I need to let you know that I will be departing immediately after this morning's Masses from St. Oliver's to go on my preordination retreat to the Benedictine monastery in Culman, Alabama. This requirement must be fulfilled under Canon Law and I look forward to rejoining my brothers in formation for one last time.**
>
> **For those of you who prayed for me and my family, especially after the death of my father Leopold, on behalf of my family, please accept our heartfelt thanks and gratitude. For those of you who sent cards**

of condolences and Mass cards to be said for him and his soul, you honor my family and my father.

At the end of my retreat, I will not be coming back to the parish but rather trying to have some quiet time with my family prior to being ordained. Over the last five years, my family has sacrificed a great deal with the greatest sacrifice being my time away from them and in studying for classes and exams. I feel it's important to them to have this quiet and private time prior to ordination.

I will be your servant for the rest of my life after ordination but for the next four weeks, I'm just looking forward to some quiet time and being Cindy's husband once again. Please keep me and my brothers in your prayers and I look forward to being your newest Deacon after February 4. Now let us stand for our final blessing.

Many of the parishioners at the end of Mass were extremely supportive. They had left messages of condolences on our home answering machine and many shared hugs of support with me. As I departed St. Oliver's to drive to Culman, I was filled with a tremendous sense of peace. It was only this one last requirement that needed to be accomplished and our pre-ordination retreat would be the final spiritual gift we would receive prior to the grace of Ordination.

I had made plans to arrive in Culman on Sunday evening because the actual retreat did not start until Monday afternoon. I needed to have this private time for my own grieving process, because I have been more concerned with the needs of other people, and I had neglected my own. After checking in the room, I made my way to the church and now knelt before the Blessed Sacrament that night.

Giving thanks to God for all He had given me, I just wanted to feel His presence once again. Not knowing if it had been just coincidence or God's divine plan that my parents both died within the Christmas season, but it seemed that their deaths were taking a special significance in light of what we had just celebrated. The birth of a child represents the continuance of human life and yet the birth of a Savior meant not just temporal life that had it in with death but rather eternal life that had no end. It was just a blessed moment to be there and just like I had always felt with my brothers in formation in the summer, there was no other place that I wanted to be but in that beautiful church that evening.

The next morning, I met one of my classmates Stuart for a late breakfast and good conversation. Stewart is a human resources manager and was actually a convert to Catholicism from Judaism. Stuart had always shared his support of my professional development but I always valued his personal insights and advice he gave to me. We both look forward to not only the coming week, but also to getting for ordination. Stuart's pastor was looking forward not only to his ordination but that of our brother José. As being the only priest in that parish, he welcomed the opportunity to have two ordained deacons join him to serve the people of Rome, Georgia, at St. Mary's.

Once we made our way back to the monastery, our classmates were arriving one by one. By two o'clock in the afternoon, we had all arrived and our director of formation stood with us. We went through the preliminary plans for a week together, and then we celebrated a memorial Mass for our brother Victor. That was a very touching moment to start our time together. Ken had taken some beautiful pictures of some of the men when they were celebrating their communion service during the year and Victor had requested some pictures to be taken at his service to share with his family back in Colombia. At the Lord's Prayer, Ken snapped a beautiful picture of picture with Victor's hands gently out-stretched reciting the "Our Father."

In addition, a book of Gospels that would have been presented to Victor at Ordination Day by the Archbishop was displayed during that week.

Our retreat master Father Dubay was an accomplished retreat master as well as an author of several different books. Our focus for this retreat was **"Deep Prayer / Deep Conversion"** based on a book that he had published by the same name. However, there were also other things that we needed to accomplish: the final determination of who would be attending our ordination, the revised seating program as well as other administrative details that needed to be done.

Always, we started our days in prayer and celebrated Mass prior to lunch. Brothers André and Brendan were constantly with us, trying to make our stay as pleasant as possible. In the afternoons, we joined the monks in evening prayer and then also had Holy Hours in the evening. All during that week, we enjoyed good conversation, deep prayer, and quiet moments of reflection.

As we approached Friday morning, another bittersweet moment would take place. The next time that we would be together was for our pre-ordination practice at the Cathedral of Christ the King in Atlanta and then when we come together on Saturday for ordination day.

I made my way back to the church one more time and prayed before the Blessed Sacrament once again. Although Christmas joy had to be deferred, now my vocation was crystal clear. Through my father's death, I felt the calling to serve in-hospital ministry and in teaching. It was in those two areas that I had felt God's presence the strongest in those utilize his talents that he'd given me the best.

As I drove home back to Atlanta that afternoon, I'd never remembered a greater time that I wanted to be home. As I said earlier, I was a wealthy man already, and I wanted to return to the greatest source of my wealth that day, my family and especially my wife. I called my brother deacons – Bill, Tom and Rafael -- from the road and they were excited about my progress. Several of them had been asked by other parishioners where I had been, some fearing that I had been transferred to another parish already before ordination! After calming their fears, they were reassured that I was, in fact, coming back but I just needed some quiet time away.

I was very grateful to my boss Jim for all of his flexibility he'd given me since I had left in mid-December. I had left on vacation on December 16th, 2005 with the expectation of coming back on January 2, 2006, but with my dad's death, and my pre-ordination retreat, I would not be back at work until January 16th. But even returning back at work, it was difficult to get back into the swing of things. Starting on February 2, I would once again be leaving on vacation for a week to have some private time and to prepare for ordination. My supervisor Jim had been raised a Lutheran but when I invited him to my ordination, he accepted and I was pleased that he did, when he hired me back in July of 2003, within two weeks of me being hired I had left to go on my annual retreat to Culman. Jim had served as an elder within his church, and always was a positive reflection of Christianity.

Therefore, once again, God had placed me in blessed circumstances: my secular career development had progressed throughout my years in formation, and now the final chapter was being prepared to come forward – to finally become an ordained servant of the people of God.

Ordination Week – February 2-5, 2006...

"**J**im, with your permission, I'm going to head on out now."

"Sure Al, go ahead. I look forward to seeing you on Saturday."

"Absolutely, I'll be there."

With that brief conversation, I left work for the final time knowing that the next time that I returned, I would be ordained.

I had made plans with Jim to take five days off, the Thursday-Friday of this week and then Monday through Wednesday of next, knowing that I would need some time, before hand but also more importantly, the time afterward to decompress. Although there is no honeymoon for ordination like there is in marriage, I talked to men that had been ordained in previous years and most of them readily agreed that you needed at least two or three days afterwards to relax and rest from the ordination weekend activities. So this time schedule represented the best way of doing it. Our workload was easy enough during this time that it would not be an inconvenience and Jim was kind enough to let me have whatever time I needed.

Over the past two years, I had the pleasure of working for this great man who himself had a vocation of service, serving in the United States Army for over 20 years of active duty service and rising to the rank of lieutenant colonel.

Jim and I, over the last three years, had talked always about various religious topics; we never let the theological differences get in the way. Although Jim was a Lutheran, he was very much a servant of his own congregation. He served as an elder in his church, did religious instruction as well as serve in other capacities as well. Occasionally, when the regular pastor was away, even he had the opportunity to preach. So, when I went to work with him in July of 2003, he knew about my current status in formation. He was extremely supportive, and was always willing to ask about my progress and what they were teaching me. Two months prior, I had asked him if he and his bride would come to my ordination and surprisingly, he said "Sure, we would love to come." So, as I prepared to leave work on Wednesday evening, in the back of my mind, I knew that things would be different when I got back.

As you can tell by the chapter title, it's a little bit longer than just your ordinary weekend, but this weekend was going to be far from ordinary. Traditionally, on Thursday afternoon, the ordination class gathers at the Cathedral at approximately 4:30 in the afternoon to go through a full rehearsal for ordination. We were lucky to have two of the senior deacons from the Archdiocese be our master of ceremonies: Deacons Ray and Whitney. Both of these men had been ordained for a number of years, and been part of the Archbishop's support team as master of ceremonies for a number of functions throughout the Archdiocese. Their collective presence in the cathedral that day served as a calming influence.

As we entered into the cathedral, some with our spouses, and others by ourselves, the cathedral itself took on a new significance. In the previous years, the men in formation had often been asked to serve as ushers and later acolytes to the upperclassmen as they were being ordained. This year, it would be our turn; however, we would now be joining a different group of men on Saturday. The Archdiocese of Atlanta has been privileged to have many men who have been ordained over the years as permanent deacons. With backgrounds as diverse as you will find anywhere, all of these men shared a common call: to be servants to the people of God within their respective parishes. The Archbishop, not only is the man who ordained them, but also serves as our spiritual father. Therefore, our ordination also represented a reunion of most of the permanent deacons here in the archdiocese. Later in the fall, there is a separate Mass of Recommitment that is held for the deacons, however, ordinations served as a special sign: acceptance as servants -- fellow servants -- to all of the people in the Archdiocese of Atlanta.

Deacon Loris had a very special guest with him as well: Deacon Dennis who would serve as the new director of diaconate personnel: essentially our new boss. Since ordination signified a new beginning, it also signified an ending: Deacon Loris would have to relinquish us to Deacon Dennis. At previous class ordinations, this was the one weak side that we got a chance to see about Loris. At the end of the Ordination Mass, he would always end with the phrase. "Now you are no longer my children, you are now my brothers." He was like the older brother that would always be kidding his younger siblings, but once the younger siblings left the house to find their own way, then he would find himself somewhat sad. The good news for Loris was that each year when the call went out for a new class, there were new siblings to be integrated into the family!

As we were milling about in the cathedral, we greeted each other warmly and enthusiastically. Typically, comments were being made like "You think you're ready now?" or "You think this is really going to happen?" However, the smiles were too big and the hugs were just too hard. We had prepared over a long five-year course of study, and now this would be the moment that we needed to focus the most attention on.

Ordination for a man is really a lot like getting married for a woman. Typically, when men get married, the bride-to-be is really in charge, or maybe the future mothers-in-law really are! The bride does the vast majority of the planning, makes practically all of the decisions, and takes a great deal of pride for her big day. With ordinations, the roles are actually reversed. In most instances, the man is responsible for figuring out who gets invited, where will they meet, and if there's going to be a reception afterward and who puts that all together. I know in my own case, Cindy did everything when we got married. When we were together the previous Christmas before we got married, she laid out everything. Acting like a typical male, I asked her was there anything that I needed to do. Her father, sitting in his big chair, dropped his paper, looked me dead in the eye and said **"Yes Al, there's something you can do. Show up!!"** So, true to form, for a Friday evening marriage mass, I was in the vesting room at 6 p.m. and waiting a whole hour, even before the priest, until I was told they were ready to start.

For my own ordination, I told my wife that I would be taking care of everything and essentially all she needed to do was show up! However, being my bride, she did do a couple things on her own for our benefit, but I really just wanted her to enjoy the day as well. She had done so much in supporting me over the past five years. When I was leaving the house at six in the morning to make a seven o'clock holy hour, she was with my two children for 13 hours plus all by herself. She was the one who gave me the free time so that I can focus on the endless papers or presentations that we had to be able to have completed before the next class. When I had to make a last-minute hospital visit, she was the one who told me to go to that person in the hospital and dinner could wait. So, the roles would be reversed for that special day and I look forward to hearing what she thought afterward.

Deacon Loris made some initial remarks and then passed the practice to Deacon Ray and Whitney. Being both casual and directive, they put us through the ordination rite as well as gave us helpful comments with respect to having correct posture and positioning. The Archdiocese of Atlanta always made a special effort for Ordinations to be videotaped and therefore it was absolutely essential not only that we looked but that we felt comfortable.

Essentially, there were five separate stages for the rite of diaconate ordination that we needed to make sure we got correctly:

1. **the oath of obedience to the archbishop and his successors,**

2. **the laying down on the floor for the litany of the saints,**

3. **the actual laying on of hands by the archbishop,**

4. **the prayer of consecration, and**

5. **Then finally the receiving of the Book of the Gospels from the archbishop.**

Although two of these actions could be done as a group -- the litany of the saints and the prayer of consecration -- the other three had to be rehearsed correctly. With one of the senior deacons playing the role of the archbishop, it was almost surreal as they went to the exact liturgical script that the Archbishop would be saying on Saturday. Each of us took that practice very seriously because in less than 48 hours, it wouldn't be just a practice but a spiritual and historical reality.

Finally, at about 5:45 p.m. we were done. In the Archdiocese of Atlanta, we have a tradition that after the rehearsal in the cathedral, we have a rehearsal dinner at a local restaurant. I was responsible for organizing that event, and of course, just like in marriages, you always get a couple of last-minute arrivals such as relatives of classmates that needed to be part of the dinner. We were lucky that we were going to a very nice Italian restaurant about 4 miles away from the Cathedral that had hosted these types of events before. As we fought traffic on a night commute filled with cars and a slight rain drizzle, we finally made it to the restaurant and tried to park our cars in a very crowded parking lot. As you walked into the restaurant, they posted a welcoming sign for all to see. The banquet room was on the second-floor and soon within a half an hour, the warm food was brought in and the even warmer conversation punctuated the room.

I said a prayer before dinner, thinking that I was brief, but my classmates agreed with one of the older deacons that I sounded more like a Baptist preacher than a Catholic deacon! Even till the end, the class rep gets no respect! Once again, the rehearsal dinner for ordination is very similar to a rehearsal dinner for marriage. Luckily, you're surrounded by people that care about you and also you are surrounded by your brothers who you shared five years of your life with. Although occasionally we got to see each other's spouses at some functions, it was rare that we got all the spouses together with their husbands. So, it was also a time for them to get caught up on what was happening as well as trading plans for Saturday and Sunday. One of the guys, David Grubbs, did a great parody on Deacon Loris. The premise was that an unknown personnel file had miraculously been made public with his hand written comments on each and every one of us.

David is an experienced screenwriter and the satire was running thick that night. However, not only did he take a shot at the boss, he satirized each one of his classmates. After a while, not only were we listening to his comments, we were adding a few of our own! The restaurant staff were extremely gracious and kind to us that night, they had been made aware of what would be going on Saturday and a few of them popped in their heads to see what was going on. But at the end of the evening, with the food that had not been eaten at the tables placed in large take-home bags, we left to return back to our parishes and our homes. The next time we would see each other would be on Saturday morning, literally a day and two wake-up calls from now.

Friday morning, February 3, would be a very full day indeed. Since I was on vacation, I made a special effort to attend Morning Mass in my parish. Typically, daily mass is at 9:00 a.m. and because of this, I could not make that mass and then get to work. But being on vacation, this was not a problem that day. My pastor, Father Jim, was serving as the celebrant for the Daily Mass and this would be the last time that we'd serve together as priest and acolyte. Normally, Daily Mass would be said in the day chapel but we moved it inside the regular church that morning. Following Mass, would be our monthly Eucharistic adoration exposition and I wanted to spend some special time with our Lord as well. Holy hours had been something that I had been introduced to just prior to me being in formation, and now I almost felt it as an absolutely essential on that day. Parishioners that would be coming in and out during the first two hours with gently slide over or a whisper in my ear "Congratulations!" or "We're very proud of you." Of course, I was extremely thankful for their support and good wishes through these years.

At about 11:30 a.m., I wanted to get some small errands done and then traveled down to the Cathedral one more time prior to Saturday. It was a beautiful bright sunny day in February and the cathedral inside with the stained-glass shone brightly. Although I worked about 5 miles away from the cathedral, I never could get the opportunity to go to Mass during lunch because mid-town traffic is so unpredictable. However, today would not be a problem. Deacon Whitney was preparing to be the Deacon for this Mass when I went up to him and just gave him a quick hug of thanks for all you done for me in the past as well is all he would do for our class tomorrow. He smiled widely and said that he was looking forward to being there tomorrow. I told him that I'd be watching his every move during Mass in order to get any last-minute tips on liturgy or posture. At that point, he simply told me to just take a seat and he would see me after Mass.

The Mass was simple and dignified. Over 50 people came in for the noon-time mass and the priest gave a very simple homily about God's love for his people. As I entered into line for communion, I glanced upon the cut stone crucifix that hangs above the tabernacle in the cathedral. Gently, under my breath, I kept repeating the words that we say prior to Holy Communion **"Lord, I am not worthy to receive you, but say the words and I shall be healed."** This would be my last communion as a layperson and as I returned to my pew to offer a prayer of thanksgiving, I can feel the tears streaming down my face and peace in my soul. So much mercy and forgiveness had I been extended through my years of life and also in formation. One of the things that made me so motivated in my vocation is that divine mercy is not a concept; Divine Mercy is the personhood of Jesus. Therefore, Mercy does have a face and His name is Jesus Christ.

After Mass was completed, I did ask Whitney if he could ask the celebrant priest to hear my confession. A consummate diplomat, when he made his way over to the priest and whispered in his ear. Father looked up, smiled, and gestured for me to come over. Although the details of that confession will keep secret, one of the most beautiful things that he told me was that a person should read both Psalms 51 and Psalm 32. Prior to making his confession, a person should read Psalm 51 to hear how David pleaded for God's mercy and in Psalm 32 how thankful the penitent is for receiving that same mercy from God. To this day, as I go to confession, I tried to follow that very good guidance that I got that day.

Departing from the cathedral, I made my way back to our home and waited for the news of our guests that would be arriving that day. We had a number of family and friends that were coming in as far as California and Massachusetts/Rhode Island and all during the day, we were getting updates on their progress. Unbeknownst to me, Cindy made plans for a nice family dinner, catered of course, for our friends and family to join us at the house. Many of them had never had a chance to see our home before and this would be a great opportunity for us to have an enormous chance to get caught up before Saturday morning. Dinner was delicious, the laughter was deep and throughout the house! As a bonus, my two young children received the best gifts from their Uncle Mike and Aunt Adele: my daughter got an iPod Nano and my son got a portable DVD player.

As the evening wore on, I kept seeing people that had never met before slowly start to become friends. They were here to celebrate with us and I was glad for their presence. Finally, around 10:30 in the evening, with the last toast offered, they prepared to leave. Tomorrow is going to be a full day for us all and a good nights rest was desperately needed.

Saturday morning started with an alarm at about 6 a.m. I decided to do the full Divine Office for that day in the morning, knowing that today would be extremely exhausting. In addition, my completion of the Office would be a requirement and really emerge as a labor of love as opposed to a duty. We had done a study of the Psalms in my aspirancy year and as I read that morning, they started to take on a new significance. As a devout Jew, Our Lord would memorize the Psalms as part of his own prayer life here on earth. As He sought the closeness of His Father through deep prayer, the Psalms inspired by the Holy Spirit and written by their authors, would have been an essential part of Christ's mission here are. So now the same Psalms would now speak to us as men completing formation and preparing for ordination.

The traffic was light through Atlanta at that morning and although the Ordination Mass would not begin until 10:30 a.m., by the time I arrived at quarter to nine, there were already people who had parked in the parking deck and inside the church. Since we had assigned seating for our invited guests, I quickly went to the third and fourth rows on the right hand side where my family would have been setting in about an hour. I made arrangements for separate transportation to be available for my guests who were unfamiliar with the Atlanta area and Cindy would be driving in with the children in her Honda.

Once I got to our assigned rows, I laid out some printed signs which each of their names on it and arranged them like they do for the Academy Awards. In addition, there was a spiritual gift for each and every one of them. Over the previous six months, I had learned how to make knotted twine Rosaries. As a personal gift to each one of my invited guests, I left a knotted twine rosary on top of their seat so that as they came in, that would be the first thing that they would see.

Deacon Loris had already arrived and was towards the front of the altar. Per his instructions, we were to lay out the Dalmatics that we had been issued as well as our Ordination stoles where our wives would be sitting. Once this was accomplished, he asked us to leave the cathedral and to go into the preparation room that he had coordinated for us to have. In that room, we would be vested with our albs and in this room after the completion of the Mass; this is where we would dress for the first time in our black clerics. Already some of our classmates were in the preparation room and once again we greeted each other with firm hugs and big smiles. We did not vest immediately, thinking that once we put on our albs, we would grow too hot! We would be in this room for approximately 1 hour and then at the appropriate time, one of the deacons would come down to get us and bring us up to the outside of the cathedral where we would form up with the rest of the procession. We tried to keep the conversation light but now was the time for some serious prayer and personal examination. We've been through so much over the past five years: we dealt with a loss of jobs, the loss of family and friends, the increased responsibility of ministering to our parishes, and the loss of our brother Victor. At about 10:10 am, we started to vest in our albs. Once we checked each other out one last time, Jim asked everyone if we could just pray one decade of the Rosary. Someone suggested that we pray the third Luminous mystery -- Jesus preaches at the Sermon at the Mount. Jim led us through that decade and then we enjoyed pure silence. At this point, I thought of my parents who are now gone from this world. Knowing that they tried the best that they could to give me all that they had, I hoped that in this one brief moment that their redemption was complete. They were in the hands of the loving Savior that in a few short minutes I would be committing the rest of my life to serving. And then, it happened.

"Okay gentlemen, it is time to go!" Deacon John McManus had been a senior when we were in our aspirancy year and was now assigned at Corpus Christi Catholic Church, the same church that I had interviewed with his predecessor, Deacon Gene. John's presence that morning was a welcome sight. With a big smile and the wave of his hand, we followed him into the corridor leading to the outside. As he led us up the stairs to the outside of the cathedral, we can see that the Ordination Mass procession that had already been formed. It was looking for its last link and we were that link. A space had been created for us and as we were looking to the west to enter into the cathedral before us, we saw a familiar figure in white. The Archbishop of Atlanta, Archbishop Wilton Daniel Gregory, a Successor of the Apostles and our spiritual father was waiting just outside the main doors of the cathedral. He glanced in our direction and smiled like a proud father does when he sees his children all gather together. At this point, it was nothing less than electric. We were getting ready to go, we could see some of our wives who would walk before us waving at us in a few trying to say "I love you" to their respective spouses. Then the music started, the voices came down to a whisper and we started to move.

The wives moved first and took their respective places in our pews, then two-by-two guided by Deacon Ray; we made our way down the narrow runway in the Cathedral. As we were going down, the words to the hymn "Here I am Lord" were being sung by the choir. At my father's funeral service, I had requested the song as the entrance hymn. But today, even with the same words, took on a different meaning for me. For as it said in the Old Testament "I knew you before you were born", now I was giving thanks to the same God for bringing me to His house. We gently bowed as we got to our designated pews and then the procession continued with all the ordained deacons following us. In each of the three deacons of St. Oliver's –Bill, Rafael and Tom -- as they passed my pew, turned their heads slightly to make eye contact and had big smiles. They had been also my spiritual brothers and they were excited for me as I was excited to have them there.

Then all of the concelebrating priests passed us by. Some of them had been our instructors in formation and they would nod to us as they passed by. Then at the base of the altar, they would bow and then take their places to the right side of the altar. Finally, all of the priests that would be our pastors came down wearing the same concelebrating vestments. It was a beautiful white silk pattern which had at the center a large gold circle that had a white dove as a symbol of the Holy Spirit superimposed on it. Finally, the Archbishop with his Deacon Master of Ceremonies made his way down to the altar. The choir still sang as the Archbishop first reverenced the altar, then received the incense from the servers, blessed the incense and incensor, and then proceeded to incense the altar, the tabernacle, and the cross above the tabernacle. Our beautiful Ordination Mass had begun.

We had made arrangements for the Mass readings to be done in the languages that represented our class: first Spanish, then Vietnamese, with the Gospel being proclaimed in English. Just like we had been at our Lady of Vietnam 27 months earlier, we had decided that our Ordination Mass had to reflect the character of our class as well as the local Catholic Church. We were truly one universal Church and the local church in Atlanta is made up of the rich diversity of its people. Finally, Deacon Rich proclaimed the Gospel of John and then the Archbishop gave his homily. He focused on the fact that we did not need to be perfect men but we needed to be faithful to the Gospel, to the Church, and to Jesus Christ.

At the conclusion of the homily, the liturgical script calls for the director of formation to testify that we have been found worthy to the Archbishop and the Archbishop accepts his testimony on behalf of the people of God. At the conclusion of this script, the people of God accept this decision and signify their acceptance by clapping of hands. To our credit, the people of God are most accepting and clapped for us loudly.

The next step was the oath of obedience. Each one of us individually knelt before the Archbishop, accepting his charge to be obedient to him and his successors. Archbishop Gregory has a wonderful voice and as he accepted our hands into his, we all made a dedicated effort to look him in the eye. Over time, his eyes were glistening, and we were making a dedicated effort to speak clearly when we all said individually "I do." Just as in marriage, we had to individually freely proclaim our fidelity and, therefore, it was essential that this oath be taken without duress or reluctance. He made a point to gently rub our hands as he was accepting our vow, like the gentle touch of an approving father holding the hands of his child.

As we returned to the center aisle, we had to be prepared to lie down on the floor as the choir chanted the Litany of the Saints. At the words "let us kneel", we lay prostrate on the floor. At the practice on Thursday, it was suggested that we bring a small towel to lie on the floor while our heads rested on the ground. Knowing that it would be warm that day, some of us assumed that it would be because we would be hot. But some of the other deacons confided in us that it was during the Litany of the Saints, they were overcome with emotion and many men would be shedding tears of thanksgiving. Being prepared, I too placed the towel on the floor and as the course of saints was being recited once again, I was overcome by emotion and joy. The flowing of tears came readily and once again I was thanking God for His mercy and His forgiveness. At the conclusion of the litany, some of us struggled to get up because we were starting to get a little drained.

As we were prepared to ascend the altar and then to the Chair of the Archbishop for the actual laying of the hands, I look to the tabernacle and almost could feel the Lord asking me one final question: **"Albert, what have you learned the most?" My answer I gave was this "Lord, you loved me**

first so now it is my choice to love all you send to me." At this point, I was standing in front of my classmate who is now kneeling before the Archbishop. Archbishop Gregory made a very profound gesture to us during that moment. During the laying of hands, he probably left them on our heads for at least five to ten seconds, as if to demonstrate to the people sitting in the pews that there should be no doubt in their minds that through his hands, the Holy Spirit was being sent upon us as it had happened to the first seven deacons as we read in the Acts of the Apostles.

As my classmate John turned to return to his place, I approached the Archbishop and knelt before him. As the Archbishop placed his hands on my head, I could feel a warm sensation that was unlike anything else. Truly, as he was a Successor to the Apostles who themselves have been ordained by Jesus Christ, I was truly feeling the hands of Christ on my head that day. As he released his hands from my head, I just felt overwhelmed with joy. I couldn't describe it, but I knew it was there. With the completion of the laying of hands, we were now ordained deacons and we returned back to our individual rows for vesting.

We, as a class, had selected a vendor to create our ordination stoles. It was a beige silk stole with the symbols of the alpha and omega as well as the Chi Rho symbol on it. Now, as our pastors came down from the altar as well as our diaconate mentors to vest us, this is where the smiles would start. Our wives would hand to our mentors the stole that our mentor would then place on us. Then, our pastors would help us vest with our dalmatic. However, in addition I had ordered a gold ring that had the diaconate stole draping over a cross with the initials "CFS" representing the words "called-formed-sent" on the left side, the numbers 2006 on the right side of the cross and then at the base of the cross the initials "CMC" representing Cindy, Michael, and Christina. I had not worn this ring at all with the exception of getting its size correctly until that day. But just as I had worn a wedding ring to symbolize my fidelity to my wife, I now wear this ring as a constant reminder of my fidelity of service.

Now plenty of hugs between our mentors, pastors, and wives were being displayed. The joy that had been in our hearts can now be shared with our immediate loved ones and the people who shared our vocation. At the conclusion of the vesting, a prayer of consecration was said as we knelt at the altar. We were being asked to perform service for the rest of our lives, to be vigilant in our prayer lives and to be prepared to do what was asked of us. Finally, at the conclusion of that prayer, we individually approached the Archbishop to receive a Book of the Gospels. While he presented the Book of Gospels to us and we held the book to receive it, he asked to **"Receive the Gospel of Christ, whose herald you now are. Believe what you read, teach what you believe, and practice what you teach."** At the conclusion of that, we individually had the opportunity to receive the Sign of Peace from our new spiritual father. As I hugged the Archbishop, I said softly "Thank you for the privilege of serving the people of God." He responded "You're very welcome." With the final book of Gospels being presented, we now were in one long line in front of the altar.

As the choir once again started singing, our new brother deacons from previous years individually embraced us for the sign of peace as well. Some of these men I knew and some of them I had just met that morning. But all of them wished us well. Of course, when my now brother deacons from my parish came to me, I embraced them with so much joyfulness. They were truly happy for me, my family, and for each other. I had sought these men's advice and counsel, and they had been generous with me. But now was a time I could embrace them in a new relationship: we would be fellow servants together.

At the conclusion of the sign of peace for the deacons, we ascended to the altar and took our place on the right side of the bishop as he faced the people of God. As I glanced out, I saw my family and my friends. These are

217

the people that loved me the most and I was so happy that they had made the journey to be there. To some extent, I began thinking "This is what truly heaven will be like; we will be together gathered around the Table of the Lamb."

The offertory was brought up by our wives with the Archbishop accepting the bread, the wine and the water for the Eucharistic sacrifice. At that point, the Liturgy of the Eucharist started.

All of the concelebrating priests came together and joined the Archbishop at the altar. There was probably over 50 priests who came in support of the diaconate. As the Archbishop presided, some of the priest took turns reading part of the Eucharistic Prayer. At the time of communion, some of my classmates got a chance to bring Holy Communion out to the people in the cathedral as well as a separate room that had the ordination mass being relayed on two large monitors that were positioned there. So even though they were not in the Cathedral, they could fully participate in the Mass and we can hear their responses to the liturgical script through the doors that were open in a hallway. The Archbishop personally served us Communion as our spiritual father and as we remained in our seats, we finally had a chance to relax slightly and to take in what we had been through.

Just prior to the conclusion of the Mass, Deacon Loris fulfilled his last function: to give thanks to all who had assisted us throughout our five years in formation, to charge us as his newest deacons to fulfill what we had promised -- to serve the people of God, and then he spoke about Victor. He said how Victor had been an inspiration to his community and his faith, and although God had brought him to the doorway of Ordination, he now was with Him. All of us, each and everyone of us had had a separate relationship with Victor, but we were all amazed that throughout all that happened to him, the unexpected death of his wife, the countless struggles to maintain a job and still attend formation classes, the endless attempts to work with the American government to get his daughter out of Colombia and into the

United States, and finally all the hard work he did in his parish. He is truly an inspiration and continues to be an inspiration of what we needed to be: a dedicated servant to the people of God.

Then the Archbishop did the very graceful thing: he personally thanked Deacon Loris for all his hard work that he had done to prepare us. At this point, Loris smiled and his eyes got misty too. Instead of being his young children, we were now his brother deacons.

The Archbishop gave us all his final blessing and we now prepared to join the procession out as ordained deacons. I made a special effort to make eye contact with my friends as we made our way out of the Cathedral. Once again, smiles were aplenty in as we reached the end of the Cathedral, we raced back on the outside to a side entrance near the altar. Even though the sun was shining, a heavy mist or sun shower was happening. It wasn't a downpour, but just like a cool refreshing mist to bring the temperature down a little bit. Since the weather was not cooperating, the alternate plan was for us to have our picture taken with the Archbishop in front of the altar after he had made his way down the aisle. But, because of all of the concelebrating priests and other deacons, by the time we made it back to the altar he was still at his chair waiting for his part of the procession to start. So silently, we waited in the back until he had cleared the Cathedral and made his way back to where we were. We were already assembled at the altar when he came in on the right side. It seems at once, a thousand photo flashes were going as friends or relatives were trying to take as many pictures as they could. Finally, the official photographer for the Georgia Bulletin, the archdiocese newspaper, asked them to stop so that he could take his pictures for the paper and they acquiesced for only a minute. But the Archbishop, being graceful as always, allowed a few more minutes before he gently told them that we had to go.

As we were leaving the altar, he was smiling at us and wished us well. We descended the back stairs to go back to the conference room where we had been just three hours earlier. At this point, we took off our vestments for

Mass, and now changed into the black clerics that we were now officially able to wear. Some of us have bought just plain black clerical shirts, while other of us vested in slightly more dressy rabbis and black suits. Within about 10 minutes, we were all dressed and preparing to leave. There was a reception for us in that same large room that had housed the people that could not get into the Cathedral. Of course, many of our friends had been waiting for us and once again smiles and hugs were aplenty. I finally found my wife and children with some of my friends. They were briefly taken aback when they saw us in our clerics. My best friend Patrick, always the comedian along with my other friend Paul, said in a loud voice "Is that you Father Albert." "No Patrick, it's just me Deacon Albert!" Once again, some hugs were shared and Patrick whispered "Congratulations."

I had made arrangements for a private reception to be held at my parish hall later on that afternoon. It was important for me to have some private time with some other people that had been extremely helpful throughout my formation but I was unable to get them into the cathedral for my ordination. After an hour of maneuvering through mid-day Atlanta traffic, I arrived back at my parish with some of my guests already there. Once again, between multiple hugs and slaps on the back, I was able to start to tell my guests individually how much I had appreciated their support and kindness. A gift table had been set up along with a real mailbox that had the words" Deacon Al -- 2006" printed on the side. Some of my friends had written to me in advance of what I wanted as a gift, and I made arrangements with them to purchase for me some of my deacon's stoles that I would be using after Ordination. Some of them had already arrived and were displayed on the table for me. For the next two hours, over 200 people arrived to wish me well. This is the part of ordination that is also like getting married -- the wedding reception -- the ordination reception; it's one in the same. It's the ability for us to gather around our friends and the people they care about us, to wish us well for the future and for us to celebrate our present. The five o'clock Mass was just concluding and I was in the back, shaking hands with some more parishioners. Their thoughts and good wishes were added on to those of the people I just left.

That evening, our friends, Keith and Lisa, posted a small informal dinner party for our guests in their home. It was a beautiful gesture on their behalf, the food was overflowing and the deserts tasted especially sweet. Just as the night before, for some of our friends that had never met each other before, this was a chance for them to get to know each other better. In addition, they also take advantage of trying to embarrass me on how my faith had not been as strong and my love for sleeping in on Sundays was greater than my love of going to Mass! However, all in all, it had been a great ending to a perfect day!

Although my first mass was not going to be until 11:15 a.m. that morning, I needed to go home that night to practice my first homily one more time. As I went for my homily, I focused on the section of the Gospel that Sunday that talked about the importance of prayer as well as being empowered to preach. For the first homily after ordination, this Gospel passage could not have been more perfect and I was looking forward to seeing how well it would be received. Deacon Alfred Mitchell, who had served as a past Director of Diaconate Personnel for the Archdiocese of Atlanta, once made a great comment about being prepared for homilies and the people's response to that homily. **"If people approach you after Mass to tell you how good your homily was, you thank them generously and then tell them this: the Holy Spirit always does great work, but sometimes He lets you help!"**

As I awoke the next morning, once again I did the full Divine Office for that day. I would be scheduled to preach at three different masses that day: the 11:15 a.m. would be my first mass, I would preach in Spanish for the first time for my Hispanic brothers and sisters at 1:00 p.m., and finally I would preach to the teens at the 5:30 p.m. that evening.

I arrived at St. Oliver's at about 10 o'clock in the morning. The 9:30 a.m. children's Mass was still going on and I was waiting in the back of the church with the ushers. Almost immediately, the ushers started working their way over and grasping my hand firmly. Many just whispered "Congratulations" or "Good job". Some of the parishioners in the back rows started to look around to see what was going on. When they finally caught on, many of them just smiled and waved.

After the post-Communion prayer, Deacon Tom was making the announcements for the parish. He then made the following announcement to the people "We're privileged to have with us a new deacon assigned to St. Oliver's. In fact, he's with us in the back and I would like him to come up and say a few words." For our visiting priest, Father Thomas, he had been with our parish many times before to say Mass as well as trying to build a new church for his own community nearby. He graciously nodded his head, and I went to the ambo to speak to the people.

I thanked them for their support for my vocation, not only while I had been in formation, but for those with sent prayers and Mass cards after the death of my father over the Christmas break. I told them that I could not be effective in being a minister to my father's family and to my own, had I not had the prayers of support from this community. I looked forward to being their servant, for the privilege of being able to baptize their children, to marry them in the Church or convalidate their marriages if they had married outside of the Church, or to be with them as a brother in Christ during their times of personal stress. At the end, they clapped enthusiastically and I left to return to the back of the church. After the Mass, they were streaming out and once again the handshakes and hugs were plentiful.

For my very first mass, I had made special arrangements with our choirmaster, Mary Jane, for certain songs be played during the Mass. She graciously pass my request to the choir and they, in turn, started the Mass with the hymn "Here I am Lord", the same hymn that we had started our ordination mass with as well as my father's funeral five weeks earlier.

With my pastor being the celebrating priest, we're also joined by a group of Boy Scouts that were celebrating their annual mass of service and recognition as well. As my family and friends were in the first four pews on the left-hand side as I looked from the front of the church, the Boy Scouts were assembled on the right hand side in the front rows. It was a beautiful sight for me. They both looked excited for me and for the parish. For many of my visitors, this would be the only time that they could see my parish community and many of them at the end of the Mass; they were overwhelmed by the hospitality extended to each of them. At the beginning of Mass, Father Jim made a specific point to say that we had a very important occasion to celebrate: that it was a Boy Scout weekend and we needed to support all of our scouts but, by the way it was also official and I had finally been ordained! This joke was not lost on the parishioners, and once again they clapped their approval!

The first two readings were finished and the Responsorial song was sung, we then stood up for the Proclamation of the Gospel. As I asked for my first blessing prior to proclaiming the Gospel, Father Jim made a very personal act of kindness: he placed both his hands on my head as he prayed for me to be able to be worthy of proclaiming the Gospel of Our Lord Jesus Christ.

With the two small altar servers with me, I approached the Book of the Gospels, lifted the book high, and then made my way to the ambo. Gazing around the church that morning, once again the feelings of joy came over me as I gently were glancing tears away for my eyes so that I could be prepared to read. At the conclusion of the Gospel, I kissed the page that I had just read, and waited for the choir to finish before I delivered, with the abundant help of the Holy Spirit, my first homily. Just prior to starting my homily, I commented that I myself had been both a boy and an Eagle Scout. Back in April 1976, I also received my Eagle Scout Award with four other scouts in my Scout Troop, Troop 64, in Trumbull, Connecticut. As I was looking out at the scouts that morning, I commented that the merit badge sash that some of the older scouts were wearing, complete with all the merit badges that they had earned to date, to some extent resembled the upper part of the deacon's stole. Therefore, by wearing their sashes of their uniforms, they were making a deliberate and public statement about their commitment to serving their families, their parish, their community, and our God. They should be prepared to look forward to a full life of service, because of the vocation they had received as young Boy Scouts today, would be the vocation that they would carry for the rest of their lives. The young boys, at first, seem surprised that I had something specifically for them, but the Scoutmaster at the end of that first Mass made a point to come over to thank me for including them.

I first started recalling on what had taken for me to get here that day. I'd spoken how through my mother's death, I had felt the first indications that I had a call and how the Rosary had influenced the growth of my spiritual development. However, now I was challenged to live out my faith, in both my personal actions as well as my own preaching. All of us, whether we know it or not preach to the world, day in and day out, about our Christian faith. Therefore, it was not a question on whether or not the world knew that we were Christians, but rather our ability to fully integrate our Christianity into every facet of our lives. If we were successful in this endeavor, then our Christianity and our love for Christ which show through to everyone that we came in contact with.

Then I issued a challenge to my parish:

"The main challenge facing St. Oliver's is not whether or not we will have to learn Spanish. The greatest challenge facing St. Oliver's is that do we have the time and the courage to learn each other's story. Because it

is only through when we learn each other stories that we start the process of being both emotionally and spiritually engaged to each other to become a better community. And just as you have five years to know me and my family and learn about our unique circumstances, so now I have the responsibility to learn your stories as well. You have embraced me, my wife and my children and I am so thankful for your generosity in doing so. So in return, I am also willing to listen and learn, if you have the courage to tell me.

For the rest of my life, I will be your servant, I will be there to hopefully baptize your children and your grandchildren, to witness the weddings of your children and friends, and if need be, provide comfort to you in your moments of anguish in the hospital or at the death of loved ones. I would rather share these opportunities with you if I know your story so that I can be a better minister to each and everyone of you. But I cannot do this unless you let me, and I am ready now to listen."

At the end of my homily, my parish community gave me a warm ovation, however, the joy in all our hearts was for Our Lord and as the Mass progressed as we are preparing to distribute communion, once again my pastor made a very generous gesture to my family and guests. My family and friends first came forward to receive communion and then once they had been served, the rest of the parish community came forward. Many of my parishioners gave me a silent but positive sign of support. Some involve just winks, some involve the slight pat on the arm and others were just whispers as they departed. As we finished the Mass, Father Jim asked the parish if there were any visitors with us today. Practically all my friends stood up in the parish and they were welcomed once again.

With the final hymn being sung, Father Jim asked Cindy to join me as we walked up the aisle together. He's always been so supportive of his deacons but he wanted to make an additional show of support for the role that the wives played in supporting their husbands and his deacons. Once again, parishioners were rich in thanksgiving and their praise. For me, I was being overcome by their goodwill and their generosity.

I would later preach in Spanish at the one o'clock afternoon Mass. Prior to ordination, I worked with a couple, Steve and Miriam, who worked on my Spanish pronunciation with translating a very simple homily that they had helped me prepare. Our Hispanic apostolate had been going for about two years now, and Deacon Rafael and I would serve together at this Mass as fellow deacons. Rafael proclaimed the Gospel in Spanish and then I preached immediately after him. People were pleasantly surprised that I could speak Spanish, but I give all the credit to my coaches who worked on my pronunciation a great deal with me. However, I will have to learn Spanish, probably in the next three or four years, I hope to be at least being much more fluent that I am now.

My last Mass of the day was at 5:30 p.m. which is our Life Teen Mass. I looked forward to this Mass because so much of my formation had been done with the teens of this parish and at my previous parish. So is the teens assembled for their Mass, many of them were pleasantly surprised to finally seen me ordained as well. I spoke to them about the importance of their prayer life and how the Rosary had influenced my prayer life for the better. Our teens are so on fire for a God, and it is always a joy to work with them because what they don't have sometimes in knowledge, they more than make up for with it with enthusiasm. In fact, several the teens have considered either the priesthood or the diaconate as a possible vocation for them in the future. I firmly believe that the example of deacons serving in the Church does positively reflect the desire for some teens to serve God in a very unique and special way. Once again, at the conclusion of Mass, the teens were enthusiastic and happy for me to be in the parish.

Finally, since it was Super Bowl Sunday, we had made arrangements to meet at a restaurant at the hotel that most of the guests were staying at. However, since the game was going full blast, we elected to just stay and watch the game and ordered in some additional food. Now, it was time to gently slip back into reality. Our friends would be leaving the following day and this would be the last night for us to spend time together. So, watching the Super Bowl, enjoying a few more laughs and hugs, again concluded with Pittsburgh Steelers winning and our friends were getting ready to leave. I can probably say that I have never hugged so many people in one weekend as I did my ordination weekend. I can say without a doubt that I have never had a weekend more filled with joy. Once again, I truly believe that this is what heaven we'll be all about: that we will be in the constant and continuous presence of the Lord and each other. They will be no separation because we will all be in one place and will have nothing but joy in our hearts. I finally got to bed, somewhat exhausted but just thankful for all that had gone on in the past 72 hours.

The following day, I had to drive one of my guests to the airport. I was wearing my black clerics because I had another appointment once I had dropped them off. So on the drive down to the airport; we talked about their children, and what plans I had to the spring. Arriving at the airport, we made our way to the Delta terminal and thankfully made it right to the curb, which was surprising considering it was Monday morning. As Paul and Sherry got out of the car, they came around to ask me a favor, "Albert, can we have your blessing?" "Of course, after all you've done for me; it is my privilege to do this for you." I gave them my first blessing that day, and wished them a safe flight home.

I returned back to the parish to try to fill out some paperwork that they had requested, but they were not finished with what they needed to do.

However, a parishioner had died and her funeral Mass would be at 11 o'clock that day. I asked Father Jim if it would be okay for me to assist at this mass and he said that it was fine with him.

So we went to the back of the church to vest together. Not even 48 hours after being ordained, I was now participating in my first funeral as a deacon. At this point, this is where my vocation really hit home. We had to be prepared to meet the people of God wherever they were in joy or their sorrow, whatever was their present state. As I read the Beatitudes for the Gospel at that mass, I was filled with hope. I had requested the Beatitudes to be read at my own father's funeral Mass and hearing those words once again, now as ordained clergy took on a new significance. Christ himself was teaching us again that God looked not to the high and mighty, but to the lowly and the hurting. As long as they still had faith in Him, He would be forever faithful to them.

As I was finishing Mass, one of the family members came up to me to thank me for being at Mass for her mother. I replied that it was my privilege to be there and then she asked me a question. "So how long have you been ordained?" I replied "Well, just over 48 hours, actually." She blinked, looking a little shocked, then smiled warmly and said "You looked like you have been doing this for years."

In retrospect, we, as a class of 15 men plus our brother Victor, had been practicing, studying, praying, ministering and learning over the past five years. But it was always the grace of the Holy Spirit that gives us the strength to love God's people so that we can be effective in our ministry and our prayer life. So has the same Holy Spirit that was present in the ordination of the first seven deacons of the Church as recorded in the Acts of the Apostles, was the same Holy Spirit that came down to rest on us in our ordination: the 15 humble and devoted men for the Archdiocese of Atlanta on the fourth of February, 2006.

So now we have been given a great opportunity – to have Almighty God's light radiate in our souls and in our minds to fulfill a sacred mission to take that light to a world that desperately needs that light to be seen– even today. It is my prayer that I always remain true to the vocation that called me in the first place, to be a man of service: to my God, my family, my parish, and to the world. The personal and spiritual rewards already have been great since that 1st Saturday in February: I have experienced a greater love from my own family, to receive the love of the people that know me and have allowed me to share in their own happiness and sorrows, and as the opportunity to be present, sometimes being able to serve sometimes absolute strangers. We, as His Deacons, follow in the image of Our Lord Jesus as the Ultimate Servant – to be generous to a fault, giving solace to those who seek or need it, instruction in the Faith to those who want it and kindness to all those who we come in contact with – all the days of my life.

Someone once asked me what I would like on my tombstone someday. The only thing that would be appropriate, a simple quotation:

"My entire life is service to God and His People – I am a Catholic deacon."

Epilogue: The spiritual gifts of your vocation to serve

[Author's notes:

I originally wrote this reflection after the death of my father as a way of being able to process all that had happened over the past two weeks – December 23, 2006 – January 07th, 2006.

My original audience for this dedicated reflection were primarily for my fellow brothers in diaconate formation who kept me in their prayers all the time I was with my dad as he was dying.

As deacons, we are frequently called to the sides of people who are sick or possibly dying. Just as my mother's sudden death had been seen as a start of my vocation call, being at my father's bedside as he slipped silently away was the final affirmation of my vocation. God would be calling me to be a calming presence for others as they were either in hospital or hospice care.

Therefore, the final spiritual gift that my father gave me was the ability to be there for other people as they faced their final moments here on earth. For me, Hospital Ministry is a joy, a privilege and a continuation of the spiritual gift my father gave to me as he was dying during Christmas time - 2005.

Deacon Albert]

On the morning of December 23, 2005, and approximately 7:38 a.m., I received an urgent phone call that many people will eventually receive but dread to take: **"Albert, this is Millie. It's about your father."**

My dad had been diagnosed with lung cancer in the early part of May of 2005. He had been a very active smoker since the time he had been a young teenager until his retirement in summer of 1989. He tried to give up smoking several times but his addiction to nicotine always forced him back. In fact, while serving as an OSHA inspector for his company, he would frequently travel through North Carolina and you can always tell at the end of one of those trips that he had taken, part in some off-duty time activity included buying cigarettes for himself and my mother. He always returned with eight to ten cartons of cigarettes in his own luggage. Of course, his rationale was that cigarettes were overly taxed, so if he could buy cigarettes as a bargain, well that was his own business.

Well, unfortunately, ever since 1964 when the Surgeon General of the United States had made his now famous statement about the relationship between lung cancer to smoking, millions of Americans have heard the guidance and either made up their own minds to continue to smoke or perhaps never started smoking in the first place because of that very warning. However, my father was one of those in the first group and ultimately, it did come back to haunt him.

My dad Leopold had been a very unique individual. He emigrated from his native Puerto Rico as a young man who intended for either studying for the priesthood or becoming a professional person. He lived with his sister in New York but was later drafted and served three and a half years in the Army Air Corps that later became the United States Air Force. He was honorably discharged, he met my mother, Francoise, who was working as either a receptionist or a secretary within a major television network in New York, and they quickly got married.

Their marriage however was not always happy. Although children came, money as well as their own personal differences became readily apparent as topics for very intense discussions. They never seem to have enough money to go around, and they never seem to share a lot of personal love for each other – at least what we saw publicly. Perhaps, they felt for the good of the family and being "good Catholics" on the outside, they would stick it out and, ultimately, they did for the family but they ended up divorcing in 1989 when I was 29. My mother remained in the family home in Connecticut until she died in 1994 from a massive heart attack and my father ended up emigrating to Florida to be with his brother, Reuben, who had retired from the United States Air Force and had started a small real estate business.

Through his brother's introduction as well is through his own initiative, he started building up a new and small group of friends that shared their own interests of grandchildren, former career occupations, as well as singing in a local men's chorus. He also developed a deep personal friendship with a local woman by the name of Millie who herself had lost her own husband, a retired US Navy Commander, a few years earlier and yet she was a very social and gregarious person. Both recognized that they could be good for each other and it was from this meeting of the minds, a deep, personal and agape friendship was formed that lasted 16 years.

The reason why all this background information is provided is not just to form a simple narrative but to recognize that we all evolve on a journey, the role of close friends to us as well as our family play in our emotional and spiritual lives.

In my own growing up, I'd never been very close to my father and I recognized that there were some things about his personality that I just did not like, and those were traits that I did not wish to emulate. My father always wanted to be accepted, respected and treated with courtesy yet somehow he could never come to reconcile the fact maybe some people would never-ever like him. He never saw how some people would treat him differently, but as I got older, I could see these nuances and slights.

He could be tremendously obsessive sometimes, always having to show that he was in control, without sometimes realizing this obsessive sense of control was actually a very negative attribute. In his younger days, he might have been considered attractive, he always sported a mustache for as long as I knew him but never really had a specific sense of fashion or style.

As I grew up to be my own man, I sometimes look to my father is being a negative example -- frequently dismissing all the things that he did as being his own choices, but not wanting to make them my own. Yet in that formation process, I actually took on some of the very same characteristics that I personally would have said I never had: **a need for control, the great desire to be accepted, and a desire to excel, to be regarded as a person to be respected and esteemed.**

Unfortunately, these attributes will sometimes drive a person to have a tremendous sense of personal self-importance, that is a polite way of saying I was full of pride. Some people would say I was full of bull stuff -- which is the polite way of saying, well you know what I mean.

However, as my dad grew older and became frequently more immobile, he relied a lot more on telephone and ultimately e-mail to try to stay in touch with his children. All of his children at that time had issues with him and went from being at best, hospitable in social settings to at worst, writing him off completely. I went the entire spectrum in and tried to reconcile with him in the end.

In fact, when I was accepted into the diaconate formation program for the Archdiocese of Atlanta, I remember a question that the psychologist put forward, since my mother had already died, she asked; **"What you think your father would say if you told him you are becoming a deacon?"**

I replied, "Frankly, it's none of his business, and if I were to tell him, my response to his reply would be that I don't need his approval, I'm not looking for his approval, because I don't need what I never had".

Unfortunately, that response caused some serious concern and she relayed my comment back to my director of formation who had a small heart-to-heart talk with me. Although I am not studying to become a priest, as an ordained minister, you may become involved in situations that need reconciliation, starting with your own prayer life and relationship with God, and those than involving other people. If I was unable to be reconciled to my dad, then obviously, we were going to have some issues. Therefore, I made the commitment that I would try to start the process of reconciliation with my dad, which I did do within the next three months after the conversation.

The initial conversation went okay, he was thankful for the opportunity to listen to his side of the story but I always got the feeling that he was somehow holding back; that I wasn't quite hearing the whole story and with the sudden and unexpected passing of my mother who never knew of my vocation, I wouldn't be able to get the other side of the story.

We all know from personal instances that when we listen to two sides of the story, frequently the truth is somehow in the middle and that is what we have to try to get to by distilling the stories. However, he was rather overjoyed that I, at least, tried to make the first step to understand at least his point of view of what happened in his life, in his relationships, and with especially with his relationship with my mother.

However, when I received a phone call on that fateful day, I felt that at some point that all that previous animosity, anger, and disbelief, had to be let go. All of these negative emotions have the spiritual equivalents of strong car battery acid on our souls. In addition, that conviction was later confirmed when I saw him sitting up in his bed in the intensive care unit at Winter Park Memorial Hospital in Winter Park, Florida. He knew that he was probably within his last days, and he cried about the fact that I was actually staying in his house that he probably would never ever see again. He had instructed the hospital staff to have a **"do not resuscitate"** order to be followed which I witnessed his signature on the document, he did not want to be placed on an external ventilator that would force oxygen into his one remaining lung involuntarily, but he was on 100% oxygen being provided on a small mask as a result of that condition, he could not be moved into a hospice situation.

However, he was healthy enough that he could be removed from the intensive care section and would be placed in a private room on the very same floor. His friend Millie had notified all the important people that he had indicated he wanted to let know, but of all his children – three boys and one girl, only the youngest sons, my twin brother and I, would be able to see him while he was still alive.

Once in early 2000, I had told my dad that I was actively pursuing my possible vocation as a permanent deacon, he did not seem surprised, but he had commented that at one point, he felt called to the priesthood. However, as a young man, he soon discovered girls instead. Even though he had been a very devout altar boy all those years, serving at both daily and Sunday Mass, he later discovered he had a vocation of marriage over the priesthood. Nevertheless, for the most part, my dad received the other Sacraments of the Church with great devotion, and he had what I would call a normal sacramental life. From a service standpoint, he served on various church committees when asked, typically either on parish council or a special committee Father might have asked him to join. However, his own marital vocation was always rocky and uneasy. If he had shared some private moments of joy with my mother, those opportunities were few and far between and rarely witnessed by their children.

I cannot recall them holding hands although they did attend many formal dance functions and they did have a common love of dancing and socializing. They never celebrated their wedding anniversary and to this date, I believe they got married in April 1952 but I could not ever find their marriage certificate to confirm it. They had a very close-knit community of friends whom shared their common interests with their own interpersonal dynamic was very complicated. My mother's own religious habits included frequent recitation of the Rosary, attending Mass on Sunday, and she always managed to make a small weekly donation to the Franciscans or to another religious order.

When my mother died in December of 1994, my father could not make the trip back for her funeral Mass but he did manage to come up to upstate New York in the following May for her actual internment and burial. So even in the latter parts of their lives, they tried to remain civil to each other but always timed their activities that they would be apart from each other.

On the interstate highway traveling south to Winter Park, I was calling my dad from the car as I approached Gainesville on the afternoon of the 23rd. You could tell by the sound of his failing voice that he seemed encouraged by the fact that someone was actually coming to see him. My dad had always been a very precise driver, and in his mental calculus he could do in his head, Leopold could always give you a very good approximation of how much time you need to take in order to get from point A to point B. The problem was with the sound of the constant oxygen rushing into his lungs through the small mask, it made talking to him on the phone very difficult. So I relied on the medical technician to pass on to him my message on where I was and when I would arrive in Winter Park.

Finally, I arrived at Winter Park Memorial Hospital and approached his ICU room at 6:30 p.m., I was a little taken aback. My dad had lost nearly all of his hair as result of the chemotherapy treaments, his eyes were somewhat sunk in and there were numerous topical blotches on his skin. He seemed to have made friends with all of the medical personnel on the floor, and especially remained being a gentle flirt with all of the female personnel, starting with his own doctor. However, as I had a chance to start talking with him about all sorts of different topics, you could tell that he had been resigned to the fact that he was not coming to his earthly home. Although we all held out hope for a miracle – for nothing is impossible with God.

He showed me all of the medical documentation about his personal wishes, and he had been very precise about his final arrangements. He had met with my brother and his bride, who is a trust officer for a bank in Atlanta, and assured me that everything that I needed to know were in those documents.

My primary concern then was not for his stuff, but was for his soul and I asked him when was the last time he had seen a priest. He said that he had seen a priest at Mass earlier in the week and with Millie who came later that night, we arranged for a priest to come visit him the next day, which would have been Christmas Eve. Ultimately, I left him at about 11 o'clock that night and returned to his place for very short night of rest.

Thus, the final earthly suffering, passion and ultimately death of Leopold J. Feliu was about to begin.

The first sorrowful mystery: the Agony in the Garden:

What goes through a man's mind when he is approaching his final days or even hours on this earth?

Probably, it amounts to a very intense and concise final general examination of conscience -- knowing that you received certain gifts throughout your life, this life gave you some circumstances that you had to endure and persevere through, that you had the opportunity to do both good and evil, you are a sinner and need God's reconciliation and forgiveness in order to give you peace in the last moments of your life.

There are very few times that I saw my dad actually very happy. Although he enjoyed a good joke as much as anything else, I never saw him in a period of sustained happiness. It always seemed that he moved from one mishap to another in his life. The kids' grades were never quite good enough, the lost promotion or the perceived professional slight, his wife did not necessarily love him enough, and we could never just do things his way were topics for his frequent criticisms that resonated in our house.

When my father was away on business trips, my mother either sewed dresses for herself or read a great deal. The local public library in the town we grew up in was a breath of fresh air for her. She loved the local library and just having her "alone time" there. For a woman that did not complete college, she was extremely well-read and could hold her own in any spirited conversation with any one that talked to her.

However, when we went to visit other relatives, especially my mother's mother and sister in Upstate New York, we as a family could actually be quite animated and hospitable, enjoying very lively discussions with our relatives and friends. In fact, going away to visit someone was actually a chance to experience some normal family life, of course, it was not our actual family life, but it was a chance to see how other people got it right.

Growing up as a young teenager, I had a very good friend who is an Italian-American, Paul, who had a very spirited but loving immediate and extended family. In fact, I would pray to God to be able to spend Christmas Eve with his family over my own because Paul's family seemed just so much better. There was real joy and love to be experienced because that was what the season is all about. Paul's mother and father were very affectionate and loving, both to each other and to their children, even though their kids were kids, but they liked each other too.

As a young man, when I met the woman who would become my wife, I frequently spent the holidays with them as well instead of being with my own family. My future in-laws expressed some concern with my wife-to-be about this, but once my wife-to-be met her future in-laws after a year we had been dating, she assured her own family that I was much better off staying with them than being with my own family.

My father always tried to keep up a very good façade about his family. Even though he felt that he had done all he could, he never quite grasped the fact that his own family circumstances were very different from others. Moreover, as he continued to spend Christmases with his new-found friends in Florida, after he left Connecticut, he gradually saw how other people and their families got along and got it right. In fact, his friend Millie allowed Leo to become an integral part of their family. Her son, Mark, had commented that he had spent the last 16 Thanksgiving and Christmases with my father and that this coming Thanksgiving with seemed quite different without him at the table. So my own sin was that my own behavior drove my father to others just as his behavior had driven me way to my friends when I was younger.

My father's personal agony also continued with the fact that his health was, in fact, declining rapidly and that he would never see his grandchildren, Christina and Michael, again in this life. He gained some comfort from the fact that his grandchildren did love him immensely, and that he loved them in return. My son Michael, who is autistic, and is the best disciple of love that I have encountered, loved his grandpa unconditionally. When Grandpa came to visit the last time, either they would sit together on the couch watching an endless cycle of Thomas the Tank Engine videos or DVD's, or he would read to my son the newest Thomas story from a large storybook.

My daughter Christina was thankful for her grandfather coming such a long way to see her dance in the Nutcracker in the winter or to go visit him and go to Walt Disney World in the spring or summertime. The kids always moved faster at the park and he tried hard to keep up. Grandpa was always an enthusiastic audience member and shared the pride of her accomplishments with anyone of his social circle that could stand to receive the latest briefings on his grandchildren. Unfortunately, because all of the rapid severity of his illness's progress, his grandchildren could not see him alive one more time. Nevertheless, I did bring some of the latest pictures of Christina and Michael to show him and he gained some emotional strength from that. Nevertheless, the agony that started in intensive care would continue in his private room.

The second sorrowful mystery: the Scourging at the Pillar

As his bed was being moved into the private room on Christmas Eve, my dad's condition was starting to visibly deteriorate. The fact of the matter was that one of the lungs; I believe the left one was completely gone and unable to hold the oxygen that he was breathing in on a constant basis. So the other lung was essentially trying to do the work of two, and in the process, his death cycle was starting.

As the body continued to fight to get more oxygen into the lungs, he increasingly became more agitated and the constant reminder of the plastic oxygen face mask strapped to his face would become a major irritant to him. So at this point, he would frequently start trying to pull the mask off his face, but in the process, he would be suffocating himself. Of course, as the body is getting less oxygen into itself, he is becoming delusional and unstable. The agony that he sought to avoid earlier that week is starting to manifest itself in his weakened body. Leave the mask on and he fights to take it off. Take the mask off and he is suffocating himself. He cannot win either way.

Each successive breath becomes more labored and painful. He had standing orders to be medicated to take the edge off the pain, but of course, he always wanted it on his schedule and his own timetable. However, he became readily apparent that the sheer force of his personal will would be insufficient for him to avoid being medicated and he started to now to feel his passion becoming a hard and bitter reality: the pain of trying to get another breath into his body and the ache in his heart knowing that his life was soon coming to an end was becoming overwhelming.

The scourge of the taskmaster's whip was not his enemy that day, it was in the heaving of his own chest to gain badly needed oxygen into his lungs and with every breath, it would become more difficult for him to breathe.

The third sorrowful mystery: the Crowning of Thorns:

His medication was provided intravenously and he was receiving a glucose drip to keep his body hydrated but his mind was becoming a battleground within himself: He was trying to maintain some semblance of control by being able to tell us what he needed or wanted, but his body was revolting by its primal need to receive oxygen in breathing. He became even more argumentative and directive: when he said he didn't want the mask on his face, he just ripped it off his face but then we have to very quickly coax him to place it back on.

His eyes continue to lose some luster while he fought to remain alert. When the pain medication kicked in, it was only then that he could relax and sleep. However, the internal battle of his spirit, mind and soul continued and we could see it manifest itself by seeing involuntary eye twitching and almost a constant low verbal groaning. But the groaning at least allowed us to provide that he was still with us; that he wasn't quite gone yet. Nevertheless, the groaning also was that of a man deeply afflicted, a man who is crying out to his God as the Psalmist recorded in so many Psalms **"My God, My God,**

why have you forsaken me?" To some extent, he was trying to atone for what had happened in his life through his suffering there. We, as Catholics, believe that human suffering is redemptive in nature, it is in that suffering we now endure joins spiritually with the sufferings of Jesus Christ at the Cross. In the final hours of his life, he was being joined to his Lord Jesus – by receiving the final three sacraments that make up the Last Rites of the Roman Catholic Church: Reconciliation, the Holy Eucharist and the Anointing of the Sick.

The fourth sorrowful mystery: the Carrying of his Cross

At the same time that I have been notified, my father's younger sister, named Esperanza whose name means "Hope" in Spanish had flown from Puerto Rico with her husband to be with her older brother. She had idolized my father when they were small children and throughout their lives. My maternal grandfather actually had two wives; my father and his sister were the children from the second wife. At that time, my grandfather was much older so his sister really looked to my father as being her father figure. She simply idolized her older brother Leopold and they had always kept in frequent contact throughout the years, typically by phone.

At this point, Leopold probably pushed himself to stay alive so that she could arrive there in time to see him one more time while he was alive. When she came into his hospital room, his eyes radiated once he understood what happened. In addition, my twin brother and his bride had also arrived to be with him. In this aspect, his current suffering had been rewarded in this life -- he had stayed alive long enough to see a partial gathering of his blood relatives surround him at his bedside. But the heavy weight of his own physical deterioration was becoming his own cross and with that cross, this physical burden became greater and greater. The final act was starting.

The fifth sorrowful mystery: the Crucifixion of Our Lord.

By Almighty God's grace, my dad survived both Christmas Eve and Day. We keep the television on in hope of seeing the Holy Father saying Mass in St Peter's Square in the Vatican. Although we had several periods that we thought we might lose him in any one of them, he did keep himself together through the day. However, as December 26th became a reality, the final stages of dying started to become readily apparent. His medications had to be given more frequently and in higher dosages to take the edge off his pain. His extremities were starting to become colder to the touch and he would frequently grasp both of the handrails of his bed as if he was trying to steady himself in some sort of spiritual flight and/or fight. His breathing became more labored and transitioned from muscular breathing of the rib cage to what is known as "belly breathing" which is more centered on the lower chest cavity/stomach and becoming more automatic.

The way that he held himself, he was enduring his own cross and his own crucifixion was well in hand. You see, as our Lord was enduring a slow and suffering death on the Cross with his own breathing becoming more labored because he could not close his outstretched hands, so my dad's spiritual cross was configured in the same manner. Earlier in the day, he could get a drink of water by sipping it through a straw. But by the 26th, he was unable to even have enough energy to sip through a straw. So instead, we had a small sponge attached to a plastic straw that we could dunk in the cold water in a plastic cup and then dab the sponge on his lips or in his mouth.

Just as our Lord cried out in his agony on the cross, **"I thirst!"**, so my dad needed to be frequently sponge-fed with cold water to ease the dryness of his throat. His throat would become parched because its rawness was being caused by the constant infusion of pure oxygen gas. His body temperature continued to declined, but his heartbeat remained strong and constant with a very firm blood pressure. It was almost by the sheer force of his will that he was keeping himself alive and by keeping himself alive, he was trying to communicate to us all that he was still very much in control.

He did receive the Last Rites of the Roman Catholic Church on Christmas Eve as well as having another visit by a priest on the afternoon of the 26th. He seemed to draw a great deal of strength from that, but you could see in his eyes that a personal and spiritual struggle was taking place. We were asking for God's grace to gently take his life but he had a look in his eyes as if he was wrestling his own angel -- he was not quite ready to go just yet.

And the women stayed:

His sister Esperanza returned with her husband and her younger daughter as well as a niece with her husband. But just as the Blessed Mother gathered the women around the foot of the Cross, so his sister gathered the other women as they prayed for him and with him. His sister does a lot of spiritual work within the Hispanic community of her own home parish. In a simple act of respect, I gave her my bilingual prayer book for her to read to her brother. She would read everything from the 23rd Psalm, which I later learned was his personal Psalm that he wanted read at his funeral to all of the significant gospel readings concerning Christ as the Way, the Truth and the Life.

Once again, his eyes were so animated and he would gently lift up his fingers as the two of them mutually acknowledged each other's loving presence: her reading the Gospels and his determined effort to spiritually drink in what she was reading to him. Frequently, her eyes became too blurry and puffy because of the overwhelming concern she had for him. Her tears were often too much as she struggled to read to him. We continued to pray for him throughout the day and a second visit of his local parish priest in the afternoon of the 26th was a welcome respite. Now he had the best of both worlds, he had gathered his family around him one last time and he had a priest to pray for him. In all of the prayers that we recite as Roman Catholics, we asked for the intervention of St. Joseph for a happy and peaceful death.

As Christ Jesus himself was probably present at the death of his foster father on this earth, so now he had everything a man wanted in the final hours of his life: his family and his faith intact.

He also started to make a very unusual action; he lifted up his gas mask and tried to position it almost as he was able to drink a cup of water out of it. It was almost like he was trying to drink in the oxygen through his mouth as opposed to breathing it. The desire for him to breathe now became the utmost concern for us. He was trying now to accomplish it as one last active control the best that he could.

As the evening became a reality, the belly breathing that I described earlier became less pronounced. The death spiral that started gently on the 23rd was now gathering momentum and as we approached midnight, we knew that we were probably within the final stretch.

Father, it is finished.

As I remained in his room for that final night, my own personal exhaustion was starting to set in. The hospital was kind enough to provide a large recliner chair that I could sleep in through the night and as Millie took the night watch at midnight, I was just resigned to thinking I could catch a few minutes of rest. As I awoke about 5:30 in the morning, I found that my father as he was reclining back in bed, had his mouth slightly ajar; almost it look like he was laughing-hard. I can see his eyes were fully closed and when I opened one eyelid, you can see that his pupils were very restricted.

But as I looked at his face, you can almost see that he was either reviewing or reliving some sort of mental tape or script that showed him in much happier times. Either his mind was now in its final preparation state or he was recounting some pleasant memories, and he was totally at peace but his breathing was much more shallow. And finally, at 7:50 a.m. on the 27th of December, 2005, he briefed his last; he finally gave himself permission to slip away.

I prayed the final Commendation of the Dead with Millie and almost felt like what it would have been like to be St. John with the Blessed Mother at the foot of the Cross - when Christ breathed His last on this earth. With his final breathe, he commended his life to His Lord, closed his eyes and then let go of his earthly life. My dad was finally at peace, no one else could hurt him, no one's opinion about him mattered except that of his God and his resting place would not be in a hospital but within the heavenly mansion Christ himself told His disciples He would be preparing for all who believed in Him-even to the end.

I called them the on-duty nurse to verify what we all believe had happened, and she replied back that he had passed away from us. The hospital had a very kind patient policy that allowed us to remain with the body and call whatever relatives lived nearby so that they could see him in the room one more time. We were able to get his sister and her husband rather quickly. Within 45 minutes, they came back to the room for one last time.

Finally, once again as his family, we prayed for his soul, asking Almighty God for His mercy and forgiveness for any sins that Leopold had committed that were still not confessed. We released his body to the hospital staff, who lovingly received and gently bathed it and placed it in their morgue for the final release to the local funeral home.

My final thoughts:

As I prepared for my father's vigil, I was reminded of the comments that I made at my own mother's funeral that died on December 15, 1994.

If we believe in the Resurrection of the Body and to see the Kingdom of God when we pass from this world to our new home in heaven, then we are able to do so because Almighty God sent down to this fragile earth His only Son, Jesus Christ, in that single event that started

our road to eternal salvation --that being His birth to Mary and Joseph at Bethlehem at Christmas time.

So we should, in fact, take comfort in the fact that Francoise has achieved and now Leopold as well - at Christmas time this year - in their passing in receiving what we all will eventually seek and find, being accepted in to the Kingdom of God, secured by the life, death and resurrection of his only Son, Our Lord Jesus Christ.

My comfort is that at this special time of the year, we remember that our salvation is a reality because He was here among us and died to pave the way to Almighty God's Glory. And their spiritual journey to be among us on this Earth, just as Francoise's and now Leopold's journey in death, started at Christmas time."

Now, his earthly pilgrimage is complete. His life has been lived and now he is in the hands of his Creator, His Son and the Holy Spirit. For those of us who witnessed his death, it is as if we were on one side of the doorway and our God is on the other.

Christ himself reminds us, that no one sees the Father except those that the Father has called to the Son, and we as ministers of the Gospel will be called many times help people pass from one side of the doorway to the other.

I can say without a doubt, that it was with that fervent prayer that I was trying to give my father his last final gift, the gift that his faith in his God would not go unrewarded, for Christ Himself called us, "wherever two or three are gathered in my name, there will I be", so it is with our prayers that give our friends the strength to let go and allows Christ to gather unto Himself those He has received by the Sacrament of Baptism.

As I was driving back to Georgia the day my father passed away to collect my own family to return to Florida for his vigil and funeral in the coming days, I had the opportunity to call several people. When I called them on the phone, they were very supportive and kind. I called Deacon

Loris, my director of formation for some fatherly guidance. My only question was "Loris, either this was God's greatest grace of my diaconate formation or it was the worst final exam God could have thrown at me". His response was equally comforting, "You know Al, it was both."

But it was through the finality of my father's death that I got the clarity of my vocation: that God has graced me numerous times to be with those who are suffering and to be the patient voice of Christ's servant and to be the one that holds their hand when they want to feel the compassion of our God. Moreover, the only way that I can fulfill this vocation is to be a man of prayer because ultimately God is the source of all good things and the way that I keep connected to him is through my prayer life with him. I never felt more connected to my Lord then when I was begging for God's mercy, not for myself, but for someone else instead. Almighty God, in His infinite mercy, answered my prayer: He gave my Father a peaceful and spiritual death, free of pain and full of hope and salvation.

So now we must commit ourselves to be greater persons of prayer, because our prayer life will give us the consolation and the strength so that those who have no one to pray for them, they will have the strength to go back to their Creator who will receive them and love them beyond our capacity to understand. We literally stand at the doorway when we are with our friends and loved ones at their final moments and we see to the future at the doorway of time.

We look forward into eternity and in return, we can see into the face of Jesus Christ with His arms wide open and saying to all of us "Welcome home, I have waited all your life for this moment."

Appendix

Example of Assignments Completed in Aspirancy through Senior Years - 2001 to 2005

Psalms Class – Psalms 110 & 114

Good morning my brothers:

As I was preparing for the presentation this morning, I cannot help but think of the many contrasting themes that run through the Holy Bible. Often, those themes are of great opposites, because one thing does not appear and exist without the other being present. Starting in the Book of Genesis, we see the creation of the beautiful world by a benevolent and loving God, yet we're also witnessed to the fall of the first man and woman to original sin resulting in death. We are passive witnesses to the Hebrew slaves, sons of Abraham and Jacob being imprisoned by hard and bitter bondage of slavery by the Egyptians and the birth of freedom through the Law and their exodus to the Promised Land of Canaan and Israel.

We're also active witnesses to the omnipresent links between the Old and the New Testaments - between the choice of God's chosen people and the adoption of the Gentiles to become co-heirs of the Kingdom of God. The wooden staff that was given to Moses as a symbol of the Shepherd of Israel proclaimed the power of an Almighty God that would set his people free.

That staff of a Shepherd would be transformed once again in the Gospel of Jesus Christ as the "Good Shepherd" of the New Testament. The wood staff that saved Israel in the Old becomes transformed to the wood of the Cross of our Lord Jesus Christ in the New. Not by a scepter of gold and silver but by His Precious Blood covering that Cross that set all men and women free from the tyranny and slavery of their sins to be reunited in the salvation and loving arms and heart of God the Father of all nations and humanity.

We seek to understand and recognize in the first Psalm in the appointment of a Royal King and a High Priest is a central element to our faith. As it was with Melchizedek in the Old Testament and with Our Lord Jesus Christ in the New Testament, the integration of both Priest and King provides salvation to people to whom he is responsible for. For without an intercessor to the Father, we could not approach God, for we are not worthy to even gaze unto His face. Without the intervention of his appointed and anointed High Priests, we could not come to share in the grace and bountiful goodness of the Father.

Both men know that the integration of their faith and their position to the people represent a constant commitment that they will provide for the needs of their people and that they will never leave their people in times of great danger or strife.

So as we prepare to read this Psalm, let us open our hearts and our minds to the Holy Spirit that guides us in our faith:

Psalm 110:

God appoints the King both King and Priest
In the Lord says to you, my Lord;
"Take your throne from at my right hand,
while I make your enemies to your footstool."
The scepter of your sovereign might the Lord will extend from
Zion.
The Lord says: "Rule over your enemies!
Yours is princely power from the day of your birth.
In holy splendor before the Day Star, like the dew I begot you."
The Lord has sworn and will not waver;
"Like Melchizedek you are priest forever."
At your right hand is the Lord, who crushes kings on the day of
wrath,
who, robed in splendor judges nations, crushes heads across the
wide earth,
who drinks from the brook by the wayside,
and thus holds high the head.

As the Psalmist tries to portraying in his words are God is a mighty God but yet He gives His power to another, we really recognize that in the person and the kingship of Jesus Christ. As it was illustrated in the Book of Genesis when God states "Let us make man in Our image", the inclusion of both God the Father and God the Son is taken further and made more pronounced in this Psalm. For it is God would say to the Son "All that you ask for I give you for all eternity, and you'll have no enemies because I will crush them before you."

The Old Testament is ripe with victories that the God of Israel provided for his people as they attempted to move from their slavery to freedom. For there is no God that is greater than the God of Israel.

The purity of the priesthood of Melchizedek, priest of Salem, is that constant reminder of a God that values and rewards above all, a constant devotion to the one that sent him and into the lands of his people. The New Testament translation to this prayer was when Jesus told those gathered in the synagogue that he must believe in Him because He comes at the command of the One who sent Him. To reject Jesus is to reject the one who sent him. However, the people around him viewed him only as the son of Mary and Joseph - unbelieving or unknowing of his works of healing and salvation.

No enemy of the Father has a safe refuge on this earth. There is no place on this earth where evil can triumph over good, and all the nations that do evil in the sight of God will be called into judgment and that evil will demand a great price. The New Testament translation to this vision is the Revelation of John to the great white throne judgment where the living, the dead, and all the nations of the earth will have their actions brought to judgment.

The image of rapid and never-ending pursuit of evil being vanquished by the forces of good portrays the everlasting desire of God to have justice delivered for the ones who have suffered under inequity and persecution.

Psalm 114:

The Lord Wonders at the Exodus
When Israel came forth from Egypt, the house of Jacob from an alien people,
to the became God's holy place, Israel, God's domain.
The sea beheld and fled; but Jordan turned back.

The mountains skeptical like rams; the hills, like lands of the flock.
Why was it, sea, that you fled?
Jordan, that you turned back?
You mountains, that you skipped like rams?
You hills, like lambs of the flock?
Tremble, earth, before the Lord,
before the God of Jacob,
who turned rock into pools of water,
stone into flowing springs.

The Exodus portrays the greatest escape on an imprisoned people to freedom. When the Israelites finally were relieved of their bondage, a nation came forth in because of their entire spirit was focused on one God and who proved himself 10 times to a Pharaoh who was himself believed to be a God. If the God of the Egypt can defeat the God of the great pyramids, the pagan gods are no match against the God of Israel.

In preparing this presentation, I must have watched the movie "the Ten Commandments" about ten times. As I watch the life of Moses developed from the time that he was believed to be an Egyptian to the time he led God's people to the edge of the Jordan River, I am still compelled to that one scene when he literally parts The Red Sea into two parts and the dry ground appears in the midst. In the one line of the old man who is blind who says that "the sea parts with a blast of God's nostril!"

Our God possesses such awesome power and in his ability to discern the need of a single man and the needs of an entire nation at the same time causes me to ponder on this mystery. How many times to you ask our God to rescue us to greatest deliverance from some real or perceived danger but yet how often do we also seek just gave him Thanksgiving and thanks for what we already have: good health, a happy family, and the ability to do good in the kingdom of God?

The trek across the desert to Mount Sinai was not an easy one, by some estimates 1 to almost 3 million people traveled from Goshen in Egypt to Mount Sinai. Without water readily accessible, people would perish in a matter of days. But yet for 40 years, even while God was angry at Israel for creating a false God, He did not neglect their basic needs of bread, food and water. And as Moses drove his staff into the rock and water burst forth, how could people of Israel doubt than the God of such wonder what ever desert them in an arid and lifeless desert? How can one in the midst of such miracles lack faith in the One that delivered them?

When Jesus was describing to his disciples the meaning of faith, he challenged them to see their faith as a mustard seed and, one of the smallest things that can be received by the human eye, yet if they were to say to mountain to move, the mountain would move because they believed and had faith.

Our faith in God combined with the spiritual water of our faith is an essential part of our faith. Instead of the life-giving waters birthed in the Sinai desert that sustained life in the Old Testament, we have the everlasting life brought forth in the waters of our Baptism and sustained by the Body and Blood of Lord through the Holy Eucharist.

That is the challenge that we face each and every single day: to renew our faith in an all mighty God that we cannot see but yet has created the universe? To we look to feel His presence in our lives every day or do we seek to find him only when we need some sort of salvation from life's troubles and hardships? I once heard in a very profound conversation that if we sought to see the face of God every day, we would always find his hand supporting underneath us. And yet, then we find ourselves doing the exact opposite trying to find hand of salvation from the calamities of this earth instead of seeking the calm strength of the One that can provide calm in the midst of any crisis.

Scripture has reported several times in the presence of God, the Earth has shook and quaked at the presence of God. He appeared in Sinai, over the Ark in the desert, in the Temple in Jerusalem and tore the sacristy veil when the Christ was crucified at Calvary. John the Baptist in proclaiming the coming of the Messiah, that the hills are leveled and the valleys laid low; that the crooked made straight and narrow to proclaim the coming of the Lord. The people of Israel who saw that miracle the on the Red Sea knew that their God was God, that he would protect all that was in His care, and he would make Israel is the chosen people. Nevertheless, God has also spoke in whispers to his people and his prophets and that is the great dynamic of this Psalm.

Our God is an awesome God and he has the ability to touch a single soul and free an entire nation because he is God. But he also loves us enough to allow us to have to free will to accept or reject his love we do not become mere creatures of his power, but loving souls to a Father in Heaven that seeks to bless and protect his people.

Eucharistic Visits to the Sick:
The Fulfillment of what Christ taught us in the Beatitudes

Requirements to be fulfilled for Social Justice Paper:

1. **The work in which they were involved.**

2. **What the experience meant to them spiritually, emotionally and physically.**

3. **What they gained from the experience.**

4. What impact this ministry had on their thoughts concerning the *preferential option for the poor.*

5. How this ministry related to the *Beatitudes.*

1 * When he saw the crowds, * he went up the mountain, and after he had sat down, his disciples came to him.

2 He began to teach them, saying:

3 * "Blessed are the poor in spirit, * for theirs is the kingdom of heaven.

4 * Blessed are they who mourn, for they will be comforted.

5 * Blessed are the meek, for they will inherit the land.

6 Blessed are they who hunger and thirst for righteousness, * for they will be satisfied.

7 Blessed are the merciful, for they will be shown mercy.

8 * Blessed are the clean of heart,   for they will see God.

9 Blessed are the peacemakers, for they will be called children of God.

10 Blessed are they who are persecuted for the sake of righteousness, * for theirs is the kingdom of heaven.

11 Blessed are you when they insult you and persecute you and utter every kind of evil against you (falsely) because of me.

12 * Rejoice and be glad, for your reward will be great in heaven. Thus they persecuted the prophets who were before you.

"Al, I need you to do me a favor. I need you to make a Eucharistic visit to a lady by the name of Marjorie. She's at Emory Medical Center in Snellville and you need to bring her the Eucharist."

"Okay Father, let me go ahead and take care of it right after Mass."

With that simple request and my short response back, my pastor gave me an assignment that started me on a journey of faith and tremendous affirmation that this is where my diaconate vocation needed to be. The date was February 27th, 2005, on a Saturday night. [1]

Eucharistic visits have been part of the Catholic faith since the beginning of Christianity. Since the Eucharistic sacrifice came to symbolize the unity of the Christian community. After Christ gave His Church the example of this memorial and death to his disciples at the Last Supper, Catholic communities have always arranged for a portion of the Eucharistic banquet to be brought to those who were sick or unable to join the entire community.

In fact, St. Tarsicius was venerated in the early Catholic Church as a martyr who died in defense of the Blessed Sacrament. While being accosted by pagans in Rome, he literally gave up his life defending the Blessed Sacrament from being defiled. The Catholic Church proclaimed him as a saint and his feast day is celebrated on August 15th. [2]

Although typically Eucharistic visits now can be made by ordained clergy or laypeople, the effort is to make sure that all of the sick or displaced parishioners are taken care of lays with the pastor. He, in turn, make sure he has trained ministers to make sure this vital spiritual need can be taken care of.

For myself, becoming a Eucharistic minister was the very first ministry I entered into after formally entering into formation. Although I always had an appreciation for what they did, it wasn't until after I started to make my first Eucharistic visits to people that were sick that I fully appreciated the value and the faith required for this vital ministry to be so effective.

I approached to Marjorie's hospital room; she was in intensive care on the 4th floor of the hospital. Marjorie was 90 years old, a cradle Catholic who had been educated by Catholic nuns and in Catholic schools at the turn-of-the-century in the east coast, predominantly in New Jersey.

She eventually became a mother of six children, four daughters and two sons. Her husband was a successful business owner and had subsequently died a while back but leaving her and her children well provided for. She had been visiting her daughter here in the Atlanta area and unfortunately slipped while taking a shower. She had broken her hip, which by itself, can be sometimes considered deadly to the elderly. But this elderly woman was a fighter.

"Marjorie, my name is Albert Feliu and I'm from St. Oliver's Parish. Can I sit with you for a bit?"

"Sure, are you a priest?"

"No Ma'am, I'm a deacon in training."

"Well good, I've been visited today by too many Protestants."

She would often turn off the TV in a room so we can have some quiet time together. And so we started to have our visits together. But quickly, we became friends. She talked about her children and her grandchildren. She spoke with almost deference to the Dominican sisters that had schooled her when she was younger. When we first visited together, she talked about some prayers used to say when she was younger. She asked for and I got her some nice prayer cards, especially with the Blessed Mother.

While I had my daily Roman Missal with me, I would gently read her the appropriate scripture for that day. And then I would give her the Blessed Sacrament. She needed a little bit of water to be able to consume the host and we would say a Hail Mary together afterwards.

She never made it back to Mass while she was sick. She was bounced around to three different facilities during her brief stay in Georgia: Emory Hospital, New London Nursing Home and Parkview Rehabilitation facility; all three facilities in Snellville Georgia. But for those two months that she was with us, she was part of St. Oliver's Catholic community. She especially enjoyed receiving the bulletins; the one for Easter was her favorite because it showed the Risen Christ coming out of the tomb.

We also discussed at length the passing of the Holy Father, Pope John Paul II, because they shared so much in common. Both were advanced in age, both have probably lived a lot longer than they expected, and yet their faith still sustained them.

261

On the eighth of May, we had our last visit together. I told her that I really drew inspiration from her and then I so looked forward to our visits together each week. Because my weekly Mass schedule changed, I always tried to make sure to tell her that I would be coming after the mass that I had served so sometimes it was in the late afternoon or early evening, but I always told her that I would be there before Sunday night. And there wasn't a single weekend that I did not make it. I came in rain, ice storms, blinding sunlight and each time it was a joy to see her.

Today on the 15th, I told her previously that I would be there in the early afternoon. When I finally got to the rehab facility, her room was bare. She had been released just an hour earlier and was en-route flying back to New Jersey from Atlanta; she would be under the permanent care of one of her daughters.

I stood in the room for a couple of minutes, made the Sign of the Cross, and then left.

So as we reflect on the Beatitudes, our Lord was challenging us to reject what the ways and norms of the world were to that community and instead to embrace each other as part of a larger family – not to a family born of bloodlines and legal obligations, but rather a family born of water and Spirit, being part of a greater family. But I can greatly appreciate the fact now that it is extremely easy for people who have to be in nursing homes to feel left behind, to become invisible in a society that values the health and vigor of the young, instead of the wisdom of the young at heart.

Marjorie was a grace to me, a gift to gently remind us that the least in the human family will be great in the kingdom of God. For each and every one of us regardless of our age, in the eyes of Almighty God, we are but just a small child. Therefore, in the arms of other children, just like in the arms of St. Tarsicius, He entrusts us to bring to other children of the same God, with the body and blood of His Son to be brought to those who need His strength, his courage and grace, and His divinity.

Marjorie by her condition would be considered defenseless. She was old, weak in her physical stature, but strong and resolved in her Catholic faith. The preferential option for the poor states that we should do everything that we can for the treatment of the poor. In making provision for the poor and helpless in this sacred ministry is to ensure that their physical absence from the Sacred and Holy Mass does not exclude them from the absence in the community.

Although she was not a parishioner of St. Oliver's, she was a member of the Universal Catholic Church and therefore it was our responsibility to make sure that she received all of the appropriate sacraments. And as each sacrament is an outpouring of God's grace, so great is the out-flowing of grace when we receive the Blessed Sacrament of because that is the premier Sacrament.

The consecrated Host and Wine that constantly reminds us that God's Son, Our Lord Jesus Christ didn't hold anything back, so what excuse can we offer when we try to hold back or try to mitigate some small request – like to visit someone for 15-20 minutes per week?

My friend Marjorie will be back among her friends in New Jersey and in a matter of time in the future: she'll will be back with her passed husband and her Eternal Creator. My only regret is that I did not know her earlier but I'm truly thankful for the time we did spend together.

"Blessed are the poor in spirit, * for theirs is the kingdom of heaven. [3]

From Diaconate Ministries Class

Diaconate Assignment: How I Pray the Mass Now
by Albert L. Feliu

I wanted to say thank you for the clarification offered by Deacon Bill for this assignment because I believe that this distinction is very important as I prepared to write this paper.

Throughout my entire Catholic education, I have never heard of the Mass being referred to as a single prayer. In fact, I would have been hard pressed to understand that the Mass was a prayer at all; it was rather a service consisting of a number of prayers interwoven between readings from the Gospel and Old and New Testaments. In the post Vatican II environment that I grow up in my home parents at St. Teresa's Roman Catholic Church in Trumbull, CT, the major distinction that I learned is that the Mass came out of being said initially in Latin and was being proclaimed in English. In fact, in most instances, I'm almost inclined to say the blessing of "In the name of the Father, and of the Son, and of the Holy Spirit, Amen" in Latin than I am in English! At least, I felt more comfortable in doing that because that's what I remember in my earliest experiences in the church.

In addition, the only other major distinction that I've seen in the Mass in my pre-Diaconate training life is that at the Sacred Consecration of the Bread and Wine into the Sacred Body and Blood of Jesus Christ is the absence of the Bells that signify the presence of the Holy Spirit descending from heaven onto the altar.

In a separate commentary, Archbishop Donahue had made a very important comment concerning the real presence of Jesus Christ in the Eucharist. His specific comments were that one of the major distinction to the second Vatican Council because when the church revised its worship involving the Eucharist; it did not replace those previous worship practices that reinforce the real presence of Jesus with anything substantial. In fact, in a recent Gallup poll that was done on practicing Catholics, only 33 percent believe that the Eucharist was the actual and divine presence of Jesus while 67 percent felt that the Eucharist only was a symbol of the divine presence of Jesus.

In addition, my only attendance in a perpetual adoration or monthly adoration of Jesus in church was only when I was in St. Oliver's, starting in April of 2000. Prior to that, my family or I had been members of 10 different Catholic churches prior to joining St. Oliver's, and never once had the opportunity to be involved in a Eucharistic adoration (outside of the Holy Mass) - and that is covering almost 39 years of me being a cradle Catholic!

I believe the greatest challenge that is facing the Mass and the Catholic Church today is the fact that we have so far removed the connection between Jesus and the Eucharist from the minds and beliefs of our Catholic brethren. What I mean in my those comments are that if you are to ask the population of a church that was under 40 years of age about the real presence of Jesus and specifically about the Eucharist, and compared those results to those Catholics that were 45 years old or older, they grew up under pre-Vatican II educational standards including the Baltimore catechism, 40 hours of Eucharistic adoration, novenas, and reciting of the Rosary, that the results might even be more disparaging than what the Gallup poll results recorded in their poll.

Therefore, the proper education of what the Mass really is becomes even more important because the influence of the church is reinforced in that Commandant that Christ gave to his disciples of the Last Supper "do this in the remembrance of Me. " If our young people do not truly and heartfelt believe that when they're receiving of the Eucharist they are encountering Jesus Christ in body, blood, soul and divinity, in their faith is in vain because they have not believed that they have received God. And if they cannot believe in Jesus, than they cannot receive the Father because Jesus reminded his disciples "no one comes to the Father except through me."

So as I approach the Mass now, I see the Mass is a totally different experience. I truly say the Mass as being special encounter with Christ; first in the reading of his word in the liturgy of the word and then in the liturgy of the Eucharist. In some instances, I almost see myself paying more strict attention to the priest role as being that visual spokesperson for Christ. For example, when I used to attend Mass in St. Teresa's, the altar was really configured as being a mini Cathedral. There were three steps just to get to the pulpit that was set in a marble stand and then from there, there was additional four steps to approach the altar were Mass was said; first in Latin and then in English. The priest was almost transcendent, in his appearance because he was so far removed from the laity.

Even if I knew the priest who is saying Mass, by the time he approached the altar, he almost took on a faceless quality to those of us sitting in the pews. The choir was situated in the rear of the church, approximately 100 yards away in a second story platform. The music quality was always a spiritual motivator; however it was so far removed from the altar it was almost considered to be secondary. I believe it was St. Augustine that was quoted as saying "when a man sings his praises to God, he prays twice." The importance of music was not understated, however, the music was sometimes so removed it appeared to be disjointed from the rest of the service.

At 16, I would than hard pressed to say that I encountered God in the Mass because my orientation was probably that I saw the priest as saying the Mass, but not being that thoroughfare to God. Now, I see the Mass as being that thoroughfare to heaven with the priest and the prayers being said as the conduit of salvation. It's almost now, I see the Mass as being that everlasting step stone to eternity, and what I see the priest doing the consecration, that's what I see Jesus as being the shepherd. Through the Eucharist, He shows me the path He wants me to follow. In addition, I also see the Mass as being that uniting factor that holds my week together.

It goes beyond just being a duty, the rather a blessed assembly of believers that gets called together to do something important. What I mean that is this, when I was in the military we had what were known as mandatory formations. Within a specific time of day or time of the week, we had either meetings or formations that we had to come together as a group. The raising and lowering of the Colors for example where the National Anthem was played in the morning, and Taps was played in the evening. Your presence was required and your absence, without unauthorized excuse, had penalties associated with that.

Translate that experience to that of the Church. You come together as a group with common bonds and beliefs, your presence is usually noted by others in that group and that if you are not at that formation, people will notice and make inquiries; "is something the matter?, was he or she sick? Has someone gone and visited them lately? Let's make sure that Father or Deacon knows so we can let them know that there in our prayers. In the first instance, the natural inclination would be that of investigating than punish if necessary; the second would be with the laity, instead of investigating, but rather to assist if necessary. So the Mass also fulfills a function of the being able to constantly reinforce a sense of community among believers.

Secondly, we need to re-educate what the function of the Mass is supposed to be in our spiritual lives. I see the Mass now as being the recharging battery of my week. Before I saw the Mass as being an hour to an hour to half out of the 168 hours of my week that I gave back to God. I got dressed, I got to church, and I took in a message, received Holy Communion, and then returned back to my life. Now, I see the Mass as being a spiritual safe haven, a place I can examine what I've done or not done during the week, received a spiritual regeneration and commitment, received Christ as I'm worthy, and then go back into the world hopefully as a better person than what I entered.

I feel more spiritually lifted by the music and definitely more attentive during the homilies. And probably one of the most important aspects is that I have gained a better understanding of what it means to be a Catholic man.

So as I approach the Mass, I see myself in so many different roles. First as a child of God; being received by virtue of my baptism, next to as being a Catholic man and husband being responsible for welfare of my wife and children, the next as a member of the Catholic laity, fulfilling responsibilities of taking care of the needs of my priest and church - financially and emotionally - by being engaged in ministries that support the church, and finally as a fellow pillar of support for others to be able to lean on as I've been able to lean on others in times of my emotional and spiritual distress. The Mass becomes the focal point of my spirituality rather than in attendance requirement. The Mass is the spiritual uplifting experience of encountering God as opposed to a rote ritual that someone told me I had to do.

So as I approach the Mass, I see the distinctions that make the experience spiritually enriching.

I see the initial procession into the church as being a re-enactment of Christ procession into Jerusalem and perhaps even the 2nd coming of Jesus back to Earth to reclaim His Church here on Earth. The opening hymn is reminiscent of the Hosannas as that the people praised and Jesus as He entered into Jerusalem on a first Palm Sunday. The kiss of the altar by the priest and the Deacon signifies their personal devotion to Christ as well as the altar simplifying the eternal banquet of the Eucharist in heaven and here on Earth.

The penitential right of "Lord have mercy, Christ have mercy, Lord have mercy" is that constant reminder in our belief that we're all sinners and in constant need of God's tender mercy. I know I constantly reflect on that point more so that I did previously. Just as the sinner who could not look to heaven as he begged forgiveness from Almighty God when the sinner was in the Temple, so we as Catholics begged forgiveness of Almighty God for our sins. During our time here on earth, God understands that we will be sinners, He only acts that we repent our sins and accept a closer relationship with Him.

As I approach the Liturgy of the Word, I am filled with the sense of everlasting truth as proclaimed by his words. Here God sends his personal reminder of his truth through his inspired word borne by the Holy Spirit and conveyed through man. The other aspect that I've been more sensitized to is the role of the Psalms in the liturgy. Before entering the Diaconate program, I never engaged in any sort of study of the Psalms as a meditative or spiritual study. So during the reading of the Psalms, I am looking more about what the theme is: is that of worship, a proclamation of love, a request for salvation, or a heartfelt request for redemption, such as David's requests after he sinned against God.

For the reading of the Gospel now provides the opportunity to reflect and understand what Jesus would say to me if He was actually proclaiming the Gospel in the pulpit. Through the role of the Deacon as being the voice of God the Son, I can here for myself what the Almighty wants out of his people and me. The Deacon becomes the conduit of God's eternal salvation your hearing of His Word. I'm often reminded of those bands that kids wear nowadays that say "what would Jesus do" or W. W. J. D. As we approach the Gospel's reading, perhaps the more appropriate saying should be "Listen to what Jesus says and then act accordingly". The word of God has not changed over 2000 years, yet to that constant repetition how can there be any doubt in terms of what God is asking of us. The Gospel then becomes a manner of being a constant reinforcement and soothing comfort for God's people. If we're complying with what he is asking of us, then there can be no doubt in terms of the status of our salvation. If we're not complying with what he is asking of us, that we must repent of our ways and seek the light that he provides for us.

The petition of prayers that is offered after the Gospel and homily forms another common moment that the community offers its prayers and patients for the benefit of others besides its self. To ask for help of Almighty God without any possible expectation of gain for you is what true Christianity is all about. I help my neighbor because I want to help my neighbor not because I seek to get a gain because of my assistance is the form of our petitions that we offer to the father. We seek his divine help so that we can become closer as a community and as a stronger community we can serve his work better than we can currently. We can our strength, both physically, and spiritually through the assistance of the father, and of the Son, and of the Holy Spirit through our asking of their assistance in our needs.

As the transition into the Liturgy of the Eucharist, this is where the Mass starts becoming almost transformational in its process.

The presentation of the offering reminds us of the constant reminder to make sure that we take care of our needy brother and sisters within the community. In earlier Christian communities, the bread offering was separated into two needs: That of the Liturgy of the Blessed Sacrifice and the needs of the community. That unconsecrated bread was distributed to the needy and the remainder used for the Christian community. The mixing of the blood and water is symbolizing the moment of the Roman centurion by the name of Longinus who pierced the side of Christ after Christ had died on the Cross. (John 19:34). We remember this mystery by the prayer of the deacon: 'The Deacon prepares the altar and prepares the chalice for the Priest. In pouring the wine and water into the chalice, the Deacon says the following prayer "Through the mystery of this water and wine, may we come to share in the divinity of Christ, who humbled himself to share in our humanity."

As we open with the Eucharist at prayer, we celebrate the unbloody sacrifice of Calvary as well as the offering of Melchisadek in the offering of wine and bread to the father. Together we as a community have the opportunity to emerge in the upper room can see the Passover sacrifice offered by Jesus before he suffered and died. We reaffirm our acceptance of our faith, as we believe those words of consecration that transformed the bread and wine into the body and blood of our Lord Jesus Christ. At that very moment of transubstantiation, we have the opportunity to reaffirm our faith through the words of St. Thomas in proclaiming "my Lord and my God" as he had the opportunity to see the risen Jesus and placed his fingers in the nail marks so to affirm his faith.

We believe that at that sacred moment, Jesus is transformed in the bread and wine and in our hearts as we accept him as our Lord and God. Again as a community, we accept this faith as a community of disciples as the original 11 less Judas accepted Jesus as a Risen Lord from the first Easter Night in the Upper Room and at the Ascension of Jesus into heaven through to the invocation of the Holy Spirit at the First Pentecost.

To move now through to the prayers of the faithful and the invocation of all the Angels and Saints in their constant intercession for the protection of the church and of God's people. It is interesting to note that when St. Teresa of Avila was dying, her fellow sisters were grief stricken and crying. Seeing their tears, she has been noted to say that she looked forward to death because she could be of greater use to them praying for their souls in heaven than she would here on earth. The intercession of the Saints and of the martyrs throughout the ages provides us a concert reminder that our time here on earth is just for a season. St. Paul states that our time on earth is like that of a mist, having no longer duration to what is absolutely necessary and then disappearing. We have a constant reminder in Ash Wednesday that goes back to Genesis that we are both dust, created initially as Adam was in then we will return to that status until we are raised from the dead and reunited both body and soul at the final judgment. So our lives here on earth are not our own, but our lives are meant to be of service to God and his people while we're here on earth. So the intercession of the Saints, throughout the span of time and eternity, provides any reinforcement aspect to our faith. Throughout any hardship at any point in our lives, we can rely on their intercession as a point us to God in Jesus because of the example of their lives because they used their lives to the service of God the father.

As we transition now into the prayer given to us on the Sermon of the Mount, the Our Father, we reaffirm the prayer that Jesus himself gave to us.

The our father is actually a collection of 7 separate petitions that we seek his intercession so that our lives can be made complete, focusing on the fact that it is our daily bread that we need, we cannot store up things are perishable for future use rather we need to make use of those things are provided everyday so that we can focus on the work of the day rather than the work of things that we may never have a chance to start. It is not mean that we do not plan for the future, rather we cannot seek to gain our security through the things that we alone can accomplish, rather we seek to gain security of God's grace through what we accomplish in our everyday actions.

The petition of "Peace be with you" and to share the Son of peace is scripturally reinforced in the Gospel's of Mark, Matthew, and Luke. When Jesus greeted his disciples after he rose from the dead, he always included the greeting "Peace be with you". This greeting serve two functions: the first being a calm to their nerves because they thought they were seeing a ghost rather than the risen Lord in both body and soul; and the second being that the disciples would receive a constant piece of Christ Jesus through the receiving of the Holy Spirit, the giver / spirit of life in the works of God's love while we remain here on earth. Christ's peace is the peace that transcends all understanding and provides us a constant comfort that our God will not abandon us even in times of great a turmoil and strife and.

As we prepared to see the blessed banquet of the Holy Eucharist, we're now invited into the table of our Lord and fulfill his direction he left with us: that we must share in the flash of the Son of man and drink his blood to gain everlasting life. For so whoever lives and believe in him, though he were dead, shall gain life everlasting. We are recalled to the rising of Lazarus from the dead, as Jesus questioned Mary and Martha in their belief in him. In addition, we're also redirected to the story of the Roman commander who came to Jesus with the faith that if he could just say the word, his servant would be healed. Even though his servant was a distance away, Christ commented that he'd never seen such faith in all of Israel. In addition, we are reminded of the faith of the Samaritan woman who begged that her daughter be healed, even though she and her race of people were not accepted by the very people they God had accepted as his chosen. In all of these instances, it was their initial or post miracle-overwhelming faith that proclaimed the greatness of God's glory. However, even in the light of these great miracles, God's chosen people still rejected the very prophet promised by God the father.

Therefore as we approach the altar of God's glory, we use this time to ask God to heal our hearts, our bodies, and our souls by asking him just say the word, our sins are forgiven, we are deemed worthy to receive the grace of Almighty God and to receive in actual form the body and blood of his son, our Lord Jesus Christ. We are not worthy to receive this banquet feast; however we are able to receive this feast because his son died for us and regained our souls through the blood of the lamb.

With the Eucharist consumed, our bodies nourished, and our souls restored to grace, we return to our seats with Thanksgiving in our hearts and peace in our souls. Our prayer Thanksgiving is directed to the one who created us, the one who saved us, and the one who lives in us until we are able to approach the throne of Almighty God at the end of our lives.

With the altar now cleared as we started, the banquet completed until we come to meet again to hear and be God's presence, we look forward to receiving the blessing of Almighty God as we again to go out to our communities and our families, and again as we started the mass, we receive his Blessing, "In the name of the Father, and of the Son, and of the Holy Spirit, Amen". "The mass never ends it must be lived, so now let's go and love and serve the Lord."

And so the great prayer is concluded until we come again in prayer and Thanksgiving.

Year 2005 Class work

Homiletics Class –1st Sunday of Lent

This Sunday's readings have a common thread and it is with the appearance of signs. As we approach once again the season of Lent, we wrestle with a possible question: **what sign am I looking from God to provide in my life?**

The reason we need to challenge each other with that question is too often in our lives, we see the situation in an initial very negative response. But if we provided ourselves with a little bit more time and a bit more reflection, perhaps a more balanced answer could be seen.

So we begin with Lent.

With the idea of fasting, we are going to complain about the possibility that we have to actually consider doing it or at least decrease our own caloric intake for a day and yet with myself, I have actually missed a meal in my lives, perhaps though not many recently.

Or we're wrestling with a personal situation and we plead to God to show us a sign: **just a small single sign so that we can know that He's really plugged into our specific plight and we're not in his Eternal spiritual holding pattern or voice mail recorded message.**

We see people around us that are seeking signs and so many of them are disappointed, not because the signs are not there but because the signs that they were looking for just didn't materialize to their liking.

In today's readings, we have two separate instances of signs that were provided for by God and yet none of them were either asked for or mirrored what the people were looking for.

A rainbow is such a beautiful image, sometimes you can only imagine that only God could have created such a thing of beauty and yet it's so fleeting and temporary.

You can't see a rainbow when it's bright and sunny by itself, like on a dry day in Arizona, you need the essential element of airborne water, thus the beauty of the reminder is God would never drown the earth again.

The rainbow is a physical and spiritual reminder sometimes we get just enough water and then He can turn off the water spigot – for now.

I'm sure people in floodplains eagerly await the image of a rainbow when the water keeps rising higher and higher and higher.

The second sign provided in the New Testament is the image of Christ proclaiming a simple message **"Repent and believe in the Gospel, for the kingdom of God is at hand."**

You know too often, you'll see a person wearing a sandwich sign either in a railroad station, or an airport, or some other large place with lots of people such as the World of Coke exhibit in downtown Atlanta with the very same message on his front or back.

Yet, countless people walk by him like they never even saw him.

Why is that, is it because the message is dated?

Is it because the earthly messenger may try to look like Christ but we know that there's only one Christ and that person is not him?

But if we believe our faith, all of us are created in the image of God and therefore if we believe in the Trinity, we are created in the image of God the Father, God the Son, and God the Holy Spirit?

Sometimes, we can't be bothered to take the time to see the image of God, His Son the Christ, with the Spirit in that person.

Maybe, it's because we don't take ourselves and our faith seriously enough because if we did, that person may have sent us the best spiritual 911 message we ever could have received and we just didn't get it or could be bothered?

With the Lenten season, we are provided with a badly needed time out in our lives, Lent provides us with the rare spectrum of 40 continuous days that we can look at ourselves, we can look at the way we are living, and maybe, just maybe, **we can do something about it to change it for the good**.

The sign that we are looking for today my brothers and sisters may not be what we're expecting but it doesn't invalidate the significance of the sign.

Because the three main attributes of Lenten observance: **fasting, almsgiving, and prayer** are powerful signs in and of themselves, because they force us to detract from earthly urges of overeating, greed, and a continuing distraction from God and instead force us to think of greater issues such as temperance, charity, and a closer relationship with God.

There is no other time within Our Church's liturgical year; we get this unique opportunity to focus on not just spiritual self improvement but truly to find a path closer to walking with God.

So maybe the sign of a lighter wallet may be the greater sign of good so today someone, that you know or don't know, will be able to eat, be housed, or be clothed because you gave money as a sacrifice to your God who has given you everything.

Or the sign of worn-out trousers at the knees may be the greater sign that is good because you're spending more time in silent prayer, giving thanks for what you do have or asking Him for His forgiveness for what you have done against Him.

St. Paul reminds us that our baptism provides us the way to the resurrection of our Lord Jesus Christ.

However, maybe the greatest sign we need to contemplate for today and everyday is the figure of battered and broken Christ on the Cross.

Because ultimately in that sign, that image, and that very action, it demonstrates truly how much God loves each and every one of us so that His Son can be offered as a sacrifice for our sins in this life so that we can be with him forever in heaven in the next.

So, what sign are you looking for God to give you today?

Or maybe yet the better question is "What sign did you get today, how did you read it and what are you going to do about it?" Amen.

Social Justice Paper

Homework- Reflection paper - how is the international community reflected in my parish - and what aspects of Catholic Social Teaching might affect this community in my parish.

Please allow me to give some specific facts about the current parish dynamics at St. Oliver Plunkett.

Our parish is supported by the Missionaries of La Salette, which is a Marian order based in La Salette, France. The Order is based upon the apparition of the Blessed Mother who appeared to two small children who were tending another person's flock of sheep in the 1850's.

The Blessed Mother, unlike at Fatima or Lourdes, had a very special symbol that she wore over her gown: she was wearing a crucifix of her Son that had two separate two distinct symbols on the crossbeam: on one side was the hammer that was used to drive the nails into her Son's hands and feet and on the other side it was a set of pincers.

❑ The hammer represented our ability to sin, the same sin that forced her Son to be die on the Cross of Calvary for Our Eternal Salvation.

❑ The pincers represent God's forgiveness and mercy, just like the pincers are used to remove the nails that were buried into His Son's hands and feet after He died on the Cross.

The message of La Salette was simple: it was Mary's urgent call for redemption for all God's children that had fallen away from the Church – the Holy Catholic Church. She is the expression "that her sons arm was heavy from holding back the raised wrath of Her Son at the disobedience of his children." [4]

From that apparition, came a religious order whose chasms from the Holy Spirit are twofold:

1. **To build a renewed sense of community, a community that was built on the Catholic faith, and**

2. **To bring a message of reconciliation because without reconciliation with God, one cannot effectively serve God or His people.**

The individual is too much at tension with his own soul cannot be an effective witness to the greatness of God's mercy. The tension is caused by too much sin and the recognition of that sin on your life. This tension causes one to retreat into oneself to the absence of being together in a larger community. It is only after one has received the gift of absolute forgiveness, can anyone be an effective evangelizer to others that he/she comes in contact with. The tyranny and millstone of sin that was holding us back has been smashed by the Wood of the Cross and the Blood of Christ.

Having said that, let me tell you a little bit about St. Oliver's. Saint Oliver Plunkett Roman Catholic Church actually started as a mission church that was based in St. Anne's in Marietta, Georgia. The Order of Our Lady of La Salette has a significant presence in the United States since the middle 1800s and the in the Archdiocese of Atlanta for over 20 years. Presently, the Lavallette's are in three churches in the Archdiocese of Atlanta – St Anne's, St Thomas the Apostle and St Oliver's. The La Salette order has produced a great number of priests from France and Ireland and one source of growth for the order has been in Central and Latin America.

The parish community of Saint Oliver's is a growing and dynamic parish -- currently at about 2,000 families are registered and we grow at approximately 150 to 200 families per year. The current church building was built in the early 1990s as a direct expansion from the first Church that was built in the late 1980s. The Church building is now the Parish Hall and is also used as the secondary church for Masses of Easter and Christmas. During those holy times of the Liturgical Year, we actually have to have concurrent masses at the same time in order to meet all of the obligations of the faithful.

Although currently we only have two priests, we currently have three deacons who range in age from the late 50s to the middle 70s. I will be the youngest deacon candidate that the parishes had ever produced -- at the tender age of 45.

Approximately 2 years ago, the current pastor recognized the need for an expansion of our parish community to include our Latin brothers and sisters. Snellville's approximate location on the eastern side of Atlanta and the State of Georgia reflects the growing communities of Snellville, Loganville, and Grayson and Walton County. In addition, Gwinnett County continues to grow in its own Hispanic population because up its robust economy, continued housing development for residential areas and business development for new buildings and structures.

We recognize that because of some of their undocumented work status, many of our Hispanic brothers and sisters are reluctant to register at a Church because of the documentation involved. For what ever it is worth, an ingrown fear shared by some that the Church could be an agent of the State does not help us in being able to register these parishioners. However, we know that they are needing to be sacramentally sound: to receive all the sacraments of Baptism, Reconciliation, Holy Eucharist, Confirmation, Marriage, and Anointing of the Sick.

The present pastor, Father James Henault, who it served as a pastor in Florida previously, recognize that this emerging Catholic population had to be served within his borders. He had recruited at very young Polish priest that was also multilingual and together they learned Spanish and recruited a Spanish-speaking deacon, Rafael Cintron and started to build their new ministry. A Spanish Mass was started at 1 p.m. every Sunday and for most holy days of obligation as well as Holy Week observances, became multilingual in nature. The Good Friday service specifically comes to mind in our efforts to diversify. As we see each of the 14 Stations of the Cross acted out, the explanation for each would either be exclusively in English or in Spanish. The 10 petitions and responses of Good Friday would be done half in English and half in Spanish. So we started to see our Hispanic brothers and sisters attending more parish events.

Finally, within the La Salette community, the present pastor signed a document of mutual cooperation and prayer with a La Salette parish based in Las Termas Rio del Hondo, Argentina. Every six months to a year, either they would send a representative from their community to Saint Oliver's or we would send a representative to Argentina. Last July, I was privileged to spend 13 days in Argentina visiting with our brothers and sisters in that faith community. I will enclose my paper on that separately because that was also a very enlightening experience.

Additionally, we encountered some of the Anglos that were not very receptive to this new outreach. They complained about the additional traffic, about the integration of new activities such as a special Mass, such as for our Lady of Guadalupe and in other new activities that had a more Hispanic flavor. Of course, from the referencing the Gospel, one only has to see that any measure to exclude for whatever reason is counter to the spirit of the Gospel as well as counterproductive to building a large faith community.

As Father Jim had made in his introductory remarks, the challenge for the Catholic Church was not to build a separate churches that were based on ethnicity only, such as the French Catholic Church, the Polish Catholic Church, or even the Spanish Catholic Church, but to build a much larger church that was more inclusive. Those churches based on specific ethnicity were either dying or being blended together. The Church of the future was to be with us all being accepting of each other but also seeing the great graces these other culture brought to the one Holy Catholic and Apostolic Church.

I remember with great fondness the celebration of the Mass of Our Lady of Guadalupe last December 2004. On that very Sunday, it literally brought the house down. We processed around the Church with a very large portrait of our Lady, singing songs, and praising God and Mary. As we entered into the Church and the Celebrant priest incensed the altar, **I remember looking out at all these people and thinking only a Mother, A Mother to all the Nations of the World, could bring together so many of her children – white, brown, tan, black and yellow.**

The Mass for Our Lady was unbelievable. Before the Mass starting, I had to give a very quick Spanish instruction to one of the other deacons – Deacon Tom Mackin -- on being able to say "the blood of Christ" in Spanish. Nevertheless, to his credit, he actually wrote the words on the palm of one of his hands so that he could extend the chalice to the person with the other hand. That was his own small demonstration of unity that he felt he could do – try to learn three words of Spanish. However, even in that small act of humility, he was trying in his own way to serve his brothers and sisters in the body of Christ as best he could.

The principal challenge that faces any multicultural church is this: with so many things that can divide us, money or the lack thereof, a common language or many languages; old versus young; devout versus occasional; practicing Catholic versus lost or withdrawn; the Catholic Church must be a symbol of unity and inclusiveness. It can be as small as people having to learn new phrases in a different language such as you're welcome – di nada, thank you - gracious, or Go with God – Via con Dios. It can be as large as trying to learn a new language so that the liturgy can be celebrated in one's native language until they learn enough English to understand.

One of most common misconceptions was that the immigrants to the United States around the turn-of-the-century all learned English first. They may have learned English first but their Catholic faith was celebrated in Latin but the preaching and the teaching was done in their native language. So they did learn English in order to be more economically viable but I am sure they prayed and sang in their native tongues. Therefore, our challenge may be to recognize that we have to accommodate them so that in our love of our Lord, we all can come together in praise the source of creation – God the Father, Jesus His Son and our Brother and the Holy Spirit – the Lord and Giver of Life.

As a personal example, I am not required to learn Spanish before my own ordination, God willing, in February of 2006. However, I know that in order to be effective in my future work as a deacon in a multicultural parish, which I will have to make some sort of firm commitment to learning the language of the people. However, even if I were to be assigned in our Lady of Vietnam, then I would have to make the commitment to learn Vietnamese. Because even though I could be successful with part of the population, the young and those that understand English, I would not be effective in servicing all the people of God. Moreover, my calling is, in fact, to be effective to all the people of God.

Therefore, by virtue of my own travels to Argentina, and to Snellville, Georgia, I recognize that we have a tremendous opportunity to serve our brothers and sisters in Christ that may not feel comfortable in formally registering in a parish. Because of their undocumented worker status, they may not come initially to worship. But at some point, when they do come to worship, it would be far more welcoming to them to hear instead of "good afternoon", to be able to hear "Buenos Tardes, senor y senora, como esta ustedes? Or even better yet, "Via con Dios" -- Go with God.

We must welcome all the people of God for Christ Himself reminds us in the Great Judgment Passage of the Gospel of Saint Matthew when asked "when did we do these things for you Lord?"

Then the king will say to those on his right, 'Come, you who are blessed by my Father. Inherit the kingdom prepared for you from the foundation of the world.

- ❑ For I was hungry and you gave me food,

- ❑ I was thirsty and you gave me drink,

- ❑ a stranger and you welcomed me,

- ❑ naked and you clothed me,

- ❑ ill and you cared for me,

- ❑ in prison and you visited me.'

Then the righteous will answer him and say, 'Lord, when did we see you hungry and feed you, or thirsty and give you drink? When did we see you a stranger and welcome you, or naked and clothe you? When did we see you ill or in prison, and visit you?'

And the King will say to them in reply, 'Amen, I say to you, whatever you did for one of these least brothers of mine, you did for me.' 5

(Endnotes)

[1] 02/27/05   Request from Father James Henault, Pastor of St Oliver Plunkett RC Church, Eucharistic Visit to Emory Northlake Hospital-Snellville GA for Mrs. Marjorie Tolland - Mother of Parishioner of St Oliver's - She broke her hip at her daughter's home; 1st Sunday Communion Visit

[2] Catholic Online Saints – as quoted at http://www.catholic.org/saints/saint.php?saint_id=322

St. Tarsicius - Feast day: August 15 Patron of first communicants

Tarsicius was an acolyte or perhaps a deacon at Rome. He was accosted and beaten to death on the Appian Way by a mob while carrying the Eucharist to some Christians in prison. The incident is included in Cardinal Wiseman's novel "Fabiola", and Pope Damasus wrote a poem about it. Tarsicius is the patron of first communicants and his feast day is August 15.

[3] Matthew 5:3

[4] As quoted from the official Website of the Missionaries of Our Lady of La Salette as quoted from http://www.lasalette.org/the_apparition.htm

The Message
The unknown Lady now spoke to the children. "We were drinking her words," they would say later, adding, "she wept all the time she spoke to us."

"Come near, my children, be not afraid; I am here to tell you great news. **If my people will not obey, I shall be compelled to loose my Son's arm. It is so heavy that I can no longer hold it.**

How long have I suffered for you! If my Son is not to abandon you, I am obliged to entreat him without ceasing. But you take no heed of that. No matter how well you pray in the future, no matter how well you act, you will never be able to make up what I have endured on your behalf."

[5] Matthew 25: 34-40.

Deacon Loris's Summer Assignments

Year 2001 -- My introduction into the Eucharist ministry

In preparing for this assignment, I had the opportunity to meet with four different people they had a great deal of input and influence into this specific ministry. I met with my pastor, Father Cliff Hasler, on two separate occasions: August 7th and August 21st for approximately one hour for each session. In addition, I had conversations with the two parish deacons, Bill Jindrich and Mike Capozza, for conversations that lasted approximately three hours total.

Why I had the opportunity to meet with the Eucharistic ministers that deliver the Eucharistic to the homebound and the sick, the person that coordinates that opportunity is Mrs. Eileen Pankow. Eileen has been performing this ministry for the past 10 years and has a beautiful story to tell about her involvement in that.

When I first met with Father Cliff, I check about the first 20 minutes to bring him up to speed in terms of what the program had done for me and what I had done for the program to date. We focused a great deal of time the importance of maintaining a good spiritual life and some of the practices that reinforce that practice. We both taught in in-depth about the divine office as well as other methods of contemplative prayer. Father Cliff has an extensive appreciation for centering prayer while I prefer the rosary as my extensive contemplative prayer. We also spent a great deal of time on the importance of developing that sense of prayer in our everyday lives.

Father and I also spent a great deal of time on the importance of the Eucharist both within the structure of the mass and outside of it. I had been heavily influenced by two experiences that brought me closer in my calling for the diaconate. First, I had an experience at a mass about a year ago involving the Eucharist that is very special in intimate. During a Sunday mass, one of the deacons as he was preparing the altar for the distribution of Holy Communion, inadvertently dropped one of the consecrated species and it just fell underneath the altar while he was walking between the Eucharistic ministers. I don't believe that he saw what had happened and literally was just ready to step on one of the host when I came out of my pew, scooped out the Blessed Sacrament and then gently placed in back into his hands.

After his first luck to of initial shock, he just smiled at me, and mouthed the words "thank you". I quickly returned back to my place in the pew, and the service resumed. After the mass had completed, I went to the deacon and asked him if I had done the right thing because it was not my intention to potentially embarrassing in front of the entire congregation. He warmly smiled and said "oh no Albert you did just fine, and thank you for your help." I left the mass and from that point on, I felt moved from the Spirit and within weeks of that event, I started the process for applying to the diaconate.

In addition, I had been the recipient of the book called "my daily Eucharist". The purpose of this block was to give 365 daily inspirational stories about a different aspect of the Eucharist. It had stories in there from the Saints, especially the story of St. Tarsis - a small boy in ancient Rome that had been entrusted with the body and blood of Christ after a community service had taken place. On the way home to bring the Eucharist to his aging parents, he was accosted by a mob of Roman boys who thought he might have been carrying gold because it was always rumored that Christians were rich. He was beaten and killed by those boys, and when they stripped his body to find the supposed "gold", the Eucharistic that he was carrying was gone, it had vanished.

Our own Lord preserved the sanctity of His Eucharist and brought into glory a young boy who sought to protect it at all costs. That story was told at my daughter's first fully communion and a homily given by Father Mike and I've never forgotten that story. So when I saw that sacred species that the floor and then realizing that the deacon was not ready or had not seen the species, it was out of that inspiration that I acted. Now I recognize that I'm not a candidate for sainthood, but I recognized in my own personal development and growth, that the Eucharist was beginning to become a greater part of my spiritual life.

My discussions with the deacons who serve St. Oliver's were also equally important. Deacon Mike Capozza served as my trainer for Eucharistic ministry back in April of this year. As a function of his training those who were there both initially and for retraining was on the importance of recognizing the sacred species was the body, blood, soul, and divinity of our Lord Jesus Christ. One of the things that we try to reinforce and the Eucharistic ministers that serve in the church is the importance of insuring that the Sacrament is never scandalized and that when the Sacrament is received, that there is a personal contact made between the recipient and the Eucharistic minister. The Sacrament is not meant to be just dispensed, but an act of physical and spiritual connection between those who act as the Lord's minister and to the Lord's people. Mike gave a great training session and I'm thankful for that opportunity because that was the exact message that needs to be conferred to all parishioners.

I had the privilege of being a Eucharistic minister at the Easter Vigil Mass for this year. Although I was not scheduled to be a minister, the need arose and I was able to fulfill that role. However the joy that I felt to be considered worthy of being His servant at that Mass was an experience I shall not forget easily. It was as if the start of my diaconate training was transforming from just purely and academic experience to a rail hands-on practical spiritual development.

My conversations with Deacon Bill were equally as involved. Bill and I share a good relationship because we're always focusing on the practical aspects of being and becoming a deacon. One of the things until I had a great deal of conversation about was what do we need to do to enhance the presence of the Blessed Sacrament. Bill and I had several times been at the same hour when the Blessed Sacrament was exposed for holy hour.

The reverence for what he can do is a powerful example to his faith and his commitment of service to the community at large. In our conversations that we've had we have focused on the need of the adults, specifically parents, to reinforce the belief that the Eucharist is the Real Presence of Jesus in our lives today. When the Eucharistic prayer is stated in the Gospels of Matthew, Mark, and Luke and when Christ said in Matthews Gospel "and behold I am with you always until the end of the age", this is the foundation that we should be able to teach our young people from that when the prayer of concentration is said, Christ is revealed a physical presence once again that we can feel and taste. In addition, in the Scripture 1/8 says unless you eat the flesh of the Son of Man and drink his blood, then you'll have eternal life with him (John 6:52--59).

I can see Bill's reinforcement of his faith in the Eucharist the way he ministers at the altar during Sunday mass. I see a great devotion and a specialness of purpose when he ministers at the Lord's Table. He moves with a deliberate purpose insuring that there are enough species and wine for the Lord's Table. And during the great Amen when he holds aloft the chalice while Father holds the large Eucharistic host, I see his determination and reverence. He is not just trained as an ordained minister; he is acting as a man a totally involved in his faith. And that's what makes the power of his example that much more special to be around. He is acting in the exact capacity that he was called to do, as a servant to the congregation and of His God.

To my final conversation was with Eileen Pankow who is responsible for the Eucharistic ministers to the sick and homebound. Eileen story is one of both great love and devotion. Eileen's personal history is that she had a mother who died of cancer who died while Eileen was relatively young. Eileen's mother was very devout Catholic and Eileen service to the sick is a method of tribute to her mother and her faith.

Eileen coordinates a core membership of people as they go to the sick and homebound. I asked Eileen about a special experience that she's had while they Eucharistic minister. She stated that one of her most poignant memory is when she was called to a home of parishioners who had a son that had suffering from cancer. And she arrived, he was in a very weakened state but he indicated his desire to receive the Eucharist. And she completed the service; she looked into his eyes and saw that he was at rest. Later that evening, she had been told that he passed on that night but he was totally at peace. She feels such a sense of personal satisfaction at being a minister of the Lord's will and his Eucharist.

In addition, she has had instances where spouses and family members who are not Catholic were so inspired by her example of service and love that they asked to become members of the church. The sheer power of her personal example and willingness to serve intern served as a powerful witness to others so that their faith may be increased. Again and again to comment on the fact that every time that she goes out to serve others she received so much more. In addition she commented that when she first started serving as a Eucharistic minister that she felt so unworthy, yet, the Scripture is loaded with examples of how the Lord does and takes those who are unworthy and makes them into powerful examples for the Lord.

Year 2002 – My Introduction to Baptism Ministry

I chose this assignment for two reasons: the first being is that this will be the one sacrament that the deacon can confirm upon the laity, and secondly, I had the privilege of being able to set up for baptism to be performed between Christmas and New Year's last year and I found to be a very deep and positive spiritual experience.

In preparing for this assignment, I had the opportunity to meet with four different people they had a great deal of input and influence into this specific ministry. I met with my pastor, Father Jim Henault for approximately ½ hour. In addition, I had conversations with the two parish deacons, Bill Jindrich and Mike Capozza, for conversations that lasted approximately 2 hours total. In addition, I had the opportunity to meet with one of the laypeople that instructs this class, Ms. Patty Ruiz as she taught the class. In this ministry, there are two lay people that each teaches a class once a quarter and then the deacon teach in the remaining months of the quarter. Upon completion, each instructor will have taught four months out of the year and therefore can make a substantial contribution to our faith community without making a tremendous time commitments as well.

In addition, during the second and fourth weekends of both July and August, I had the ability to help set up and then observe the actual Baptismal rite being performed by the deacons with some of the parents that had been in the class previously and actually scheduled to have their children baptized.

The class format is relatively straightforward: there is an academic class period of approximately 1 ½ hours for two sessions over two separate Sunday afternoons. The first session covers two main topic areas on building a foundation and establishing tradition. The next session focuses on becoming a new creation and belonging to a community. Since most of the parents that are taking these classes have newborns as their children to be baptized, frequently the newborns to attend the classes or to parents.

Their baby's presence in the class by itself as a powerful statement to witnessing knowledge of the faith but also understanding the almighty presence of God in their lives. A common reference point when discussing about their understanding of God knew at the birth of their children, they all felt the benevolent love of God in their lives. In the act of expanding their families, each of the couples expressed a desire to enhance the love that they felt for each other but also to enhance their understanding of the faith.

It was interesting to note that there is somewhat a disparity in terms of what the faith teaches versus what they personally believe. For example, the concept of sin always was brought up as being something that was either bad or evil but yet on a personal note it was still difficult for them to talk about except in some wide academic sense.

One of the other topics that brought some spirited discussion was actually the intent of the church in welcoming small children in the assembly of Mass. Although our church physically has a crying room that allows for parents with small children to be to attend Mass, one consistent theme is that some parents felt that they were physically separated from the rest of the community and therefore by the fact that they had small children, the community physically separated them from their worship.

Some people almost felt compelled to view the crying room as being some sort of spiritual penalty box as opposed to being able to sit with the main body of the assembly in the sacristy. I believe part of this was driven by discussion of Matthew's Gospel when Jesus beckoned the small children to be able to approach Him and yet the disciples pushed the children away as being a nuisance.

I personally felt that this is a real issue that we should be able to address as the faith community because I've personally witnessed some of the older parishioners be less than tolerant to parents with small children, yet, at some point in our lives involved in contact with small children that have to be less than hospitable and yet I've also dealt with adults that have acted the same.

Finally, I would like to make a recommendation that would enhance the confidence of the young adults and parents of children who have their small babies or small children baptized. As much as we would like to think that adults are growing in their faith and knowledge of Catholicism, the reality is that many adults in our faith community have probably not made an intelligent study of their faith since they left their CCD days and possibly high school or college.

Of course, as they have grown older, they have either integrated their own thoughts about the teachings of the church into their own opinions, which sometimes are dramatically different from the official teachings of the Roman Catholic Church. In other instances, people do have a profound lack of understanding of what exactly the church teaches as the Truth and how we as Catholics are supposed to act in defending the Faith.

My specific recommendation would be at the conclusion of the actual Baptismal rite as the first gift of the parish in the faith community a current copy of the Catechism of the Catholic Church, what I affectionately call the "Green Book". It is interesting to note as we ask the parents of the child to be the first teachers of the Faith to the child, we take it on faith that they mentally and physically possess those attributes that would be instrumental in them teaching the faith. However, wouldn't it be a more powerful statement that we give to them, as a faith community, the first tool to be able to teach the faith to their children or at least provide them with unavailable resource for them to be about to read before they tried to answer the questions of their children.

If we are to accept the fact that most of our adults are not fully prepared to have all the answers about the faith, wouldn't it makes sense to be able to give them a ready reference to make that task easier for them to accomplish instead of them trying to rely on their memory or a flawed understanding of what our faith to teaches?

The actual cost of the book is less than $12 a copy and would be a tremendous investment in making sure that these parents feel comfortable enough to be able to complete the act of being examples of the faith to their children but also being able to teach their children what our faith actually is before their children enter into CCD classes. If the presentation of this material could not be done at the end of the baptism, then it should be done at the end of the second-class when the training is considered complete and the paperwork is submitted for the actual Baptismal date with the church support staff.

I know for my own spiritual formation that it took me until I was 40 to finally read the Catholic Catechism and understand exactly what my faith was about.

Although I had heard of the Baltimore Catechism when I grew up as St. Teresa's Roman Catholic Church in Trumbull CT, I don't remember seeing physically the Baltimore catechism and I can assure you I probably don't remember reading it as a child as well. Therefore, I think this might be something that we could take immediate action and, at least to make an outward sign from their Church to the parents, as an additional level of support for them to grow in their own faith journey and to feel comfortable enough that they can actually teach what the Church professes to be the Truth.

Year 2003 – Initial Interview with your Pastor

On Thursday, August 6th, 2003, I had the pleasure of meeting with my pastor, Father Jim Henault – of the Missionaries of our Lady of La Salette, for the approximately an hour to discuss my current formation process as well as my progress in formation till ordination.
What his perception(s) is of your formation;

As we reviewed the five years of formation, his perception of my formation is that things were progressing as expected. His specific instruction to me when I started formation was for me to be able to totally focus on my studies and to work with my diaconate mentors in the parish. In addition, he instructed me to find a good spiritual director to assist me in answering questions about our faith as well as to assist me in developing a stronger prayer life. I am privileged that I have a very good spiritual director as well as two very good diaconate mentors that can help me in that aspect.

What his expectations are of your formation;

His specific expectation on my formation is that my education provides me to be a competent member of the parish liturgical leadership team as well as to be able to function fully in my capacities as a Deacon. Therefore, I have to be fully qualified and trained to perform the liturgical functions assigned to deacons; such as the ability to perform baptisms, funeral wake services, graveside services, Eucharistic Adoration, as well as to be able to assist for larger liturgical assemblies such as Christmas and Easter vigils, confirmations, and like liturgical functions.

How he envisions incorporating you into ministries and liturgy during you last two years of formation;

I was privileged to be asked, at his request, to serve as Master of Ceremonies for the Holy Thursday Mass this past year and at our parish's 25th anniversary Mass that was concelebrated by the Archbishop of Atlanta with present and past priests assigned to the parish. In addition, I assisted and worked with the other deacons during the Christmas Eve and Day masses. It was at his specific instruction that I was available all Masses during Holy Week of this year, in case other assigned ministers did not show up and I had to be able to the step in that is needed – such as being a Eucharistic minister. This request alone was probably the best practical experiences that have received to date because it allowed me to see the complete flow of Holy Week.

Father Jim has been extremely generous in his support of his current deacons and he is equally committed to my development so that I can be a seamless addition to his current staff. This commitment also spills over to the other priest assigned to St. Oliver's. Father Peter has been actively working with one of the other deacons on improving his preaching skills. In short, both of our priests support the ongoing and continuous development of the deacons assigned in our parish.

With regards to me, it will be in his discretion and direction when he will start allowing me to perform in a greater liturgical capacity or teaching capacity.

What he may have in mind for you upon ordination.

Although we discussed ordination in a general sense, it was both agreed-upon that it represents a significant day in the distant future, but there's still a great deal of work to be done in the present and that should be our main focus of activity.

However, as I stated earlier, it is his desire that my formation provides me with the faculties in the

instruction to be in a competent member of his parish leadership team as well as an effective instructor in the faith. My previous summer assignments focused on those ministries that would be directly related to the diaconate: the sacrament of baptisms as well as being able to effectively proclaim the word of God.

Therefore, it will be his expectation and my fervent desire to continue to build on those activities that are directly related to my diaconate ministry and to work with others in the parish community that can assist me in that effort.

For example, he has asked me to start working with the RCIA Ministry which is something that I've never had specific contact with but something that will be extremely important to me in the future as a Deacon. Therefore, we have to start taking the steps now in order to make that happen in that is what we're planning to do.

I had made the personal commitment to him that I plan to learn Spanish, initially in the capacity of being able to fulfill the various liturgical rites of our faith to a newly and expanding segment of our faith community: the Hispanic community.

Earlier this year, we initiated a 1 p.m Spanish-language Mass to the church schedule. Although we currently have Spanish -- speaking Deacon, Deacon Rafael, assigned to St. Oliver's, I felt it was personally important that if I was going to be a man of faith in our community, I had to at least be able to address the needs of all the people I would serve. And if this meant having to learn a third language, I have to be fully prepared for that commitment. I am privileged that I've enlisted the assistance of a Spanish voice coach by the name of Angel Concepcion, who'll work with me my senior year on being able to correctly pronounce the prayers of the church in Spanish.

Currently there are liturgical manuals that have the rites written in both English and Spanish on opposite pages so that I can follow along the rite of the Church by being able to correctly read the appropriate prayers or intercessions. This was not made mandatory or even suggested by my pastor but I made a commitment for myself as a return commitment to his greater commitment of serving all the people which his parish is assigned regardless of language or nationality.

Generally, address what his expectations are for you in the parish.

His chief expectation is to fulfill the Ministry of my vocation: to be a servant of Christ within my parish community: to preach the faith, by example of voice, action, deed, and example, the gospel of Our Lord Jesus Christ, to provide comfort to those who are sick and dying, to be a witness of Christ in my workplace and in my community, and to be a man of prayer and faith.

Therefore, the next 30 months to ordination, our chief challenge will be to look at those opportunities that will allow him to observe me, to challenge me to grow in faith and while providing patient guidance and instruction in those areas where I need assistance in prior to ordination.

Working with other members of the parish staff as well as other members of our Faith, I look forward to the lifetime opportunity to fulfill my vocation and to serve Christ.

Year 2004 – Interview with Deacon Bill Jindrich

Background:

William "Bill" Jindrich has been an ordained deacon in the Roman Catholic Church since May 16th, 1987. He was in his early forties when he started his formation with a number of gentlemen from the Archdiocese of Atlanta, GA. In fact, his brother in Christ, Deacon Tom Mackin was in the same ordination class with Bill. Recently, Tom has come out of retirement to assist his brother Bill in as an active deacon at St. Oliver's in Snellville, Georgia. After the untimely death of Deacon Mike Capozza in November of 2003, Tom was asked by the Archbishop of Atlanta to help us in our hour of need. Deacon Rafael Cintron – Class of 1989 -- is our other Deacon. His main area of responsibility is with the Hispanic apostolate as well as doing religious education for our Hispanic Brothers and sisters. Rafael came to us from St. John Neumann where he was a deacon there for a number of years.

Bill has a very unique and interesting history. Prior and during his diaconate formation, he has worked with the Dominicans -- the Order of Preachers as well as the Missionaries of La Salette and for eight years served at Holy Cross -- a diocesan church. Bill has also been married to his bride Linda for well over 30 years and between them, they have children and ultimately grandchildren as well. Bill is truly the family man at heart as well as in action. I'll talk more about Bill and Linda's relationship later in this paper.

The best way that I can describe Bill is that he is truly a "gentle giant". Standing well over 6'5" in stature and with hands that can easily palm a NBA basketball, Bill has both patience and a sincerity that is rare in most men. He also has a ready smile that he shares generously with all he comes in contact with. I have known him since I joined Saint Oliver Plunkett's in August 1998 and it was with Bill that I had my first serious inquiry about the diaconate.

In terms of the hierarchy within the parish, Bill is, in fact, the senior servant of the people of God. Both priests, Father Jim Henault-pastor and Father Peter Jandaczek will lean on Deacon Bill for guidance and input and he is perceived by the parish community as being any person can easily approach and talk to. His homilies are always well-prepared, in fact after one homily, it was remarked by the director of music ministry that we had a prophet within our midst. Therefore, it is my pleasure to present his responses to your questions as well as some additional insights that he was able to provide to me at this point of my formation.

The Matrix below shows his ministries and areas of responsibilities:

❑ Parish liturgy committee	❑ Cancer survivors ministry	❑ Respect to life committee	❑ Chief trainer altar servers
❑ Spiritual director – St. Vincent de Paul Society	❑ Primary instructor, baptismal preparation	❑ Sacrament of matrimony preparation	❑ Annulment caseworker
❑ Minister for wake services	❑ Homiletics preparation	❑ Catholics returning home presenter and facilitator	❑ Minister – stations of the cross during Lent
❑ Minister – holy hours	❑ Diaconate formation and mentoring		

For the next three questions, I'll be referring to this matrix of above to help illustrate Bill's extensive involvement with St. Oliver's community.

1. **Regular weekly routine for with the Church;**

Bill has a rather full schedule with his work at St. Oliver's. Starting with Sunday Mass, each of the deacon's as well as the deacon candidate in formation is committed to two masses per Sunday. Currently, Deacon Tom Mackin is recovering from the replacement surgery and will be out of action until the first week of October. And it is not uncommon to have to arrive approximately 30 minutes before the start of your assigned mass and stay to at least 20 minutes after mass is terminated to fulfill all your assigned duties therefore, time management skills are essential. **It is Bill's expectation that he doesn't spend more than 20 hours a week doing church or ministry related activities.**

However, he also has a very good rule that he will not combined days in succession with church business. For example, when we had our appointment tonight, he would not make another appointment for tomorrow night as well. His bride Linda has had multiple sclerosis for a number of years and her care is a primary interest of Bill. **Therefore, he is made it a priority to make sure that he splits his time between his family responsibilities and Church.** However, he also stated that it was a blessing that members of the parish community can assist him in Linda with some of the treatments that she must have. Therefore, instead of having to take a day off from work so he can be with her in a medical treatment, a parishioner can transport Linda to her treatment and then that preserves some of Bill's vacation time for quality time off together as a family and as a couple.

2. **Monthly routine with the Church;**

The monthly routine probably would mark coincides with the liturgical year that we follow as Catholics. Clearly at this time, in Ordinary Time, we face a slightly less time intensive schedule than we would if we were either in Lent or in Advent. So when this happens, there are other activities have a tendency to fill in or at least be able to have a better focus. Of course, now this is also the time that the deacons like everyone else try to take some sort of vacation so we rely on the other deacons to help pitch in. For example, because as a possible strike between BellSouth and the Communication Workers of America, Bill was able to fill in for my masses and I was able to fill in for his masses the week prior. Although we don't keep score, it is part of our collective attitude that we do the best we can to help each other out because things to happen. Mike's untimely death was a sad example of this principle. But the parish ministry schedules tend to relax in the summer and then pick-up in the fall.

3. When and how does he make time available for his family;

One of the things that he focuses a great deal of attention on is being a dedicated husband, father and grandfather. Again, some more personal information, Bill is had to deal with family illnesses throughout the entire time that I have known him. In addition to Linda and her MS, his daughter has had a bout with breast cancer and he also lost a nephew to a severe illness. He has born all of this anguish over time and yet he never seems to lose fact of his family's importance in his life. He is a very faithful follower of the principle of Family, Career, and Church but he is also a deep man of faith and it's my observation that it was his faith that got him through these difficult circumstances.

But, he also commented that when Linda and he were younger, they both were active in parish ministry and frequently to do ministry together as a couple. Therefore, it wasn't a question of sacrificing one aspect for the other, but it was the ability to combine the two into both quality personal time and being able to be a benefit to others. However, Linda does serve from time to time as a lector at Mass and frequently will be at the same Mass as Bill. His granddaughter Taylor is an altar server and also is sometimes with her granddad serving together at the Altar of the Mass. But from a personal standpoint, it is a pleasure to relieve him at Sunday Mass so that he can go home to his bride, just like I want to go home to my bride when I'm done with my responsibilities as well.

4. How does he resolve conflicts with family, work and Church;

Bill had a very good answer for this question: you must constantly plan and try to minimize as much as possible any possible conflict that may arise from an imbalance between these three critical elements. By being mindful of how much he spends at church, he makes sure that he does not throw the other two elements out of kilter.

5. What is his working relationship with other members of the parish clergy?

There is also another valuable tip that he shared with me. While he was at Holy Cross, he did not enjoy the same level of positive relationship with the clergy that he had with the Dominicans or the Missionaries of La Salette. But instead of getting dismayed, his attitude was to constantly focus on the people and their needs and to provide respect and tolerance to the leadership of the parish. Therefore, he did not break his vow of obedience and there was no discord demonstrated.

6. What is his working relationship with lay leaders of the parish?

To quote Bill, "everything works". In discussing this question further, he recognizes that he is very approachable and that parishioners will sometimes try to gain his support for a specific item. But, Bill is also very aware that he is part of the parish leadership team and that many of those decisions are not his to make but he is faithful to being the servant of his community. Therefore, his frequent comment to those who have a genuine disagreement with either one of the priests is to "make an appointment to see them and discuss your grievance personally." If there is something that needs be brought up to the pastor, Bill will bring it up to him in a private conversation. In the military, we are taught this action as "praise in public and criticize in private". This is a very smart method for dealing with people. The reason why I bring this topic up is that already in my formation, I have been approached by people asking for my opinion on certain liturgical topics and decisions within the parish. I have been able to deflect their request by stating that I'm under obedience to my pastor and therefore, it is his decision to make and my action to complete. Bill was very supportive of that response; we recognize that we are servants of the people of God, but we are also under His and our pastor's authority.

Year 2005 – Submission of Personal Information for Ordination

Bio Information for Albert Linus Feliu

Age: 45

Date of Birth: August 9th, 1960

Place of Birth: Brooklyn, New York

Spouse/Children: Married to the former Cynthia Ann Lapadula, Bristol, CT for 21 years, married on June 15th, 1984. Two children: Christina – 14, Michael 11.

Education (if college, include type of degree(s) and year(s) received):

❑ Candidate -- Masters in Project Management; Keller Graduate School of Management – Online University, Oakbrook Terrace, IL, Estimated completion Date: June 2006.

❑ Masters in Telecommunications Management; Keller Graduate School of Management – Online University, Oakbrook Terrace, IL, June 2004.

❑ Masters in Organizational Management; University of Phoenix-Online Campus, Phoenix, AZ; March 2000.

❑ Masters of Business Administration - Concentration in Finance, University of Hartford, West Hartford, CT: December 1991.

❑ Bachelor of Science - Engineering Concentration, United States Air Force Academy, Colorado Springs, CO: May 1984.

Work Experience:

Currently a Project Manager with BellSouth Telecommunications -- Account Receivables Management in Atlanta GA. Previously served in management positions in areas dealing with Corporate and Geographical Area Marketing, Information Technology, and large team Call Center Management from 1995 – present.

Previously worked in the Personal Insurance and Financial Services industries as marketing and quality consultant as well as the Department of Defense while serving as a Commissioned Officer in the United States Air Force respectively.

Primary Hobbies and Interests: Reading, Teaching, writing and being with close friends. Currently writing a book about his experiences being in diaconate formation over the past five years.

Parish: St Oliver Plunkett Roman Catholic Church, Snellville GA.

Pastor: Father James "Jim" Henault, Missionaries of Our Lady of La Sallette

Parish Ministries: Chaplain – St Oliver's Men's Club, Occasional instructor for Sacramental Preparation for Confirmation, Catholics Returning Home, and Altar Servers, 1st degree – Knights of Columbus, Eucharistic Minister to the Sick and Homebound.

Particular Ministries of Interest: Liturgy, Sacrament Preparation for Baptism and Confirmation, Lector Training, Life Teen, Visitation to the Sick.